The Essential
Smith Wigglesworth

Donnie,

May his mantel fall upon you.

Cheryl
7/22/99

The Essential Smith Wigglesworth

Selected Sermons by
Evangelist Smith Wigglesworth
From Powerful Revival Campaigns
Around the World

WAYNE WARNER
and JOYCE LEE

SERVANT PUBLICATIONS
ANN ARBOR, MICHIGAN

Vine Books is an imprint of Servant Publications especially designed to serve evangelical Christians.

Published by Servant Publications
P.O. Box 8617
Ann Arbor, Michigan 48107

Cover design: Paul Higdon
Cover photo: Courtesy of Flower Pentecostal Heritage Center, Springfield, MO

99 00 01 10 9 8 7 6 5 4 3 2 1

Printed in the United States of America
ISBN 1-56955-071-9

LIBRARY OF CONGRESS CATALOGING-IN-PUBLICATION DATA

Wigglesworth, Smith, 1859-1947.
The essential Smith Wigglesworth : selected sermons by evangelist Smith
Wigglesworth from powerful revival campaigns around the world / [edited by]
Wayne Warner and Joyce Lee.
     p.   cm.
Includes bibliographical references.
ISBN 1-56955-071-9 (alk. paper)
1. Pentecostal churches—sermons.   2. Sermons, English.   I. Warner, Wayne E.
II. Lee, Joyce, 1945 -   III. Title.
BX8762.Z6W544   1999
252'.0994—dc21   98-51430
                                                                 CIP

Contents

International Narratives

Dedication

To the memory of
R. Bryant Mitchell (1905-97)
whose Christian character and ministry
continue to challenge me.
Wayne Warner

To Jay,
my encouragement and inspiration.
Joyce Lee

Introduction

American pentecostals were looking for someone like Smith Wigglesworth in 1914.

The pentecostal experience—which includes being baptized in the Spirit with the evidence of speaking in tongues (Acts 2:4)—had received wide promotion beginning in 1901, but critics and persecutors had discouraged many and caused others to take a less than enthusiastic role in the movement. Persecutors burned pentecostal buildings and tents, interrupted meetings, and physically abused ministers and laymen. Inside the movement, growing pains, moral failure, doctrinal disputes, and other struggles brought divisions. Even when some farsighted thinkers called for the creation of organizations, many independent-minded pentecostals unfortunately misread their intentions and wrote and preached against the efforts.

Persecutors and internal strife threatened to destroy or render powerless the movement many believed God had raised to spread the last message just prior to the coming again of Christ. True, there were many respected and strong leaders in the vanguard of the movement—people such as E. N. Bell, Florence Crawford, G. F. Taylor, A. J. Tomlinson, Maria B. Woodworth-Etter, and others. But the movement needed another Apostle Paul or a Winston Churchill to rally the troops. Smith Wigglesworth, the previously little-known English evangelist, hardly had the antidote for all of pentecostal's ills. But he came preaching a blazing, no-holds-barred, powerful gospel straight out of the book of Acts. He was a man of character. Some even called him the "Apostle of Faith" because of his legendary and fearless prayer for the sick—and even for the dead. "All things are possible; only believe," became his boldfaced motto.

Surrendering to God and having one's life cleansed was Wigglesworth's answer for people who wanted to move from the ordinary to having power with God. "When God brought me into a deeper experience with him," he said, "he spoke by the Spirit making me know I had to reach the place of absolute yieldedness and cleansing so that there would be nothing left." And he added, "That meant a clean sweep."

One of the principal publications during the formative years of American pentecostalism introduced the then 55-year-old Wigglesworth to its readership during his first visit to the U. S. in June 1914. "He lays no claim to learning," the editor of *The Latter Rain Evangel* wrote. "God took him out of one of the humbler walks of life, anointed him with a heart of love and compassion for the sick and the suffering and put His Spirit upon him."*

Believers and unbelievers alike responded to Wigglesworth's powerful ministry in 1914 and during his subsequent visits to America. In 1922 he returned to Chicago and preached at a big union meeting of pentecostal churches—purportedly the first joint meeting among pentecostal churches in the city. And his visits to other international ports of call gave the English plumber-turned-evangelist legendary qualities.

Now, more than fifty years after his death, his popularity continues as attested by many of his sermons still in print.

Who is this man who threw down his pipe wrench, packed his suitcase, and began preaching a powerful salvation-healing

---

*Miracles of Healing Wrought in England," *The Latter Rain Evangel,* June 1914, p. 6. The magazine was published by The Stone Church, one of Chicago's early pentecostal churches—now located in Palos Heights, Illinois. Wigglesworth jokingly calling attention to his lack of education, said God took him to North America in 1914 "to teach him geography."

message around the world when most men his age were thinking about retiring?

Smith Wigglesworth was born into a poor family in Menston, Yorkshire, England, in 1859. Like so many other children of his day, Smith had little time for school. At the age of seven he was working in a woolen mill twelve hours a day. As a result he never learned to read and write well until he became an adult.

At the age of eight, Smith was converted in the Menston Methodist Church and in 1872 he was confirmed in the Anglican church. Later, after he moved to Bradford, he worked with the Salvation Army and the Plymouth Brethren. Always interested in the poor, Smith took the gospel and food to deprived children in Liverpool, supporting himself with his plumbing business.

Smith married a Salvation Army officer, Mary Jane "Polly" Featherstone, and in 1889 the two founded the Bowland Street Mission in Bradford. Polly would preach while Smith minded the children and helped in other ways. It would not be until 1907, when Smith was baptized in the Holy Spirit at an Anglican church in Sunderland, that he began to preach.

"Before his Sunderland experience," Norman Armistead wrote, "Smith usually sat meekly alongside his wife, Polly, as she preached. However, soon after he returned from Sunderland, he was on his feet speaking from the text, The Spirit of the Lord is upon me, because he hath anointed me....(Luke 4:18)."*

During the next few years his ministry broadened, and he was soon conducting meetings in other countries, preaching and praying for thousands of people. Countless people testified that they had been converted and healed in his meetings. At his

---

*Norman Armistead, "Comment," *The Flame*, Gloucester, England. May-June 1997, p. 3. Used by permission.

death in 1947, James Salter, his son-in-law, wrote that following his 1914 visit to North America his gifts "made room for him." Salter, who often traveled with Wigglesworth, wrote, "New Zealand was swept, Colombo in Ceylon shaken, Sweden roused, Switzerland stormed, Norway inflamed, and California stirred to its depth as God confirmed His Word through this Mantled man."

Wigglesworth preached the 48 sermons in this book around the world, and then Christian editors published them in magazines of the day. The topics in this collection cover the Wigglesworth essentials: salvation, holy living, worship, evangelism, the baptism in the Holy Spirit, healing, and, of course, faith. His old friend Donald Gee observed that Wigglesworth could preach the subject of faith from any text he chose—the reason his contemporaries called him the Apostle of Faith.

In addition to the selected sermons, we have added anecdotal readings relating to Wigglesworth's life before and during his international ministry. The photographs illustrate the ministry of one of the 20th century's outstanding evangelists. You can also track his life with the Time Line on page 399.

Wigglesworth would not take credit for two books that bore his byline—*Ever Increasing Faith* (1924) and *Faith That Prevails* (1938)—explaining that others had taken his sermons in shorthand and published them. The two books have remained in print. Today his sermons can be found in as many as a dozen books, including five published by Servant Publications. Several of these are in languages other than English.

Even though Smith Wigglesworth was nearly 88 when he died in 1947, he still accepted preaching invitations. About the time of his death in England a telegram arrived inviting him to take part in the 40th anniversary of a large New York church, Glad Tidings Tabernacle. The pastor had not forgotten Wigglesworth's pre-World War II meetings there and wanted the congregation to hear the old warrior's faith-building words once again. No doubt had he lived long enough to make the trip to New York, the anniversary crowd would have enthusiastically joined with him in his favorite chorus taken from a song by another evangelist, Paul Rader:

> Only believe! Only believe!
> All things are possible,
> Only believe.

I hope and pray that these chapters Joyce Lee and I have selected—a sort of recycling of the Wigglesworth anointed preaching—will bless you and others with whom you share this book.

Wayne Warner
Springfield, Missouri
November 2, 1998

Preparing for an International Ministry

A Tale of Encouragement From Childhood

My father was very poor and worked long hours for little pay in order to support Mother and us three boys and one girl. I can remember one cold frosty day when my father had been given the job of digging a ditch seven yards long and a yard deep, and filling it up again, for the sum of three shillings and six pence (about eighty-seven cents). My mother said that if he would only wait a bit, it might thaw and his task would be easier. But he needed that money for food, for there was none in the house. So he set to work with a pickax.

The frost was a full yard deep, but underneath the hard ground was some soft wet clay. As he threw up some of this, a robin suddenly appeared, picked up a worm, ate it, flew to a branch of a nearby tree, and from there sent out a song of joyous praise. Up to now, Father had been very despondent, but he was so entranced by the robins lovely song of thanksgiving that he took fresh courage and began to dig with renewed vigor—saying to himself, If that robin can sing like that for a worm, surely I can work like a father for my good wife and my four fine children.

Smith Wigglesworth in Stanley H. Frodsham, *Smith Wigglesworth, Apostle of Faith* (Springfield, Mo.: Gospel Publishing House, 1948), p. 10. Used by permission.

1
Living in the New Realm Now

We are glad for cathedrals and churches, but God does not dwell in temples made by hands; he dwells in the heart. "God is a Spirit: and they that worship him must worship him in spirit and in truth, for the Father seeketh such to worship him" (Jn 4:23, 24). The church is the body of Christ; its worship is a heart worship, a longing to come into the presence of God. God looks at our hearts. He delights in his people (see Is 62:4). He wants us to come to a place of undisturbed rest and peace. Only simple faith will bring us there. Jesus said, "Except ye be converted, and become as little children, ye shall not enter into the kingdom of heaven" (Mt 18:3). Not that we should have the child's mind, but the child's spirit, meekness, and gentleness. It is the only place upon which we can meet God. How my heart cries out for living faith, with a deep vision of God. The world cannot produce it. It is a place where we see the Lord, where when we pray we know God hears; asking God and believing for the answer, having no fear but a living faith as we come into the presence of God, knowing that in his presence there is fullness of joy and at his right hand are pleasures for evermore (see Ps 16:11).

Being a Good Testimony
God is looking for a people through whom he can reveal himself. I used to have a tremendous temper, getting white with passion. I was difficult to please at the table. My wife was a good cook, but there was always something wrong, according to my

judgment. God knew his child could never be of service to the world unless he was wholly sanctified. After God sanctified me, I heard my wife testify in a meeting that, from that time, I was pleased with everything. I wanted to be a good testimony to the men working for me. One day they waited after work was over and said to me, "We would like to have that spirit you have." It is our human spirit that has to be controlled by the Holy Spirit. There is a place of *death* and *life* where Christ reigns in the body. Then all is well.

This Word of God is full of stimulation. The Lord would have us come into a new place of grace, that all may see us new. *"Behold!"* What is it? The Holy Ghost arousing our attention. He has something special to say. *"Behold"*—if you will believe you may be sons of God! In likeness, in character, in spirit, in longings, in acts, until all shall know you are a *son of God*. You can reach this altitude only by faith. No man can keep himself. The old nature is too difficult to manage. You have been ashamed of it many a time. However, God can change you; he will operate upon you by his power and make you a new creation if you will believe. Then you will have the testimony, "Kept by the power of God!" The Almighty will spread his covering over you, and you will know what it is to be able to do all things, for all things are possible to him that believeth.

Separation From the World

"Learn of me; for I am meek and lowly in heart: and ye shall find rest unto your souls" (Mt 11:29). The world has no rest, it is full of trouble; but in him there is peace which passeth understanding, with an inward flow of divine power changing your nature until you live, move, and act in the power of God. Therefore the world knoweth not, because it knew him not. I will give you an illustration. I have lived in one house fifty years.

I have preached from my own doorstep; all around know me. They know me when they need someone to pray, when there is trouble, when they need a word of wisdom. But when they call their friends, do they call me? No! Why? They would say, he is sure to want a *prayer meeting* but we want to finish up with a *dance.* Wherever Jesus came, sin was revealed, and men do not like sin revealed. Sin separates from God forever.

You are in a good place when you weep before God, repenting over the least thing. You may have spoken unkindly, but you realize it was not like the Lord, and your conscience has taken you to prayer. It is a wonderful thing to have a keen conscience. It is when we are close to God that our hearts are revealed to us. God intends for us to live in purity, seeing him all the time. "Beloved, now are we the sons of God, and it doth not yet appear what we shall be: but we know that, when he shall appear, we shall be like him; for we shall see him as he is. And every man that hath this hope in him purifieth himself, even as he is pure" (1 Jn 3:2-3). Our Lord who died for us, who became poor that we might be made rich—what an offering!—who suffered for us, who was buried for us, who arose and is living for us—how we love him!—he is coming again. You may be a son of God *now.* "As many as received him, to them gave he power to become the sons of God, even to them that believe on his name" (Jn 1:12). When we *believe,* we *receive* him; anything may take place, for all power is given unto him.

Paul prayed for the Corinthians. "That ye come behind in no gift; waiting for the coming of our Lord" (1 Cor 1:7), that the testimony of Christ might be confirmed in them unto the end. Wherever I am, whether traveling by train or ship, I preach to the people; it is God's plan for me; it is in order. The captain hears, the stewards hear—"Oh! they say, another on board!" The world thinks there is something wrong with you if you are full of zeal for God. On this ship they had scheduled an entertainment, and I said I would take part. It was the strangest thing for me; I said I would sin. I saw men dressed as clergymen entertaining the people with foolishness. I was troubled. I cried out to God. Then came my turn, just before the dance. A young woman came to take my songbook; she was half-dressed. She said, "I cannot play that." "Never worry," I said. Then I sang, "If I could only tell you how I love him, I am sure that you would make him yours today!" There was no dance. They began to weep, and six young men gave their hearts to God in my cabin.

The New Realm

No man that sins has power. Sin makes a man weak. Sin takes away his dignity and power. Sin dethrones, but purity strengthens. Temptation is not sin; the devil is a liar, he will try to take away your peace; you must live in the Word of God—"There is therefore now no condemnation to them which are in Christ Jesus, who walk not after the flesh, but after the Spirit" (Rom 8:1). If Christ condemn you not, who is he that can condemn you? Don't condemn yourself. If there is anything wrong, come to the blood. "If we walk in the light, as he is in the light, we have fellowship one with another, and the blood of Jesus Christ his Son cleanseth us from all sin" (1 Jn 1:7). You can come into a new experience in God, with all fear gone; you can live in a new realm—sons of God, with power. "If our heart condemn us not, then have we confidence toward God. And whatsoever we ask, we receive of him, because we keep his commandments, and do those things that are pleasing in his sight" (1 Jn 3:21-22).

Paul went to impart some spiritual gifts. Did Paul give gifts? No! No man can give a spiritual gift; such gifts are given by Jesus through the operation of the Spirit.

Before leaving home, I received a wire asking if I would go to

Liverpool. There was a woman with cancer and gall stones, very much discouraged. If I know God is sending me, my faith rises. The woman said, "I have no hope." "Well," I said, "I have not come from Bradford to go home with a bad report." God told me to establish her in the fact of the new birth. When she had the assurance that her sin was gone and she was born again, she said, "That is everything to me. Cancer is nothing now. I have got Jesus." The battle was won. God delivered her and she was free, and up and dressed, happy in Jesus. When God speaks, it is as a nail in a sure place. Will you *believe*? Life and immortality are ours in the gospel. This is our inheritance through the blood of Jesus—*life forevermore!*

From *Glad Tidings Herald* (New York City), May 1936, pp. 1–2. Sermon delivered as "Now! Now! Now!" at Colombier, Switzerland.

2
The "Go-Ye" of the Holy Spirit

The Word of God is wonderful, and I believe that God wants to fill us with his Word. He wants us to be so filled with it that no matter where we are, the Word will be lived out in us. The Word is power, the Word is life, the Word of God is faith, the Word is Jesus, and the Word of God is everlasting life to him that believeth. "He that heareth my word, and believeth on him that sent me, hath everlasting life" (Jn 5:24).

We Need Spiritual Power
And we need to be careful in reading the Word; I believe it is too precious to rush over; we have need to "rightly divide the Word of Truth." I want to speak to you tonight from Acts 1 of the power given by God. Oh, the power of the Holy Ghost! The power that quickens, the revealing power, the travailing power! The power that lives and moves! The power that brings about exactly what Jesus said: "Ye shall receive power" (Acts 1:8).

I love to think that Jesus wanted all his people to have power, that he wanted all men to be overcomers. Nothing but this power will do it. Power over sin, power over sickness, power over the devil, power over all the powers of the devil! I know that Jesus revealed by his Word these truths—"ye shall receive power."

I think there is nothing more beautiful to look at than to look at the Jordan in our experiences. The moment that Jesus was baptized in the Holy Ghost there was a manifestation that never appeared in the world before or since. Right there by the

Jordan was the Son of God, directly on the Son was the Holy Ghost in the form of a dove, and in the heavens above was the voice of God. It is beautiful to think of how the Trinity is interested in humanity.

Why have we power when the Holy Ghost comes? Because the Holy Ghost reveals Jesus; and Jesus, being the Word of God—in that Word there is all power. In order to understand what it means to have all power there are two things necessary; one is to have ears to hear and the other is to have hearts to receive it.

I am sure that everyone should know this truth that God sent the devil out of heaven because he was weak; if he had been strong he would not have sent him out. You never find anything that is impure get purer, but always viler, and Satan when he was cast out became weaker, viler, and more impure. Every born saint of God, filled with the Spirit, has a real revelation of that truth, "Greater is he that is in you, than he that is in the world" (1 Jn 4:4). I say this with as much audacity as I please.

I know evil spirits are in abundance and in multitudes; Jesus cast them out as legion. Satan and his angels were cast out of heaven and it seems to me that he had power to make evil spirits, but these are never as strong as Satan himself. Because of purity, holiness, and righteousness, they that are strong shall become more and more righteous; and equally so, Satan and his emissaries become viler and viler. But the believer, because of the Spirit that is in him, has the power to cast out the evil spirits. It must be so; God wants us to have this power in us; we must be able to destroy Satan's power wherever we go.

Using the Power

When I received the Holy Ghost, all the people thought that I had gone wrong; but we have to live to prove things. It is a strange fact, but the people of this world seem to be in a dilemma and don't know what to do. One day as I came into the house, my wife said, "Which way did you come?" I answered that I had come in by the back way. "Oh," she said, "if you had come in by the front you would have seen a man there in a terrible state. There is a crowd of people around him and he is in terrible straits."

Then the doorbell rang and she said, "There he is again. What will we do?" I said, "Just be quiet and still." I rushed to the door and just as I was opening it the Spirit said, "This is what I baptized you for." I was very careful then in opening the door, and then I heard the man crying outside. "Oh, I have committed the unpardonable sin. I am lost, I am lost." I asked him to come in and when he got inside, he said again in awful distress, "I am lost, I am lost." Then the Spirit came upon me and I commanded the lying spirit to come out of the man in the name of Jesus. Suddenly he lifted up his arms and said, "I never did it." The moment that the lying spirit was out, he was able to speak the truth.

I then realized the power in the baptism of the Holy Spirit. It was the Spirit that said, "This is what I baptized you for," and I believe we ought to be in the place where we will always be able to understand the mind of the Spirit amidst all the other voices in the world.

After the Holy Ghost has come upon you, you have power. I believe a great mistake is made in these days by people tarrying and tarrying after they have received. After you have received, it is "Go ye." Not "sit still," but "go ye into all the world, and preach the gospel." We shall make serious havoc of the whole thing if we turn back again and crawl into a corner, seeking something we already have. I want you to see that God depends upon us in these last days. There is no room for anyone to boast and to say, "Look at me, for I am somebody." They are of no value whatever. God is done with that man altogether; he will have a people to glorify him. He is doing what he can with that which he has, but we are so unwilling to move in the plan of God that he has to grind us many times to get us where he can use us.

Jesus was so filled with the Holy Ghost that he stood in the place where he was always ready. He was always in the attitude where he brought victory out of every opportunity. The power of the Holy Spirit is within us, but it can be manifested only as we go in obedience to that opportunity which we have before us. I believe if you wait until you think you have power after you have received the Holy Ghost, you will never know you have it. Don't you know that the child of God who is in possession of the baptism is inhabited by the power of the Spirit?

You will remember one time when they tried to throw Jesus from the brow of the hill, that he pressed through the midst of them and as soon as he got through he healed the man with the blind eyes. Pressing through the crowd which was trying to kill him, he showed forth his power. Some people might think that Jesus should have run away altogether, but he stopped to heal. This thought has comforted me over and over again.

One day, as I was waiting for a car, I stepped into a shoe-maker's shop. I had not been there long when I saw a man with a green shade over his eyes, crying pitifully and in great agony. It was heartrending, and the shoemaker told me that the inflammation was burning out his eyes. I jumped up and went to the man and said, "You devil, come out of this man in the name of Jesus." Instantly the man said, "It is all gone; I can see now." That is the only scriptural way, to begin to work at once, and preach afterwards.

You will find as the days go by that the miracles and healings will be manifested. Because the Master was touched with the feeling of the infirmities of the multitudes, they instantly gathered around him to hear what he had to say concerning the Word of God. However, I would rather see one man saved than ten thousand people healed. If you ask me why, I would call to your attention the Word, which says, "There was a certain rich man ... and [he] fared sumptuously every day" (Lk 16:19). Now we don't hear of this man having any diseases but it says, "*In hell* he lift[ed] up his eyes" (v. 23, emphasis added). We also read that there was a poor man full of sores who went to heaven. So we see that a man can die practically in good health but be lost, and a man can die in disease and be saved; so it is more important to be saved than anything else.

The Abundant Life

But Jesus was sent to bear the infirmities and the afflictions of the people and to destroy the works of the devil. He said that the thief (which is the devil) comes to steal and to kill and to destroy; "I am come that they might have life, and ... have it more abundantly" (Jn 10:10). I maintain that God wishes all his people to have the life more abundant. We have the remedy in the Word of God! Jesus paid the full price and the full redemption for every need, and where sin abounded, grace can come in and much more abound, and dispel all the sickness.

When I was traveling from England to Australia on January 6, [1922], I witnessed for Jesus, and it was not long before I had plenty of room to myself. If you want a whole seat to yourself just begin to preach Jesus. However, some people listened and began to be much affected. One of the young men said to me, "I have never heard these truths before. You have so moved me that I must have a good conversation with you." The young man told me that his wife was a great believer in Christian Science but was very sick now and although she had tried everything she had been unable to get relief, so was seeing a doctor. But the doctor gave her no hope whatsoever. In her dilemma, and facing the realities of death, she asked that she might have an appointment with the man in second class who was preaching, because, she said, "The things he says make us feel he is real."

So they made an appointment and when I got to her I felt it would be unwise to say anything about Christian Science so I just said, "You are in bad shape." She said, "Yes, they give me no hope." I said, "I will not speak to you about anything but will just lay my hands upon you in the name of Jesus and when I do, you will be healed." That woke her up and she began to think seriously.

For three days she was lamenting over the things she might have to give up. "Will I have to give up the cigarettes?" "No," I said. "Will I have to give up the dance?" And again I replied, "No." "Well, we have a little drinking sometimes and then we play cards also. Will I have to give—?" "No," I said, "you will not have to give up anything. Only let us see Jesus." And right then she got such a vision of her crucified Savior and Jesus was made so real to her that she at once told her friends that she could not play cards anymore, could not drink or dance anymore, and she said she would have to go back to England to preach against this awful thing, Christian Science.

Oh, what a revelation Jesus gave her! Now if I had refused to go when called for, saying that I first had to go to my cabin and pray about it, the Lord might have let that opportunity slip by. After you have received the Holy Ghost you have power; you don't have to wait.

The other day we were going through a very thickly populated part of San Francisco when we noticed a large crowd gathered. I saw it from the window of the car and said I had to get out, which I did. There in the midst was a boy in the agonies of death. As I threw my arms around the boy I asked what the trouble was and he answered that he had cramps. In the name of Jesus I commanded the devils to come out of him and at once he jumped up and, not even taking time to thank me, ran off perfectly healed. We're God's own children, quickened by his Spirit, and he has given us power over all the powers of darkness; Christ in us, the open evidence of eternal glory; Christ in us, the Life, the Truth, and the Way.

We have a wonderful salvation that fits everybody. I believe that a baptized [in the Spirit] person has no conception of the power God has given him until he uses that which he has. I maintain that Peter and John had no idea of the greatness of the power they had, but they began to speculate. They said, "Well, as far as money goes, we have none of that, but we do have something. We don't exactly know what it is, but we will try it on you: In the name of Jesus of Nazareth, rise up and walk" (see Acts 3:6). And it worked. To make yourself realize what you have in your possession you will have to try it, and I can assure you it will work all right.

Acts Still Being Performed
Some time ago I told a man that the Acts of the Apostles would never have been written if the apostles had not acted, and the Holy Spirit is still continuing his acts through us. May God help us to have some acts. There is nothing like Pentecost; and if you have never been baptized, you are making a big mistake by waiting. When God saved you, he meant for you to witness to others. And for you to think that you have to remain stationary and just get to heaven is a great mistake. The baptism [in the Spirit] is to make you a witness for Jesus. Thank God the hardest way is the best way; you never hear anything about the person who is always having an easy time. The preachers always tell of how Moses crossed the Red Sea when he was at wits' end. I cannot find the record of anyone in the Scriptures whom God used who was not first tried. So if you never have any trials, it is because you are not worth them.

God wants us to have power. When I was traveling in Sweden at a certain station early in the morning, a little lady and her daughter got into the train. I saw at once that the lady was in dreadful agony and asked my interpreter to inquire as to the trouble. With tears running down her face, she told how her daughter was taking her to the hospital to have her legs amputated. Everything that was possible had been done for her. I told her Jesus could heal. Just then the train stopped and a crowd of people entered until there was hardly standing room; but friends, we never get into a place that is too awkward for God, though it seemed to me that the devil had sent these people in at that time to hinder. However, when the train began to move along I got down, although it was terribly crowded, and putting my hands upon the woman's leg, I prayed for her in the name of Jesus. At once she said to her daughter, "I am healed. It is all different now; I felt the power go down my leg," and she began to walk about. Then the train stopped at the next station and this woman got out and walked up and down the platform, saying, "I am healed. I am healed."

Jesus was the *firstfruits* and God has chosen us in Christ and has revealed his Son in us that we might manifest him in power. God gives us power over the devil and when we say "the devil" we mean everything that is wicked and not of God. Some people say we can afford to do without the baptism of the Spirit but I say we cannot. I believe any person who thinks there is a stop sign between Calvary and the glory has made a big mistake.

Originally published as "After Ye Have Received Power" in
The Latter Rain Evangel **(Chicago), November 1922, pp. 2–5.**
Preached at Stone Church, Chicago, October 19, 1922.

Preparing for an International Ministry

Smith Receives Jesus as Savior

My grandmother was an old-time Wesleyan Methodist and would take me to the meetings she attended. When I was eight years of age there was a revival meeting held in her church. I can remember one Sunday morning at seven o'clock when all those simple folks were dancing around a big stove in the center of the church, clapping their hands and singing:

> *Oh, the Lamb, the bleeding Lamb,*
> *The Lamb of Calvary,*
> *The Lamb that was slain,*
> *That liveth again*
> *To intercede for me.*

As I clapped my hands and sang with them, a clear knowledge of the new birth came into my soul. I looked to the Lamb of Calvary. I believed that He loved me and had died for me. Life came in—eternal life—and I knew that I had received a new life which had come from God. I was born again. I saw that God wants us so badly that he has made the condition as simple as he possibly could—"Only believe." That experience was real and I have never doubted my salvation since that day.

Smith Wigglesworth, in Stanley H. Frodsham, *Smith Wigglesworth, Apostle of Faith* (Springfield, Mo.: Gospel Publishing House, 1948), p. 12. Used by permission.

3
The Danger of Deceiving Voices

I want to speak to you this morning on the subject of the gifts. These are days when all the saints need to be furnished with the graces and the gifts of the Spirit, and we must keep in mind that it is impossible to find the gifts of the Spirit made manifest without the graces. They always work harmoniously, and the person filled with the power of the Spirit will find that the one will help the other to strengthen the person in the needy hour.

A Purpose for the Gifts

We need a clear knowledge of the Word of God; we cannot put too much emphasis on that. Then I want to say also that God demands of every believer who has been baptized in the Holy Spirit that he should have some "acts." If you do not have them, you had better get face to face with God and demand from him your acts. When I was baptized in the Holy Ghost I received from God an utterance, as all people do when they receive the baptism; it was not an earthly language, but heavenly, and I was satisfied that God had granted unto me the Comforter, the Holy Ghost. But for nine months after that I never spoke in tongues, and then God gave to me the gift of tongues. I cannot say that I was very anxious or very hungry in asking for this, as I was longing more that I might speak as the Spirit gave utterance, but God knew what I needed to be able to help others along this line.

The next evening after I had received the gift of tongues, I was walking down the road, loaded with bundles, and God came upon me mightily and tongues began to come forth in terrific force. I walked down the road without stopping, but soon I began to realize that this had no intelligence in it for me and neither was it a profit to anyone else. There were some men working in a garden nearby and as soon as they heard this peculiar noise they stuck their heads through the fence to find out where it was coming from. Right then I said to God, "I will not leave till you give me the interpretation. You have poured forth a language, now you must interpret," and suddenly God gave the interpretation and that message has been fulfilled to the very letter over and over again. Since that time I have always claimed the right to have the interpretation.

I believe God wants us to be definite and I don't want you to run away with any wrong impression; if you come out on anything else but a definite side then God has not spoken. I am not here to make children but men and women of you, men and women after the mind of God; in spirit we must be children but in understanding we must be men and women. So if God says to us that we must understand spiritual gifts, you put your name right under that "must" and apply it as your very own. I believe as long as you dwell in the Spirit it is impossible for you ever to become twisted. Scripture clearly says that no man can call Jesus "Lord" except by the Holy Ghost, and every man who has the Holy Ghost believes all the Bible. The man who is filled with the Holy Ghost is filled with that which gave the Bible; he is filled with the very matter of the Bible, for the Word is Christ and the Holy Ghost has come to manifest Christ.

Preparing for the Gifts

You will always find that all the blessings and all the manifestations of the power of God which you receive, come always on the line of faith; every saved person is saved by faith, and saving faith is not something which you can take down and then hang up again. The saving faith of God is a permanent thing which God gave and which will remain with you. It is a gift, and because of that I know that everyone in this place can choose that gift, but you have to come into that blessing under the shadow of the blood and claim your rights in the Scriptures. I want to say, however, that no man can come to God and claim his blessings if he knows that God can put his finger on any sin in his life. God never will hear sinners, and if you expect any blessings don't come to him with sin in your life. When a man repents, God is gracious and full of mercy and forgives all sin, and that man can begin from that moment with the knowledge that God has removed the past from him.

There are two points in the twelfth chapter of 1 Corinthians which have helped me more than anything else and I am sure they will help you; one is this—Paul prayed for a keen conscience and also that he might not have his conscience seared. Do you know that a keen conscience is the greatest blessing anyone can have? A keen conscience is one which is easily disturbed, one which is easily broken and brought to repentance before God, one which will not permit you to sleep until everything is made right with your brother; a keen conscience is the place where God reigns supreme as a refiner of fire.

What is a seared conscience? It is a conscience which once was keen but the person got out of the will of God and failed to repent after committing a sin. God could not come in before that sin was undone, and the person went on sinning until he got to the place where he thought he had a right to sin. This is the most horrible place to be in. I pray that God will keep us in the place where we may hear his voice and heed it.

I want you to notice that I am trying to show you, by the grace of God, that if you keep in the fullness of the Spirit you will have such a revelation of the Word of God in your life that it will save you and keep you from stumbling. "The angel of the

Lord encampeth round about them that fear him, and delivereth them" (Ps 34:7). And, "The steps of a good man are ordered by the Lord" (Ps 37:23). He shall hide thee in the secret place, in the cleft of the rock, and in the time of adversity he shall raise up a standard against the enemy. It is the Lord who reigns supreme over his household whose house ye are, his establishment, and ye shall not be moved. This means that God establishes his kingdom in you and in me. Oh, how we need to be filled with the joy of the Lord which is our strength and to have a fresh inflow of his life and love!

A man who is filled with the Spirit must have three things flowing through him: the ministration, the operation, and the manifestation of the Spirit. It is to your detriment if you have not these three working in your life. If you are to keep your path all clear and bright you must remain steadfast, unmovable, always abounding in the work of the Lord. We must abound in hope, rejoice in tribulation, and then God will make straight paths for our feet. The man who has faith is never ruffled; he does not run off as if he had been shot but he is always resting, knowing that God is over all. We must understand these principles because faith is God. Faith is the knowledge of God. Faith is that which lays hold, which will not let go. Faith is inwrought God, faith is God inwrought; faith is that which brings heaven on earth and lives in it.

Gifts of the Spirit

The word which God would bring before us this morning is found in the tenth verse of the twelfth chapter of 1 Corinthians: "To another the working of miracles; to another prophecy; to another discerning of spirits; to another divers kinds of tongues; to another the interpretation of tongues." The first we have to deal with is the discerning of spirits. Perhaps this is the most necessary thing in this present day. In connection with this we must speak on the different kinds of voices, for so many people are disturbed by voices. They have an idea that it is the voice of God but begin to find themselves in difficulty as a result of obeying that voice. We are told in the fourth chapter of the Epistles of John that we must be able to discern the spirits. "Beloved, believe not every spirit, but try the spirits whether they are of God" (1 Jn 4:1). So God would have us know the difference between false prophecy and the spiritual, divinely appointed prophecy.

There are voices of all descriptions. I have for some time had to deal with people along this line. If ever you find a person under the power of the Evil One, you will find that that spirit will never acknowledge that Jesus came in the flesh; so if you want to test any spirit you can tell by that, because often the voice will come right out and say, "No, Jesus did not come in the flesh," and every spirit that confesseth not that Jesus came in the flesh is not of God. In the fourth chapter of Luke we see how Jesus dispelled the power of Satan. If you test a false spirit by the inward presence, it will disturb the peace of God and you will know it is of Satan. Make that thing worship the Christ within and the devil will flee. No person need be captured at any time with an evil thought, because we are to understand the wiles of the devil. Many people are disturbed with thoughts, evil thoughts which usually come early in the morning; but if these are tested, the person will always find that they will deny that Jesus came in the flesh. Perhaps some will ask, "Is not that a gift of the Spirit to discern the spirits?" Yes, it is a gift, but I want to say right here that if you are living in the fullness of the Spirit you will have this gift at any moment when needed. It will not be an abiding gift, just a gift for the needy moment. Every one of you without exception will find that as you go on and on with God you will have to be in the Spirit of God or you will be a failure. It is not possible to love the present evil world and have the

Holy Ghost within; you cannot love carnality and have the Holy Ghost. When the Holy Ghost comes in, every evil power will be dispelled till your whole body is free from sin and death. Oh, you need to be filled with the Holy Ghost to be ready at any moment for Satan's power!

Deceiving Voices

I want to show you how terribly deceiving these voices can be. One time when I was ministering in a certain place, two young ladies came into the room about five o'clock in the afternoon and instantly we perceived that something had taken place. One of them had on white kid gloves, which were spotted with blood. The excitement of these two ladies was such that one could see there was no peace abiding within. If ever you get out of the will of God and Satan comes in, you will find there is no rest. I have learned that if anything disturbs my peace it is always satanic. Neither one of these girls was willing to tell us what had happened. Now that is another way to test voices; God never reveals anything that you cannot tell on the housetop; everything God says to you, you can preach out. And if you feel you dare not tell what you have heard this voice telling you, you may be sure it is evil. I know people pride themselves that God speaks to them differently from everyone else; if ever you get to that place, you are on the wrong track, you are going one notch downward. It is the false pride of the devil. Some people seem to believe that the devil comes around only with horns and a long tail, big ears, and big eyes. Don't you believe it; the devil was turned out of heaven because of his pride and you must never forget that he is called the "angel of light." He has never lost that pride. And to you ministers I would say that whenever a person comes to you and says, "I never heard a man preach like you," you can make sure that is the voice of the devil every time.

These two girls were working in a telegraph station and Satan came as an angel of light to one, saying, "If you will obey me, I will make you the biggest and best preacher in the world." Now God never speaks that way. The girl became so excited about this and was sure it was the voice of God. She asked off from work for an hour and she became more excited as the voice repeated those words over and over; she got so worked up that she dug her nails into her flesh until the blood came. Then the voice further said to her, "You go to the station at 7:30 and a train will come in. Buy two tickets. Don't tell anyone what I have said except your sister. You will find a train leaving for Glasgow at 7:32. When you have purchased the two tickets you will have six pence over." Sure enough, after she had the two tickets she had the six pence left.

"Oh," you say, "that surely was the Lord speaking to her." Then another part of the message came true, for the train came in exactly at 7:32. She was to find in one of the coaches a gentleman sitting with his back to the engine and this man was to have all the money that the girl wanted and was to have it deposited in a certain bank. It needed only brains to think it out, but the people who get to that place do not use their brains and will not let anyone else think for them. They say, "Don't you try to stop me, for no one can stop me. You do not need to talk to me, you have not had the Lord speak to you." This is a dangerous place.

These two girls went up and down the coach, the full length of the railway train, and failed to find anyone fitting that description. Someone said she had better come down for the next train, so they stayed there until nine o'clock. Then the voice said to her, "Now that I have found you will obey me, I will make you the best and biggest missionary in the world." You have no idea what it took to get those two girls out of that awful delusion, but God prevailed and both are now on the mission field, doing good work. Never be unwilling to take advice, for God has other people who know his voice and you must be willing to learn.

While ministering in another place I had a letter from York, England, saying that they had about fourteen people who were seeking to be filled with the Holy Spirit. They were asking me to come and give them a few addresses on this important subject. So I went, and upon arriving I heard the best news anyone could wish to hear. The people said, "We have had one of the finest men to join us that you have ever seen; he is a fine teacher. We will just wait and see if he received the baptism and then we are thinking of keeping him here as pastor." That was all very good. The preaching went on and God manifested himself; the power of God came down and people began seeking. About 10:30 that night we saw this promising young man laid out under the power of God. The saints could hardly keep quiet, they rejoiced so over God's dealings. They would say, "Now we have him; when he receives his baptism we will have the best man," and they were so jubilant. Everything went well and then about 11:30 the power of God slew him and divine utterance came forth and we were all glad and had a good time praising God.

When he was getting ready to go home the saints came around and said, "Oh, we are so glad you got through! You certainly are the best teacher." And then one woman went up to him and said, "I shouldn't wonder if you were not the second John the Baptist." That night, while on his way home, the devil came to this young man and said, "I shouldn't wonder if you were not the second John the Baptist." But he was able to throw if off and would have nothing to do with the voice. But listen, in the middle of the night the devil awakened him: "You are John the Baptist. Arise." He was unable to shake that off, and the next day he went up and down the street, shouting "I am John the Baptist."

Who spoiled him? The saints. Who was to blame for his

downfall? Those people who should have had more sense. Never tell a preacher how wonderful he is. He knows he is nothing if he is in the right place, and don't you try to make him something. If you do, you will get out of the will of the Lord and get him out too.

Is there deliverance for these people? Oh, how we need to distinguish the voice of God from that of Satan. We need to know that God the Holy Ghost has a better plan for us than that. I have met such wrecks. I came across one of the finest men in the ministry, such a good teacher who had been blessed to all the assemblies. It makes me weep now to think of it. You couldn't teach him anything, and if you spoke to him he would tell you that God had not spoken to you as to him, adding, "Don't you know that God has made me a prophet?" You couldn't move him.

Discerning of Spirits
The important question is, How can we tell the difference between the voice of Satan and the voice of God? It is very simple. *If you don't aspire to be something you will never get into that dangerous place; it is when your own heart desires it that the devil can switch you there.* Never desire to be anything, for in the true Christian's life no man wants to be anything but desires Christ to be his all and in all; it is to live only for the glory of God, to be filled with the power of God, to be kept at all times in that place where you know you are nothing and can do nothing but for the grace of God. If you ever think you are anything of importance, consider Jesus, and if you consider Jesus you will find there is no room for exaltation, only brokenness of heart and contriteness of spirit. The kingdom of God is brought forth in righteousness and truth. What is truth? Truth says that Jesus is the Way; truth says that Jesus is the ideal for us, and we must be like him; no man who truly follows Jesus and reads the words in

Philippians can say any more about himself. Jesus who was the Son of God made himself of no reputation, took on himself the form of a servant, and humbled himself even to the death of the cross.

Discerning of spirits: how much we need it! Sometimes I have been shut in for weeks with demon-possessed men and in the middle of the night watches these evil spirits have jumped upon me, but in the midst of it I have held my ground for God and prayed the man right into perfect deliverance. I am especially reminded of one man. I was shut in for weeks with him, and every time an evil spirit was cast out of him it leaped on me. The last one to be cast out laid hold of me so that I had to deliver myself first before I could deliver anyone else. In this case the evil spirits used to come out of this man and bind me so that I had to stand still. I couldn't move and the man who was possessed would stand and look at me. As I commanded the evil spirit to leave I would be free again. That man today is perfectly delivered and preaching the gospel. It took someone who would lay hold of God and not let go until the work was completed.

I have learned many things by experience; and if I can make you see this morning that you never will be anything, I will be able to get something done here. Anything that is not done for the glory of God is not worth having. God sees in secret and will reward openly; we will have to have secret power with God. We will have to meet God face to face in the closet and then we can come out strong for him.

From *The Latter Rain Evangel* (Chicago), December 1922, pp. 5–9. Preached as "The Gift of Discerning of Spirits: Beware of Deceiving Voices" at the Union Pentecostal Meeting, Chicago, November 3, 1922.

Preparing for an International Ministry

Report From Bradford

Bowland Street Mission, Bradford, has had many days of God's right hand and has won many trophies of the cross and seen much of the working of the mighty hands of God. But none of the past days resemble those of the present.

Thank God, we are in the midst of that which might be called the soul's awakening. Those that were lifeless and helpless (having to be carried), are now full of life and prepared to carry others from the cold, indifferent, normal life to be red-hot, Spirit-filled saints, speaking and singing in tongues. They have clear witnessing power and discernment, and can be counted upon for any real, active, vigilant work. They are full of love and kindness, desiring, longing, earnestly seeking, and beseeching God to open the windows of heaven and pour out a real revival power to awaken and shake England and the world. We fully believe we are in the last days, and before the Lord comes we trust to see the mightiest revival the world has ever seen or witnessed.

We have seen demons cast out, and the very devil of disease rebuked, and the continual power and blessing fully resembling Mark 16:17. All glory be to God.

Smith Wigglesworth, "Report from Yorkshire," *Confidence*, April 1908, pp. 6–7.

4
The Gift of Prophecy: Its Use and Misuse

I believe the Lord will impress us with the necessity of under-standing the gifts of the Spirit, why and when and where we should manifest them. I have been trying to impress upon you the importance of being filled with the Holy Ghost, but I do not want you to think that you can understand or use gifts apart from the Giver. I know that the Holy Ghost has nine gifts to minister, and I know that Jesus has gifts, and you will never find that the gifts of the Holy Ghost and the gifts of Jesus clash. They are perfectly in order.

In the fourth chapter of Ephesians we read that Jesus went up on high and received gifts for men, and the most remark-able of all is that he received gifts for the rebellious. Paul knew that, because God had been ministering to him gifts, and yet he was the most rebellious of all. When you look at that calling and see the remarkableness of his life and see how he persecuted the church; and then in his examination of his own personality, his weakness, he calls himself the chief of sinners. And in that revelation, realizing how God had been gracious to him, he writes here, "even the rebellious also."

Gifts Are to Glorify God

So all Spirit-filled, without exception, are eligible for the gifts. It is not what you were or are, it is what God will do for you, and you must see that by the power of God all things are pos-sible. He wants every person in this place to know that he is not and never will be pleased with a fig tree that bears nothing but leaves. Jesus was disappointed in it. Never think that gifts can ever be of any source whatever, only on the lines they have to be exercised, wrought out by the power of God. You must never allow yourself to be led into any trap to use a gift. If you do, you will surely have trouble in your life.

You must understand that all the gifts are to be made manifest only for the glory of Jesus. Everything that you have come heir to since you came into the fact of salvation, everything from that day, without exception, has been and must continue to be for the glory of God. If it is not, you will find yourself amongst the wood and the hay and the stubble. There is nothing going to be of any importance to your life or any other lives, only that which is gold and silver and precious stones, something that cannot be destroyed by fire. And so God would have us this morning to have an inward revelation that we have been delivered from the corruption of the world, so that the powers of Christ may rest upon us, that the glory of God may be seen, and that we may be inwardly and outwardly always bearing about in our body the dying of the Lord, that the life of the Lord should be always eminently manifested to the glory of God.

Message in tongues with interpretation: *The Lord of glory came from the heights thereof to dispense of his graces in the world, in the church to establish and bring forth a ministry of power that should permeate the earth, and bring to naught the things that are.**

---

*Here and in other chapters, Wigglesworth gives a "message in tongues" (or in an unknown language) and then interprets into English. An introduction to and regulations for use of these gifts are given in 1 Corinthians 12 and 14.

Being Channels for Him

One of the reasons Jesus came was to make in the world new orders in the Spirit. We must this morning see our vocation in the Spirit. We must under all circumstances understand that God has something far in excess of that day when we first saw the light. You must see that he took your sins only for one purpose, that you might be channels for the covenant of promise.

The fourth chapter of Ephesians is very distinct on this line, that Jesus went up on high, and he made prophets, apostles, evangelists, and teachers, and it was for "the perfecting of the saints" of which you will see the need. God has nothing in his ministry for us on any lines, only perfection. God is a cleanser. All the mighty movings of God are always to purge you, perfect you, make you holy, make you see that he can dwell in you mightily, and move in you by the Spirit gloriously. We have to be insulators, as it were, of the mighty power, the saving power in the world. There is such a thing as a preserving power; God wants us to be a preserving power in the world, that sin may have no place where we are; God controlling everything we touch.

Did you hear me say that you must not expect gifts until after you have received the Holy Ghost? Gifts are the property of the Holy Ghost, and they do not clash, as I said, with the gifts of Jesus. If you are filled with the Holy Ghost, he will drive you, from day to day and hour to hour, to the truth. Jesus is the Way, the Truth, and the Life, and the Word of God is the power of the Christ and the life of Christ.

It will be no comparison, however you are filled with the Spirit, however you are filled with joy, whatever peace you have, and whatever conditions are in your life, to your leaving out the Word of God. If you do, you will leak out and become weak; your peace will fade and your joy will leak out. The Word of God brings one into a place of fact. We must be in a place where we know what we know, and the baptized believer knows what he doesn't know. He has forgotten a lot that he used to know and that is a blessing.

Now, beloved, we dealt with the word of wisdom, and we must clearly understand about the power of the Holy Ghost within the body. Paul says, "I would not have you ignorant, brethren, of spiritual gifts." We must examine ourselves and see if we are in this faith, for I reckon that all the spiritual revelations of God are on the lines of faith, and you cannot have faith without you have the Word, for the Word of God is faith. If you will turn to Hebrews 12:2, you will find that Jesus is the author and finisher of our faith; so if you have Jesus you have faith. You will have the Giver within you. And as you let the Word of God move in your life, you will find you are living in the real place of the personality of Jesus Christ.

Essentials to Ministry

In the first place, the Holy Ghost must make within you ministrations; in the second, it must be in operation; and the third essential is the manifestation. If you are afraid of manifestation you haven't come into operation, and if you are afraid of operation, it is because you never had ministrations. The same Spirit will bring you these three effects; and when they are in your heart and life, you will find God takes you and moves upon you just as he did upon Moses and Aaron and Samuel and the prophets. The difference between the dispensation of the Jews and the dispensation of grace to the Gentiles is this: in the days of the prophets the Holy Ghost was upon them from time to time. The Spirit of the Lord was upon Samuel from time to time; the Spirit of the Lord came upon Moses, upon Samson; it came upon Ezekiel and the prophets. These operations were types of the greater dispensation of things to come. Remember, this is an important matter, because if you hear the Word of

God and do not take heed you will come into the line where God uses the Gentiles to perfect the Jews. Without us, the Jews cannot be made perfect. So we are living in a great day; we are in the dispensation of the grace of God, with the fullness of the revelation of the inward power, personality, and presence of the Holy Ghost. And so we are in a greater day in every way than the Jews were. Not that the day isn't coming for the Jews; it is, but we are in a greater day than the Jews have had heretofore.

No Spiritual Mixture

God has an appointment with every baptized soul, and his appointment is that we are in the earth for the specialty of witnessing and bringing out the glories of the cross. No baptized soul who is going on with God can ever again enter into worldly things as long as he lives. And God will strip him of all superfluities and of foolishness. If you are not stripped of worldliness there becomes a mixture in the church instead of a perfect place in God. Mixtures are always bad; that is why there was to be no mixture in the priest's garment; it had to be pure linen and pure wool. I find that the world is becoming worse and worse on these lines because she is full of mixtures. When you go to shop you never know whether you will get the pure article or adulteration. The Spirit of God is no mixture. If, after you have received the Holy Ghost, you go back into carnal lines, the people will know it. The man who is going on with God can tell it in a minute. You cannot deceive him. Language is not Spirit, and noise is not Spirit, and you cannot get it that way. The power of God is Presence. Moses said, "If thy presence go not with me, carry us not up hence" (Ex 33:15).

If the gifts of the Spirit are not in the church, you can call it what you like, but it is a black-letter church, less than what God intends. You can be baptized in water a thousand times; it will not make the Spirit move. You will have to have something better than water baptism. You will have to have fire. You will have to have the inward presence of God. Where the Holy Ghost comes, the gifts are manifest, unless the church has backslid, and "Ichabod"* is over the door. Oh, you can backslide, and there is not a grace that you cannot forfeit! "Let him that thinketh he standeth take heed lest he fall" (1 Cor 10:12). There is only one way for every one of us to keep faithful and that is, down in humiliation, brokenness of spirit, living victorious over the natural, and having the light of life in our being.

I have had people say to me, "You know I once had the gifts of healings and I haven't them now." I never believe it, whatever they say, for the simple reason that when the gift is manifested, that is a permanent gift; it is always there. But I would go so far as to say you may be so filled with the Holy Ghost that a gift may be manifested because of the fullness of the presence of God in your body. If you lived in the place where the power of God was upon you and the virtue of Christ passed through you, and if you haven't that fullness now, it is because you have passed out of the depths of God. Do not say you do not know how it happened. You always know. A stranger can never enter into your heart. "The heart knoweth his own bitterness" (Prv 14:10), but a stranger can never enter into its recesses.

We Must Live in the Spirit
I warn you that if you want to continue to have the power of God manifested through you, you have to live in the Spirit continually—not occasionally, not once a day—but always. Oh, beloved, at any cost, pay any price to live in it, for it is worth the world. I would rather speak five minutes under the unction of the Holy Ghost than have a thousand dollars given to me. I thank God we may live in the Spirit and walk in the Spirit, and

*Meaning "the glory has departed."

be continually filled with the Spirit. Then the gifts of healings will be manifested on these lines, and you will find that when God gets you to that place he will make you definite. For instance, I was speaking in a meeting in a place, and as I sat in that meeting I saw a man there in a state of terrible pain. I said, "Brethren, you must allow me to deliver this man so he can enjoy the services." He came on the platform. It is a wonderful thing when the Spirit of God comes upon you and you are not touching a person in fear, not experimenting, but are in a place where you know. I told the people this man would be healed the moment I laid my hands upon him. Upon the pledge of God's truth to me, I rebuked the thing and the man was perfectly free, to all the people's amazement.

Here is another instance: I just received a letter from Springfield, Missouri, about a man for whom I prayed. His mouth was filled with cancer, and he was in pain all the time. I said to the people, "This man will be delivered of this cancer and be made free within a few days. From the moment I put my hand upon his mouth he will have no more pain." The moment I did that, instantly the pain lifted. Now I have this letter: "You will be interested to know about the man with the cancer. One day he spit out half of the cancer and the next day the balance. He lost about a quart of blood and is weakened as a result, but God has surely undertaken."

Believe the Word and Keep Humble

Now gifts of healings, miracles, are identical with what God's Word says. It is not what we think, it is not how we feel: it is what God's Word says. Dare you believe it? Jesus, speaking expressly to the seventy who went out and came back saying what wonderful things had happened, said, "Behold, I give unto you power to tread on serpents and scorpions, and over all the power of the enemy: and nothing shall by any means hurt you" (Lk 10:19). But let me say this: No man will go forward with God if he gets proud. To keep in touch with God he must continue humble. You will never find that God can use a man who is proud. His Word says, "My soul shall make her boast in the Lord: the humble shall hear thereof, and be glad" (Ps 34:2). And you will find that God is preparing the hearts of the humble to receive his Word. "The rich he hath sent empty away"—the people who feel they can manage without God—but "he hath filled the hungry with good things" (Lk 1:53).

And so God would not have us under any circumstances to think that we are in the place of blessing when we are not in the place of humiliation and humbleness. It cannot be. Jesus, our blessed Lord, was the most meek, the most lovely, and the most beautiful in character. You never find him like this: "Stand aside now. I am a man who has the gifts!" You never find that in Jesus, but he was so moved with compassion that he could raise the widow's son. We will not have had compassion except by the inward power of God moving us. Everybody can be humble. It costs nothing except your pride and ugly self to be put out of the way.

What Is a Miracle?

A miracle is where the power of the Spirit of God comes to absolute helplessness, where no human aid can reach, but where God alone comes and performs the supernatural, when God comes and the body is made whole in a minute—not in an hour or a week, but in a minute—that is a miracle.

I was going into a big meeting in London one day and a man who stood in the doorway said to me, "Don't you know me?" I said, "No, I do not recognize you just at this moment." "Don't you know my daughter?" he said. "No." "Nor my wife?" They all stood there. "No, I seem to have lost recollection of you." "Well," he said, "I am Smith from Brighton." Then I recognized them. "Now," he said, "look at her," turning to his daughter, a beautiful young woman. They had brought her to me stretched out in a carriage where she had been for years and years, helpless, had to be lifted about; and in a moment, as soon as God's touch came upon her, from the crown of her head to the sole of her foot, there wasn't a weakness. She was perfect and has been walking ever since. No man can do those things. There never has been a man living who could do it, only the Man, Christ Jesus, and if we wish to be used in that way we shall have to have him, know him, and understand him, for he is the Holy One.

A Venture in Faith

The ministry of healing became so mighty in Australia that in some places I had to give up a day to minister to the sick, beginning at nine and continuing until four o'clock in order to get through, praying with nearly seven hundred people. There is a chance for a lifetime. You talk about opportunity; I would not take the world's worth for the opportunity, and we ought to buy up our opportunities. You never will know what you have until you experiment upon what you have in faith. Every man that has ever done anything for God was amazed to find God respond the first time he ventured out in faith. I say all these things to you to move you into a living faith in God, for what will it profit me without some of you are turned into flames of fire. What will it profit me if I turn from these meetings and you have only heard my voice and seen me? God would never have John and Peter and James to move up and down the world and leave people where they found them. They were to make disciples of all nations, and in the name of Jesus I am here, as it were, to make disciples; to create within you a deeper thirst and a longing for deeper things of God. If this is not my object I ought not to be here. We have a higher calling, a nobler calling, than to be fascinated with things of ourselves. It is not the fascination of ourselves, it is the inward fire that burns by the power of God that attracts.

The Gift of Prophecy

A very important gift is the gift of prophecy. I reckon no man can work miracles without he has gentleness, and no man can ever be a prophetic utterance for God without he is good. You will find that those gifts are in perfect conjunction with the graces. First, *the word of wisdom,* you will find love controls the word of wisdom, and you will find *the word of knowledge* is controlled by joy; *faith* coincides exactly with peace, and you will never have faith if you have not peace. Peace comes from an unmovable, established position on the Word of God. Now you could not have *gifts of healings* without you knew something about long-suffering, and you could not have the *gift of miracles* without you knew something about gentleness; nor *prophecy* without you knew something about goodness.

We must never despise prophecy, but I will tell you what you must do. You must always judge it, and you will find that a person who refuses to have his prophecy judged is wrong inwardly, and his expressions are wrong outwardly. I know people think discernment is a wonderful gift, and this is striking, the people who have discernment. I will tell you what would be a fine thing: If those who *think* they have discerning of spirits would display it upon themselves, they would get such a revelation of themselves in twelve months they would not be harsh or critical of others. God does not want us to be harsh or critical of others. He means us to be filled with the Spirit.

Prophecy causes more trouble than anything else in the world. If you will turn to the Old Testament you will find prophetic utterances. Prophetic utterances beginning in the flesh and ending in the flesh are wrong. People do it because they like to be heard, and it destroys confidence. There are men who believe they have power to go up and down and make prophets. It is unscriptural, and I can prove it to a very ordinary man. The man who would make a man a prophet is in a bad way, and the man who is willing to be made a prophet is in a worse way. No man can save you, no man can baptize you in the Spirit, no man can give a gift. Turn to Ephesians 4:8, "Wherefore he saith, When he ascended up on high, he led captivity captive, and gave gifts unto men."

Who is he that ascended up on high but Jesus? "He gave some, apostles; and some, prophets; and some, evangelists; and some, pastors and teachers" (Eph 4:11). No man has ever had the power to give these offices. The most you can do is to lay hands on a person to receive the Holy Ghost, which is a perfectly scriptural thing to do. I have seen hundreds receive the Holy Ghost while I have had my hands upon them, but was it I? No, but you may have the power of God so upon you and through you and in you, until from you will flow the healing virtue as from the body of Jesus; and when you touch people, they will be healed. I have touched people who were dying, and they have been instantly healed from head to foot. I remember one night going into a house where a woman lay dying. Her husband came to me and said his wife would like to say just a word before she passed away. I went in and took hold of her hand, and she said, "Sam, I am healed. The virtue from Smith is going all over me." She was perfectly healed in that touch.

I believe, too, that if you are filled with the Holy Ghost you will create a desire for the Spirit, an inward thirst for God, and with the laying on of hands, the gift of the Spirit will be moving in that man. You do not bestow the gift, but the power of God works through you, and remember there is never a baptism of the Holy Ghost but that God is there. It is the promise of the Father. You never have a baptism of the Holy Ghost without Jesus is there, for he baptized; you never have the baptism of the

Holy Ghost without the Holy Ghost comes in, so you have the Trinity there. Every touch of God that I get makes me see how I need more of him all the time. I hope none of you in this meeting will ever be so foolish as to allow any person to make you anything, but that you will all be willing to let God make you something.

Is prophecy real? It is just as real as anything else. When you have prophecy, be sure that the Spirit of God gives it; and when it is given, be sure it is nothing personal. There are foolish and ridiculous things taking place in some parts. I think a man ought to have the choice of his own wife, but when prophecy goes forth that you are to have a wife of their choosing, you are on dangerous ground. When prophecy goes forth that you are to have a certain house on a certain street, you know that is carnal. All these things make our position one of ridicule and a laughingstock in the eyes of the people. God save us from foolishness and from ignorance. How will he save us? When we are humble enough to be taught.

True and False Prophecies
The deceptiveness of the devil is shown in prophecy tremendously. When prophetic utterances from the Lord go forth they are of great blessing to everybody, but where is the mistake? It often lies in people going up to the one who has given the message and saying, "Oh, I got so blessed through that prophecy. It was wonderful. We must have it written down," and you spoil the people who give the prophecy. It is a very serious thing because prophecy is a gift, and the seriousness of the thing is to use a gift without the power of God upon you. They begin to say, "Thus saith the Lord," and go on forever.

Now listen: If the prophecy is not given in the unction of the Spirit, it will be damnation. It is blessed when clear prophecy comes through, because a person may have prophecy who knows very little of the Word of God and yet have perfect prophetic utterance. If you turn to the seventh chapter of the Acts of the Apostles and read the prophecy that Stephen utters, you'll see it is most sublime. As he prophesied under the power of the Spirit, the power of the devil came upon those people; they couldn't stand it. It meant his death but it was in the power of the Spirit.

There is something about prophecy that makes you know it is God. Here is a man in the assembly who starts in to pray. He has prayed many times in the assembly and you have been blessed, but suddenly you catch fire and you feel the inspiration as the Spirit prays through him, and you know when God has finished and when he begins his own prayer. The lesson to learn in Pentecost is when to finish, for it is a serious thing to go on after the Lord has finished. You begin in the Spirit and end in the flesh. The same thing is true of prophecy; they begin in the Spirit and end in the flesh.

Then there are some foolish people in the world who when they know someone has the gift of prophecy, go around to his house and try to find out something by prophecy. That is as bad as going to a medium. Do you think you can get a prophetic message on those lines? Now listen: Wisdom is justified by her children, and if you do not keep in wisdom, nobody wants anything to do with you, so do not work along those lines. If you want to know the mind of God, get it in the Book; you do not need a prophet to tell you. God is his own interpreter.

I was saved when I was a boy eight years old, and I have never lost the witness. I never went to school and so I had no chance to learn to read. When I got married, my wife taught me both to read and write, though she could never teach me to spell, but I do the best I can. I so love the Word of God I do not remember spending any time but with the Word. Papers and books have no fascination for me. The Word of God is my meat and my drink. I get a fresh breath from heaven every time I read it. It is full of prophetic utterances that make my soul rejoice.

Originally "The Use and Misuse of the Gift of Prophecy," in *The Latter Rain Evangel* **(Chicago), January 1923, pp. 17–21. Preached at the Union Pentecostal Meeting, Chicago, November 2, 1922.**

Preparing for an International Ministry

The Pentecostal Experience

The story of Smith Wigglesworth, the Bradford plumber who became a world-renowned evangelist, has often been told. Alexander Boddy, the vicar of All Saints, Monkwearmouth, Sunderland (1886–1922) had been deeply influenced by the Welsh Revival, the Azusa Street, USA, meetings, and T.B. Barratt, in Norway. The Pentecostal movement, as it later developed in Britain, can be traced to meetings in Sunderland led by Barratt.

Smith Wigglesworth was amongst many believers from all over the country who visited Sunderland seeking the baptism in the Spirit. He was counseled by Mrs. Boddy who led him into the experience.

Before his Sunderland experience, Smith usually sat meekly alongside his wife, Polly, as she preached. However, soon after he returned from Sunderland, he was on his feet speaking from the text, "The Spirit of the Lord is upon me, because he hath anointed me..." (Lk 4:18).

Such was the impact of his sermon that his wife was moved to cry out, "That's not my Smith, Lord, that's not my Smith!" Truly her Smith was not the same man as before. As he spoke, she witnessed the beginning of a ministry that was to take her husband around the world.

Pentecost! Acts 2! Power! Witnessing! These are words which create a longing for a revived Church. More and more prayer groups are committed to prayer for revival. Samuel Chadwick reminded us that "The Church is the creation of the Holy Ghost. It is a Community of believers who owe their religious life from first to last to the Spirit. Apart from him there can be neither Christian nor Church. The Christian religion is not institutional but experimental."

Back in the 1940s, when my father spoke of acquaintances who had moved to "Pentecost," he usually meant that they had joined one of the classical Pentecostal churches which resulted from the events in Sunderland.

But Pentecost (as the Christian churches understand the term) is not a denomination; it is an experience available to every Christian. The "promise of the Father" (Acts 1:4) is for all who repent of their sin and are baptized in the name of the Lord Jesus for the forgiveness of sins. Far more than the return of a "feel good factor," it is an experience of cleansing from sin and empowering for service. It is a gift for effective witnessing, increased holiness of life, and dedicated service.

Major Norman Armistead, in "Comment," *The Flame*, May-June 1997. Published by the Flame Trust, Gloucester, England. Used by permission.

5
The Active Life of the Spirit-Filled Believer

These are the last days, the days of the falling away. These are days when Satan has a great deal of power. But we must keep in mind that Satan has no power only as he is allowed. And we must never think that Satan has power over the believer. If I could only establish that fact in your hearts, it would be something living all the time. Satan has no power over the believer. "That wicked one toucheth him not" (1 Jn 5:18). So we must understand that all things that fall to our lot are according to the mind and will of God. "All things work together for good to them that love God" (Rom 8:28). We may be chastised by God, but it is only because he wants us to have his holiness. We may have any amount of correction, but it will only be the touch of the Lord to bring us nearer to him, that we may be at all times more than conquerors.

I want you to clearly see that the day will come when the Evil One will have a great power. And you can imagine that just as that day draws near the believer is more greatly insulated with divine revelation and more power. You will find the saints will become more holy and will have more liberty and more power. As Satan has power, the saints will have greater power. And just as the day comes for the saints to be caught away, we shall have mighty power on all lines, and the last great power will take us out of the world. Know this fact: that God is always revealing himself on every line and thought to keep the believer at such a standard of victory that he is in the place where he never need be defeated.

Being Ready to Do God's Work

There is nothing helping me so much in these days as the fact that God is loosing me. It is a great thing to know that God is loosing you from the world, loosing you from a thousand things. You have to have the mind of God on all things. If you don't, you will stop his working. I had to learn that as I was on the water en route to Australia. We stopped at a place called Aden, where they were selling all kinds of ware. Amongst other things were some beautiful rugs and feathers, ostrich feathers in great quantities. They were very lovely for those who wanted feathers, but I had no room for them. However, there was a gentleman in the first-class section who wanted feathers, and it appeared that he had bought one lot, and the next lot put up was too big; he did not want so many. He said to me, "Will you join me?"

I knew I did not want feathers, for I had no room or use for them and wouldn't know what to do with them if I got them. However, he pleaded with me to join him. I perceived it was the Spirit as clearly as anything and I said, "Yes, I will." So the feathers were knocked down for three pounds. Then I found the man had no money with him. He had plenty, but of course it was on the boat. I perceived it was the Spirit again, so it fell to my lot to pay for the feathers. He said to me, "I will bring the money and give it to one of the stewards." I replied: "No, that is not business. I am known all over the ship. You seek me out."

The man came and brought the money. I said, "God wants me to talk to you. Now sit down." So he sat down and in ten minutes' time the whole of his life was unhinged, unraveled, broken up, so broken that like a great big baby he wept and cried for salvation. It was the feathers that did it. But you know, friends, it seems to me we will never know the mind of God till we know the voice of God. The striking thing about Moses is that it took him forty years to learn human wisdom, forty years to know his helplessness, and forty years to live in the power of God. One hundred twenty years it took to teach that man and sometimes it seems to me it will take many years to bring us just where we can tell the voice of God, the leadings of God, and the lines of God, and all his will concerning us.

But I am speaking to people this morning who ought to know the mind of the Lord because God wants us thoroughly furnished unto all good works and always ready to give a good account of the hope that is within us. We must always be ready as the accountant keeping the books and ordering for a business. We must be ready with all the mind of God, for the day is at hand and we must clearly see that nothing shall come against us but that which shall be on the line of profit. Everything we touch shall be definitely for the operation of God's thought for a world's need. It will be so.

Knowing the Mind of God
Beloved, every one of us ought to know the mind of God on the gifts. I notice in particular that the manifestation of the Spirit of God is given "to profit withal." I want you to know that my addresses from time to time cannot be in any way less than on the baptism of the Spirit because I see in that baptism all revelation, all illumination, everything for which God in Christ was to be brought forth into perfect light, that we might be able to see right into that holiness of his which was filled with all the fullness of God. Then we will understand that he was the firstfruits on every line so that we may live the same, produce the same, and be in every activity a son of God with power. It must be so. We must not limit the Holy One. And we must clearly see that God brought us forth on natural lines to make us supernatural, that we might be changed all the time on the line of supernatural basis, that we may every day live so in the Spirit, that all of the revelations of God are just like a great big canvas thrown

before our eyes, and we see clearly step by step into all the divine will of God.

There are three things in particular that we must understand concerning the baptism of the Spirit. Any assembly, I don't care what it is, that puts its hand upon the working of the Spirit will surely bring trouble to that assembly. The assembly must be as free in the Spirit as possible, and you must allow a certain amount of extravagance when people are getting through to God. I notice that unless we are very wise, we can easily interfere and quench the power of God which is upon us. It is an evident fact that one man in a meeting, filled with unbelief, can make a place for the devil to have a seat. And it is very true to fact, that if we are not careful we may quench the spirit of some person who is innocent and is incapable on the line of innocence to help himself. "We then that are strong ought to bear the infirmities of the weak" (Rom 15:1). You must be careful in that. If you want an assembly full of life you must have an assembly in which the Spirit of God is manifested. And in order to keep at the boiling pitch of molted heat, of that blessed incarnation of the Spirit, you must be as simple as babies; you must be as harmless as doves and as wise as serpents.

In this I always ask God for a leading of grace. It takes grace to be in a meeting because it is so easy if you are not careful, to get on the natural side. The man who is a preacher, if he has lost the unction, will be well repaid if he will carefully, inwardly repent and get right with God and get the unction back. It never pays us to be less than always spiritual, and we must have a divine language always on the line, and the language must be of God. Beloved, if you come into the real perfect line of the grace of God, one thing will certainly take place in your life. You will change from that old position of the world's line where you were judging everybody, and where you were not trusting anyone, and come into a place where you will have a heart that will believe all things; where you will have a heart that under no circumstances reviles again when you are reviled.

I know many of you think many times before you speak once. Here is a great word: "For your obedience is come abroad unto all men. I am glad therefore on your behalf: but yet I would have you wise unto that which is good, and simple concerning evil" (Rom 16:19). Innocent. No inward corruption or defilement, that is full of distrusts, but just a holy, divine likeness of Jesus that dares believe that God Almighty will surely watch over all. Hallelujah! "There shall no evil befall thee, neither shall any plague come nigh thy dwelling. For he shall give his angels charge over thee, to keep thee in all thy ways" (Ps 91:10-11). The child of God who is rocked in the bosom of the Father has the sweetest touch of heaven, and the honey of the world is always in it.

Heart-Burning Religion

Oh, if the saints only knew how precious they are in the sight of God they scarcely would be able to sleep for thought of his watchful, loving care. Oh, he is a precious Jesus! He is a lovely Savior! He is divine in all his attitude toward us, and makes our hearts to burn. There is nothing like it. They said on the road to Emmaus, "Did not our heart burn within us, while he talked with us by the way, and while he opened to us the scriptures?" (Lk 24:32). Oh beloved, it must be so today.

It will greatly help you to see three things: First, the ministration. The Holy Ghost is full of ministration. Then again, don't forget about the operation of the Holy Ghost. And always keep in your mind the fact that the Holy Ghost must bring manifestation. Let us take the first thought now which is bearing on this great plan. We must understand that the Holy Ghost is breath, the Holy Ghost is Person, and it is the most marvelous thing to me to know that this Holy Ghost power can be in every part of your body. You can feel it from the crown of your head to the soles of your feet. Oh, it is lovely to be burning all over with the Holy Ghost! And when that takes place, there is nothing but the operation of the tongue that must give forth the glory and the praise.

You must be in the place of magnifying the Lord. The Holy Ghost is the great magnifier of Jesus, the great illuminator of Jesus. And so after the Holy Ghost comes in, it is impossible to keep your tongue still. Why, you would burst if you didn't give him utterance. Talk about a dumb baptized soul? Such a person is not to be found in the Scriptures. When the Holy Ghost comes he must be a power of ministry. That is his office. The power of ministry through the revelation of the great ideal of Jesus!

When the Holy Ghost becomes a ministry in the life, what will happen? Why, beloved, if we can get lost in God only once in a year, to be divinely imbued with this power, it will be worth a world to us. Talk about preaching! I would like to know how it will be possible for all the people filled with the Holy Ghost to stop preaching. Even the sons and daughters must prophesy. After the Holy Ghost comes in, after that operation by the Spirit, a man is in a new order in God. And you will find it so real that you cannot help it, you will want to sing, talk, laugh, and shout. We are in a strange place when the Holy Ghost comes in.

The Outflow of the Spirit
If the incoming of the Spirit is lovely, what must be the outflow? The incoming is only to be an outflow. I am very interested in scenery. When I was in Switzerland I wouldn't be satisfied till I went to the top of the mountain, though I like the valleys also. On the summit of the mountain the sun beats on the snow and sends the water trickling down the mountains right through to

the meadows. Go there and see if you can stop it. Just so in the spiritual. God begins with the divine flow of his eternal power which is the Holy Ghost, and you cannot stop it.

We must always clearly see that the baptism of the Spirit must make us ministering spirits.

The next thought then is that it must be on the line of operation. You will find that if you really get full of the Holy Ghost, two things must happen: ministry and operation. I want you to notice Peter and John had been baptized only a short time. Did they know what they had? No. I defy you to know what you have. No one knows what he has in the baptism of the Holy Ghost. He has no conception of it. You cannot measure it by any measuring line of human standards. It is greater than we can comprehend.

Consequently Peter and John had no idea what they had received. For the first time after they were baptized in the Holy Ghost with this order of the Spirit, they came down to the Gate Beautiful. There they saw the man sitting who for forty years had been lame. What was the first thing after they saw him? Ministration. What was the second? Operation. What was the third? Manifestation, of course; it could not be otherwise. You will always find that this order in the Scripture will be carried out in everybody. In these meetings we are having you must have one set purpose. I believe that God has me here for this purpose: to make you all actors. There are so few actors; therefore, so little is done. I want you to notice that there is a great deal of difference between your acting and the acting upon the stage. On the stage in the theater they tell me that they take fiction and act it so it produces a fact before the people. We have a fact, let us not work as if it were fiction. If we do it will be very serious, but we must work out facts in the name of Jesus.

Here I am on the platform this morning. I had no idea what God had given me till I began to act. As I began to act, then

God began. You cannot have results, manifestations, operations, the truths of the Spirit, the working of the ministry, and the gifts of the Holy Ghost, without you begin to act. I clearly see that we ought to have spiritual giants in the earth, mighty in apprehension, wonderful activity, always having a wonderful report because of their activity in faith. I find instead that there are so many people who have perhaps better discernment than you, better knowledge of the Word than you, but they have failed to put it into practice. So these gifts lie dormant. I am here to help you begin on the sea of life with mighty acts in the power of God through the gifts of the Spirit. You will find that this of which I am speaking is out of knowledge, I can truly say, of a wonderful experience in many lands, having seen so many things that have waked me up. The man who is filled with the Holy Ghost is always in an acting place. Jesus was always in the act. You read the first verse of the Acts of the Apostles: "Jesus began both to do and teach." He began to do first, and so must we.

Beloved, we must see that the baptism of the Holy Ghost is an activity with an outward manifestation. When I was in Norway, God was mightily moving there, though I had to talk by interpretation. However, God always worked in a wonderful way. One day as we were going up a hill, we met a man coming down who stopped the three men I was with, one being the interpreter. I was walking on but I saw that the man was in a dilemma, so I turned back and said to the interpreter, "What is up?" "This man," he said, "is so full of neuralgia that he is almost blind and he is in a terrible state. He is asking us if we know the nearest help." As soon as they finished the conversation, I said to the spirit that was afflicting him, "Come out of him in the name of Jesus." And the man said, "It is all gone! It is all gone! I am free." Ah, friends, we have no conception of what God has for us in the world!

I will tell you what happened in Sydney, Australia, the other day. A man with a stick passed a friend and me. He had to get down and then twist over, and the tortures of his face made a deep impression on my soul. I asked myself, "Is it right to pass this man?" So I said to my friend, "There is a man in a terrible state; he is in awful distress and I cannot go further. I must speak to him." I went over to this man and said to him, "You seem to be in great trouble." "Yes," he said, "I am no good and never will be." I said, "You see that hotel. Be in front of that door in five minutes and I will pray for you, and you shall be as straight as any man in this place." This is on the line of activity in the faith of Jesus. I came back after paying a bill, and he was there. It wasn't a stick but an umbrella that he had. I will never forget him, wondering if he was going to be trapped, or what was up that a man should stop him in the street and tell him he should be made straight. I had said it [in the Spirit], so it must be. If you say anything you must stand with God to make it so. Never say anything for bravado, without you have the right to say it. Always be sure of your ground, and that you are honoring God. If there is anything about it to make *you* anything, it will bring you sorrow. Your whole ministry will have to be on such a line of grace and blessing it will turn the whole thing. We helped him up the two steps, passed him through to the elevator, and took him upstairs. It seemed difficult to get him from the elevator to my bedroom, as though Satan was making the last stroke for his life, but we got him there. Then in five minutes' time this man walked out of that bedroom as straight as any man in this place. He walked perfectly and declared he hadn't a pain in his body.

Oh, brother, it is ministration, it is operation, it is manifestation! Those are three of the greatest principles of the baptism of the Holy Ghost. And we must see to it that God is producing through us these three. Beloved, I want you to notice this, that except you stand with God it is impossible for God to manifest his power.

The Bible is the Word of God; it has the truths, and whatever people may say of them, they stand stationary, unmovable. Not one jot or tittle shall fail of all his good promises. His word will come forth. In heaven it is settled, on earth it must be made manifest that he is the God of an everlasting power.

Begin Acting in His Name

God wants manifestation and he wants his glory to be seen. And he wants us all to be filled with that line of thought that he can look upon us and delight in us in the world subduing the world unto him. And so you are going to miss a great deal if you don't begin to act. But once you begin to act in the order of God, you will find that God establishes your faith and from that day starts you on the line of the promises. When will you begin? In a place in England I was dealing on the lines of faith and what would take place if we believed God. Many things happened. But when I got away it appeared one man who worked in the coal mine had heard me. He was in trouble with a stiff knee. It was the first time he had heard me, I think. He said to his wife, "I cannot help but think every day that that message of Wigglesworth's was to stir us to do something. I cannot get away from it. All the men in the pit know how I walk with a stiff knee, and you know how you have wrapped it around with yards of flannel. Well, I am going to act. You have to be the congregation." He got his wife in front of him—"I am going to act and do just like Wigglesworth did." He got hold of his leg unmercifully, saying, "Come out, you devils, come out! In the name of Jesus. Now Jesus help me. Come out, you devils, come out." Then he said, "Wife, they are gone! Wife, they are gone. This is too good. I am going to act now." So he went to his place of worship and all of his mine friends were there. It was a prayer meeting. As he told them this story, these men became delighted. They said, "Jack, come over here and help me." And Jack went. As soon as he was through in one home he was invited to another, loosing these people of the pains they had gotten in the mines.

Ah, brothers and sisters, we have no idea what God has for us. We must only begin! But oh, the grace we need! We may make a mishap. If you do it outside of him, if you do it for yourself, and if you want to be someone, it will be a failure. We shall only be able to do well as we do it in the name of Jesus. Oh, the love and expression that God's Son can put into us if we are only humble enough, weak enough, and helpless enough to know that except he does it, it will not be done! "What things soever ye desire, when ye pray, believe that ye receive them, and ye shall have them" (Mk 11:24).

The Gift of the Word of Wisdom
The first of the nine gifts which must be manifested is the gift of the word of wisdom (see 1 Cor 12:8). I am positive this morning that there isn't anything that an assembly needs so much as wisdom, the possession of which will save us from many foolish things. When you are at a crossroad, and don't know which way to go concerning buildings or alterations or otherwise, a word of wisdom for your assembly would be such a manifestation of God's love that you would never forget it. But you will always find that wisdom never comes on any lines but the lines of love. That is the first grace of the Spirit. The love of God is shed abroad in our hearts by the Holy Ghost and the fear of the Lord is the beginning of wisdom. And perfect fear is joined up with that divine love. I want you to see clearly that if you are where the love of God is the very nature of your life, you have no place to live as it were, only in God. You can trust God to give you the word of wisdom because it is a needed word for us through our pentecostal order. If we were not balanced by other qualities, we

should jump over the traces,* the Spirit of the life of Christ is so mighty within us. And so we need wisdom.

The word of wisdom from the Lord would save us from a lot of trouble. We all have to pay a big price for our learning; I have paid some big prices. I remember one time I was in great difficulty and needed help. I was walking on the road one day and met a man who lived opposite me, who said, "Smith, I have been thinking about selling my house. I cannot think about anyone buying it but you." "Strange thing," I replied, "I have no money. But how much do you want for it?" He mentioned the price. "I will buy that house," I said, "if you will just turn it over to me for the money without having to bother with the lawyers." "All right," said he, "I will."

I had given my word without thought. That was a mistake. There were a thousand mistakes on this job; the thing I needed at that time was just one word of wisdom from God. It didn't come because I was so active. You can be too active and if you act outside of God you will always be in trouble. If we are not well balanced, and deep down in God, we make a thousand mistakes because we are too much in a hurry.

I told my wife what I had promised. "How will you manage it?" she asked. "I have always managed it so far," I said, "but I don't know how to get through this." I thought, "Can I take it out of the business?" No, I couldn't. So I set on a human plan; I wasn't in the divine plan on this. I was in God's service, but you can be in God's service and still get out of his plan. That is where we make a mistake, getting outside the plan of God.

Well, I had some rich relatives and thought I would borrow some money, but none of them seemed to have anything to spare; everybody was in difficulties. I had made a foolish appeal,

---

*Traces are straps or chains, part of a draft horse's harness. Jumping, or kicking, over the traces is "to shake off control; to show insubordination or independence."

so after I had tried them all, I said to my wife, "It is strange, I have tried everybody about this business but it doesn't seem to come off." Then she said, "You have not been to God yet. When you go to God, you will get it all." I went to God, saying, "Father, I have been very foolish and I have gotten into a hole. If you will help me out, I will never ask you on the same line again." Here comes the word of wisdom. Oh, that word of wisdom! God gave it. In two minutes the whole thing was settled on God's side but not on mine. How could it be? So I came down to my wife, saying, "What do you think he told me? 'Go to Brother Webster.'" Brother Webster was about the poorest man I knew, and yet he was about the richest man I knew—for he knew God. Off I went early the next morning. "What brings you this morning?" Brother Webster asked. "Why," I said, "I was talking to the Lord last night, and so I came to see you the first chance I had." "If it is a matter like that," he said, "we will go down to the house and speak about it." We went down to the house. "I promised to buy a house from a man," I began, "three weeks ago and I am short one hundred pounds. I have tried to get this money, I believe not in the Lord's plan, and I have been tried about it." "How is it" he asked, "that you have only come to me now?" "Because I only went to the Lord about it last night." "Well," he said, "It is a strange thing. Three weeks ago I had a hundred pounds. I put it between the mattresses. I have put it in all sorts of places in the house. I could not have any rest so I took it to the bank. If it will be as great a blessing to you as a trouble to me, you shall have it." So we went to the bank and he got the money and said, "Take it and be off."

Oh, to know God! Oh, to go in the way that God would have us! Oh, to cease from our own planning and our own arranging! Oh, to have the word of God! The word of wisdom! Oh, to believe the word and to enter into this treasury and hear him say, "Do this," and do it! When we get there God will surely, as divinely as we are human, have a divine plan for us and bring us right into line where there will be no trouble, no trial, and sorrows will be at an end when we get to know God.

Being Led by the Spirit
Beloved, I pray that as we go forth into these gifts of the Spirit that God will show us there is a way for us, and that it is his way. If we turn to our way we shall surely make great mistakes and shall be filled with trouble. I desire to impress this thought upon you. Live in the Spirit, walk in the Spirit, walk in the communion of the Spirit, talk with God. Apart from this there is no security for you, but on these lines all else is for you. All leadings of the divine order are for you. I pray that if there are any who have turned to their own way and have made God second as I did in that matter, they will come to repentance on all lines. Separate yourself from every earthly touch and touch ideals. Begin with God this moment.

From *The Latter Rain Evangel* (Chicago), February 1923, pp. 19–24.

6
The Word of Knowledge by the Same Spirit

Beloved, I believe that God wants to take us further into his revelation and I beseech you to hear, because there are none so deaf as those who will not hear. We ought to have ears to hear and the hearing of faith because the Word profiteth nothing unless it is mixed with faith in them that hear it. If you want the plan of God made real in your hearts you must take it all as "Thus saith the Lord." Then God will be able to put you on the foundations which cannot be shaken. God has the only plan, and that plan is so perfect that it has no flaws in it. You will find that it always comes out right to the place where you can build upon it. "There is no other foundation than that which is laid," and that foundation is Christ Jesus. He is not only the Cornerstone, but he is also the Head of the Corner. We must see that everything is perfectly dovetailed together, and that we are all members in particular of that body so that it may be fitly joined together in perfection in all its glorious beauties, just like that wonderful city which will come right down out of heaven and will surpass every city that ever was made in all the world. Billions and trillions of saints, far more than the human mind can give expression to because they will be innumerable as the sands on the seashore—the Bride of the Lamb—will comprise that wonderful city which will come down out of heaven. And so I believe that God has a wonderful place for us.

When I read the Scriptures and see that blessed truth that

Jesus said to the sons of Zebedee, "To sit on my right hand and on my left hand is not mine to give; but it shall be given to them for whom it is prepared" (Mk 10:40), I believe there will be innumerable seats there for those prepared for that place. And every time I preach I try to get people prepared for that wonderful place at the right hand of God. I do not want to think that anyone will come short of the adornment which only the Holy Ghost can give, the adorning of the beautiful grandeur of our Lord Jesus Christ which is for us all.

Yesterday morning we spoke about the word of wisdom. And truly that word of wisdom is very essential for all to know. This morning we will launch out further and take the next word which is so profitable unto us at this time, *"the word of knowledge, by the same Spirit"* (1 Cor 12:8). So I want you to keep in mind the same Spirit and the word of knowledge.

Jesus was always on a future tense condition, but he was in the present tense of it. It may be a future tense to many in this room this morning, but nevertheless, God intends that you should be so quickened by the Spirit that you should come into a present tense of all the glories of the Scriptures. It was right for the Lord to speak to the disciples and show them the future tense, but beloved, he was in it and he manifested it.

As certain as possible am I that the world is ready for all the truth of God, and I am satisfied that there is nothing stopping the flow of God except the believer. When the believer is sanctified, then the heathen shall know; but till all the saints come into the fullness of the manifestation of the power of God there will not be the revival for which we are looking. Revivals spring from wholehearted conditions, from inward power moved by the powers of God. God can only work upon the material and if the material is not fully yielded in the hand of the Potter, there will always be some marring of the vessel. And the flow of all the powers of God will not get right through us till we are wholly and entirely purged from all dross and made pure gold in his presence.

Jesus declared unto us in John 16:8-9 that when the Holy Ghost comes in us, "He will reprove the world of sin, and of righteousness, and of judgment: of sin because they believe not on me." Then he goes on to say, "The prince of this world is judged" (Jn 16:11). And we know that as we are filled with the Holy Ghost we judge the world. God would have us so that everything we touch is either destroyed or quickened. Oh, there must be something in this blessed way of life that shall surely make manifest his power till the heathen must know that he is God!

Message in tongues with interpretation: *The Spirit quickeneth the mortal body and bringeth us into likemindedness with Jesus till the whole heart and mind are transformed and so made pure that God can bring into us all his revelation, all his life, and all his purity; till everything we move amongst is changed. As he was, so are we in the world, to glorify and magnify the Lord of Hosts amongst the heathen.*

The Word of Knowledge Brings Joy

Beloved, I see that this gift of knowledge by the Spirit always brings *joy*, which is the second fruit of the Spirit. And knowledge is that which comes from above. We will look into the perfect liberty of God where we have the unfolding of the majesty of heaven where Christ is so revealed in all his divine fullness that we see from the beginning to the end one ideal through the whole canon of the Scriptures. God hath set him over all. And God is manifesting in us himself, for in us all this truth has to be; and the truth is that we should know the Scriptures which make us wise unto salvation, which open the depths of the kingdom of heaven and reveal all his divine mind to us, which strengtheneth by the might of his Spirit in the inner man till the whole man is changed. The mysteries are by the Spirit revealed unto us and we know that God is bringing us into this glorious fact of having the mind of Christ and the knowledge of God.

The word of knowledge is, like all the gifts, great. It has been said and written by many people when they wanted to underestimate the baptism of the Spirit, that tongues is among the least of the gifts and the last of the gifts. There is no "last" with the Word. The last may be first, and the first last. It takes just the same divine power to manifest tongues and interpretation, as healing and faith, as prophecy and discernment and other gifts. We must never say that anything is small in God's Word. We must always clearly see that there is no such thing as small things. Every gift is by the Spirit, and is worked by the Spirit. And every gift is made manifest, so we must clearly see that unless we have the Holy Ghost, we cannot have this glorious inward revelation of the mightiness of God to us. But, hallelujah, we are by the Spirit brought into likeness that we may have a peep right into the glorious hidden mysteries of the kingdom of his righteousness.

Beloved, you cannot say that all the truth is contained in the Gospels, nor in Acts, nor in the law of Moses, nor in any one part of the Bible. It takes the whole of the Scriptures to contain the truth of God. The more you know of the Scriptures, the more you know of the mysteries of redemption. There are thousands of people who know the Word of God, but it isn't quickened to them. There is little life, though there may be any amount of activity because the church bells ring. And there may be any amount of seeming religious order, but beloved, the Word is a dead letter except by the Spirit, and you can only be quickened by the Spirit. So we must see that this word of knowledge of the Word of God can never be vital and powerful in us without it is by the Spirit. As surely as anything, when the Holy Ghost gets ahold of any person, his conversation is in heaven, for our citizenship is there, our Head is there. We are not like the Romans, whose head was in Rome. Our Head is in heaven. When we are quickened by the Spirit, we pray and sing in heavenly places.

And we must clearly see that God is all the time loosing us by the Spirit. When God gets us loose, we are ready for any association. No matter what ship I travel on, people are always saved on that ship. And if I go on a railroad journey, I am sure there is someone saved before I get through. It isn't possible for me to live without getting people ready for dying. I believe we have to live in a new spiritual realm of grace where all our mind, our walk, and everything is in the Holy Ghost. Beloved, the Spirit alone can do this. You can never reach these attainments under any circumstances in the flesh. "Ye are not in the flesh but in the Spirit." May God help us to see our destined position.

Thirsting for the Word

I say, and I will never draw it back till God shows me differently, that the child of God ought to thirst for the Word. The child of God should know nothing else but the Word and he should know nothing amongst men save Jesus. He can never know God through a newspaper, and very little through books. You will find that books will disturb your mind and cause all kinds of ruptures in your ordinary communion. God has shown me that I dare not trust any book but the Word of God. In fact I have never read a book but the Bible and I am as satisfied as possible. It is the only Book, and it is the only food for the believer. "Man shall not live by bread alone, but by every word that proceedeth out of the mouth of God" (Mt 4:4). And we are of his substance. We are his life. There is something in humanity that God has made for all his divine attributes, that man can receive of God and walk up and down insulated through and through by this God-indwelling presence. Ah, it is lovely! And it is all because of the word of knowledge by the same Spirit that gave the word of wisdom.

A Right Relationship Brings Peace

The next word also is a great word, especially among pentecostal people, who seem to be hungry for it more than anything else now, "*another faith by the same Spirit.*" You will find that, coupled right along with this, is peace. And it could not be otherwise. You cannot find any man who has a living faith who is in trouble. You will never accomplish anything on any line except when you are in peace. It may be a blessing for you to know that if ever I have trouble and my peace is destroyed on any line, I always know it is satanic; it is never God under any circumstances. If I am not at peace, there is something wrong somewhere, and I must get to know what it is, because they that keep their minds stayed upon God shall be kept in continual peace. When I find where the leakage is, I shall be able to put my hand upon it and say, "That is healed." Beloved, God wants to take us into that solid peace. It will make a difference in our prayers; it will make a difference in our reading and in our conversation when we are at peace with God and with one another. All the blasts of hell's furnace when-ever they come cannot touch you. For those who pass from death unto life there is perfect peace, and yet we cannot have peace unless we have faith. God wants all his people so built on this groundwork of faith that everybody that sees you will be impressed, they will be moved. You will never move the world if you are in trouble. But show the world that there is a peace that brings a joy, that there is a joy that brings a song, that lifts you up; and it will lift all that gather round you.

The children of God must see clearly that they do not belong to this world. "Ye are not of the world" (Jn 15:19). "If any man love the world, the love of the Father is not in him" (1 Jn 2:15). Therefore, you must be delivered from the world, be strengthened by the power of God, and be new creatures every day. Let us get down to this solid place of faith because there is something in it for us all. Faith can so rest in God's plan and thought that whatever is going on in the world will make no difference. If your house was on fire and you were really at peace with God and resting in faith, you could laugh.

One of our workers said to me at Christmastime, "Wigglesworth, I never was so near the end of my purse in all my life." To which I replied, "Thank God, you are just at the opening of God's treasures." If you get hold of the true principles of God, there is no person in this place who can ever be poor. Even in his deepest poverty he is made rich. When he has nothing at all, he has more to give than he ever had before, making many rich because he has reached a place of poverty. When you possess nothing, it is just the time when you possess all things. That is a seeming contradiction, but there are many apparent contradictions in the Word of God to the mind who has not looked into the perfect law of liberty. But the child of God who goes in the perfect law of liberty sees that there is no binding; it is all liberty. You will never have liberty unless you have peace and you will never have peace unless you have faith. There are three things which always work correctly and they are on those lines. You can never have *feeling* make a fact, but you can have *faith* make a fact that will bring feeling.

Beloved, God has a plan for these days, and when he comes

in, no flesh can stand against him. Faith always works a faith. It always brings a peace; it is always in the clear light of God perfecting and being perfected. There are two things we must know; every principle of this twelfth chapter of 1 Corinthians is based upon gifts. When I speak about "gifts" I speak about the gifts which are brought into the human heart and abide there, for "the gifts and calling of God are without repentance" (Rom 11:29). Just like the Holy Ghost, when he comes in he never leaves. He may be grieved and he may be quenched to such an extent that it may seem all was dormant, but it will always be because the life is not in submission. When the life is submissive to God's power, taking hold of that body, that body never loses its unction but goes on further and further to know more of the mind and will of God.

The Gift of Faith

The difference between a gift within you and a gift administered through you because of the Holy Ghost unction, is that one always takes you into a place beyond where you were before you received the gift. For instance, all men who are saved have faith, saving faith. But the "gift of faith" is much different. That faith always abides. That is the reason we may take for granted the security of the believer because we are not saved by works; we are saved by faith. And your position in Christ is according to where you are on the lines of faith. As I said the other day, no man in the place is any better than his faith. If his faith is perfected, he is being perfected in every way. If he sees Jesus even though his faith is imperfect, the same perfection in Jesus will be perfected in him. If he sees Jesus in all his divine glories, attributes, and gifts, he will find that he will come into the divine position where Jesus exchanges his robe for that man's. If he can believe it, it is true.

If you have no limitations, God has a plan to lift you into all his divine plan.

God has no place for anybody who is not thirsty. You are unusable. The Holy Ghost has no movement in you. But the Word of God, which we receive when we are born again by the incorruptible Word, abides. And if you don't interfere with it but nurture it, you will find it has the power to make a perfect Christ in you because it is the seed of God.

There is a great fullness in being a child of God. As God was in the heavens, seeing Jesus in the water, having come down there with John—just as he came to the place where they were, there was perfect surrender. Then God burst through the heavens, saying: "This is my beloved Son, in whom I am well pleased" (Mt 3:17). What was it that pleased him? That which will please him in every one of us: meekness, submission, a full condition of surrender. When he, the King of Kings, the Lord of Lords, submitted to water baptism by John, that perfect yieldedness brought him to a place where God said, "This is my beloved Son." If you follow Jesus, you will see that from that time he claims his eternal destiny, his authority. From that time on, he lives and proves himself to be the Son of God. You will find there is the same position in destiny for us; our destiny is always pre-position. We must see that God begins with us by the Word and finishes us by perfecting us as sons. "But as many as received him, to them gave he power to become the sons of God" (Jn 1:12). They were not sons, but they had power to become sons. And every person in this place has a perfect right to rise up to perfect sonship, where God indwells, flows, works through him, and manifests him in the world as a son. It is a big subject and seems to get bigger as we talk about it. It is one of those things to which there is no end because God has no end.

Human and Divine Faith

Let us turn to this line of faith, the difference between our faith and the faith which the Holy Ghost gives. I might go into the Epistles, but I think if we keep on the lines where Paul was at first brought into these things, that will help us more. Let us come to the Acts of the Apostles and see the difference of that growth in the Spirit. Paul had a revelation just as he entered into the new life with Jesus. If you read the twenty-sixth chapter, you will see that his revelation had to be increased on conditions. The increase of the revelation was this, that Jesus was showing himself unto him and said he would yet show further things unto him just as he was developed. If you want to know the great climax and finish of that condition, read the fifteenth chapter of Romans, and see there how he never preached on another man's ground and yet signs and wonders followed. Just as Joshua closed up his ministry by saying, "That not one thing hath failed of all the good things which the Lord your God spoke concerning you" (Jos 23:14), so this man of God in the latter times came to us like a refined fire out of the mint of God's order. When Paul was speaking to Agrippa he said, "I was not disobedient unto the heavenly vision" (Acts 26:19). Every touch of that vision was made more real every day till God could take him through. The baptism of the Spirit took him into the place that was impossible to be shaken.

There are many things that describe this double faith. One night I got home about eleven o'clock from an open air meeting. And when I got home, I wanted to see my wife. I loved her so much, she was everything to me. Men, love your wives as Christ loved the church. There is something in a wife that is brought to you by the gift of God that you will never know her equal. I stand on this platform because of a holy woman, a woman who lived righteousness, poured her righteousness into my life, so transforming my life from wayward indifferences of all kinds, and so shaping my life, that she was practically the means of purging me through and through. A holy wife is worth more than gold. And I say, wives love your husbands. Let nothing come between. It is the stimulus of your lives; it is the hope of your home; it is the destined eternity which is fixed in the homes.

"Where is she?" I asked. And straightaway I was told that she was down at Mitchell's. Mr. Mitchell was very ill. I had seen him that day and knew that without a tremendous change he would not last the day out. He and I had been brought up together and I loved him very much. When I was nearing his house, I heard a great cry, so I felt that something had happened. I passed his wife on the staircase and asked, "What is up?" "Mitchell has gone," she said. My wife was inside and I went in. As soon as I saw Mitchell, I saw he had passed away. I couldn't understand it and began praying. "Oh," my wife exclaimed, "Don't, Dad! Don't, Dad!" But the faith I had seemed to be a faith God helped me with and I find that God gives us this faith in a place where God can undertake. I continued praying, and my wife laid hold of me, saying, "Don't, Dad. Don't you see he is dead?" My wife was always afraid that I should have a dead person on my hands some day and there I should be, but I was never afraid of that. When I got as far as I could with my faith, then God laid hold of me. Oh, it was such a laying hold I could believe for anything! I came down from that place shouting victory. But my wife said, "Don't, Dad. You see he is dead." "He is alive," I replied. "Glory to God!" My wife laid hold of me, weeping, "Oh Dad, don't." "He is alive!" I said. And he is living today. Ah yes, our faith and God's faith! We must see that God has a plan for us and the plan is that the end of you is the beginning with God. But we must go in to possess all the glories of the attitude of the Spirit till we live and move in God. And nothing, by any means, shall ever discourage us. We shall always have a face like flint. We shall not be afraid of their faces neither in any way shall we be dismayed. And as God was with Joshua and Moses, he is with us today.

From *The Latter Rain Evangel* (Chicago), March 1923, pp. 17–21.

Preparing for an International Ministry

A Brand From the Burning

God gave me a great zeal in soul winning. Every day I sought to bring someone to Christ. I was willing to wait an hour any day to have an interview with anyone about his soul's salvation. At one place I waited an hour and a half, asking God to direct me to the one of His choice. The road was filled with people but I kept saying to the Lord, "I want the right man." After awhile I was somewhat impatient in my spirit and I said, "Lord, I don't have much time to waste." But God did not call it wasted time. After an hour and a half, a man came along with a horse and cart, and the Lord spoke to me just as He spoke to Philip when He told him to join himself to the chariot of the Ethiopian. I got up in the cart beside the man and was soon talking with him about his need of salvation. He growled, "Why don't you go about your own business? Why should you pick me out and talk to me?"

I wondered whether I had made a mistake. I looked up to the Lord and said, "Is this the right man, Lord?"

He said to me, "Yes, this is the right man." And so I continued to talk to him and plead with him to yield his life to Christ. By and by I saw that he was shedding tears, and I knew that God had softened his heart and the seed of the Word was entering. After I was sure a true work of grace had been wrought, I jumped down from his cart, and he went on his way.

Three weeks later my mother said to me, "Smith, have you been talking to someone about salvation?" "I am always doing that, Mother." "Well, I visited a man last night. He was dying; he has been in bed for three weeks. I asked whether he would like someone to come and pray for him. He said, 'The last time I was out, a young man got into my cart and spoke to me. I was very rough with him but he was very persistent. Anyhow, God convicted me of my sins, and saved me.'" My mother continued, "That was the last time that man was out. He passed away in the night. He described the young man who talked with him and I could tell from his description that you were the one."

Smith Wigglesworth, in Stanley H. Frodsham, *Smith Wigglesworth, Apostle of Faith* (Springfield, Mo.: Gospel Publishing House, 1948), pp. 28–29. Used by permission.

7
The Applause of the World Versus
the Approval of God
(Communion Service)

This is a very blessed time for us to gather together in remembrance of the Lord. I want to remind you of this fact, that this is the only service we render to the Lord. All other services we attend are for us to get blessing from the Lord, but Jesus said, "This do in remembrance of me" (Lk 22:19). We have gathered together to commemorate that wonderful death, victory, and triumph, and the looking forward to the "glorious hope." And I want you, if it is possible at all, to get rid of your religion. It has been "religion" at all times that has slain and destroyed that which was good. When Satan entered into Judas, the only people that the devil could speak to through Judas were the priests, sad as it is to say it. They conspired to get him to betray Jesus, and the devil took money from these priests to put Jesus to death. Now it is a very serious thing, for we must clearly understand whether we are of the right spirit or not; for no man can be of the Spirit of Christ and persecute another, no man can have the true Spirit of Jesus and slay his brother, and no man can follow the Lord Jesus and have enmity in his heart. You cannot have Jesus and have bitterness and hatred, and persecute the believer.

It is possible for us, if we are not careful, to have within us an evil spirit of unbelief. And even in our best state it is possible for us to have enmity unless we are perfectly dead and let the life of the Lord lead us. You remember Jesus wanted to pass through a certain place as he was going to Jerusalem. Because he would not stop and preach to them concerning the kingdom, they refused to allow him to go through their section of the country. And the disciples which were with Jesus said to him, "Shall we call down fire from heaven upon them as Elijah did?" But Jesus turned and said, "Ye know not what manner of spirit ye are of" (Lk 9:55). There they were, following Jesus and with him all the time, but Jesus rebuked that spirit. I pray God that we may get this out of this service, that our knowledge of Jesus is pure love, and pure love to Jesus is death to self on all lines, body, soul, and spirit. I believe if we are in the will of God, we will be perfectly directed at all times, and if we would know anything about the mighty works of Christ, we shall have to follow what Jesus said. Whatever he said came to pass.

Many things happened in the lives of the apostles to show his power over all flesh. In regard to paying tribute, Jesus said to Peter, "Then are the children free" (Mt 17:26). Even so, he instructed them to pay. I like that thought, that Jesus was so righteous on all lines. It helps me a great deal. Then Jesus told Peter to do a very hard thing. He said, "Lest we should offend them, go thou to the sea, and cast an hook, and take up the fish that first cometh up; and when thou hast opened his mouth, thou shalt find a piece of money: that take, and give unto them for me and thee" (Mt 17:27). This was one of the hardest things Peter had to do. He had been fishing all his life, but never had he taken silver out of a fish's mouth. There were thousands and millions of fish in the sea, but one fish had to have a piece of silver in it. He went down to the sea as any natural man would, speculating and thinking, "How can it be?" But how could it not be, if Jesus said it would be? Then the perplexity would arise, "But how many fish there are, and which fish has the money?" Brother, if God speaks, it will be as he says.

Knowing the Mind and the Word of God

What you need is to know the mind of God and the Word of God, and you will be free. The more you know of the mightiness of revelation, the more does everything in the way of fearfulness pass away. To know God is to be in the place of triumph. To know God is to be in the place of rest. To know God is to be in the place of victory. No doubt many things were in Peter's mind that day, but thank God there was one fish, and he obeyed. Sometimes to obey in blindness brings the victory. Sometimes when perplexities arise in your mind, obedience means God is working out the problem. Peter cast the hook into the sea, and it would have been amazing if you could have seen the disturbance the other fish made to move out of the way, all except the right one, just one among the millions of fish God wanted. God may put his hand upon you in the midst of millions of people, but if he speaks to you, that thing that he says will be appointed.

On this occasion, Jesus said to Peter and the rest, that when they went out into the city they would see a man bearing a pitcher of water, and they should follow him. It was not customary in the East for men to carry anything on their heads. The women always did the carrying, but this had to be a man, and he had to have a pitcher. (One day I heard a man preaching and he said it was quite all right for Jesus to go and arrange for a colt to be tied there, and another preacher said it was quite easy to feed all those thousands of people, because the loaves in those days were so tremendously big, but he didn't tell them it was a little boy that had the five loaves. Unbelief can be very blind, but faith can see through a stone wall. Faith when it is moved by the power of God can laugh when trouble is on.)

They said to the man with the pitcher, "Where is the guest chamber?" "How strange it is that you should ask," he replied. "I have been preparing that, wondering who wanted it." It is marvelous when God is leading how perfectly everything works into the plan. He was arranging everything. You think he cannot do that today for you? People who have been in perplexities for days and days, he knows how to deliver out of trouble; he knows how to be with you in the dark hour. He can make all things work together for good to them that love God (see Rom 8:28). He has a way of arranging his plan, and when God comes in, you always know it was a day you lived in God. Oh, to live in God! There is a vast difference between living in God and living in speculation and hope. There is something better than hope; something better than speculation. "The people that do know their God shall be strong, and do exploits" (Dn 11:32), and God would have us to know him.

The Appointed Hour

"And when the hour was come, he sat down, and the twelve apostles with him" (Lk 22:14). "When the hour was come"—that was the most wonderful hour. There never was an hour, never will be an hour like that hour. What *hour* was it? It was an hour of the passing of creation under the blood. It was an hour of destruction of demon power. It was an hour appointed of life coming out of death. It was an hour when all that ever lived came under a glorious covering of the blood. It was an hour when all the world was coming into emancipation by the blood. It was an hour in the world's history when it emerged from dark chaos, a wonderful hour! Praise God for that hour! Was it a dark hour? It was a dark hour for him, but a wonderful light dawned for us. It was tremendously dark for the Son of

Man, but praise God he came through it.

There are some things in the Scriptures which move me greatly. I am glad that Paul was a man. I am glad that Jesus was a man. I am glad that Daniel was a man, and I am also glad that John was a man. You ask why? Because I see that whatever God has done for other men, he can do for me. And I find God has done such wonderful things for other men that I am always on the expectation that these things are possible for me. Think about this. It is a wonderful thought to me. Jesus said in that trying hour—hear it a moment: "I have desired to eat this passover with you before I suffer" (Lk 22:15). Desire? What could be his desire? His desire because of the salvation of the world. His desire because of the dethronement of the powers of Satan. His desire because he knew he was going to conquer everything and make every man free that ever lived. It was a great desire, but what lay between it? Just between that and the cross lay *Gethsemane!* Some people say that Jesus died on the cross. It is perfectly true, but is that the only place? Jesus died in Gethsemane. That was the tragic moment! That was the place where he paid the debt. It was in Gethsemane, and Gethsemane was between him and the cross. He had a desire to eat this Passover and knew Gethsemane was between him and the cross.

I want you to think about Gethsemane. There alone, and with the tremendous weight, the awful effect of all sin and disease upon that body, he cries out, "If it be possible, let this cup pass from me" (Mt 26:39). Oh, could it be! He could only save when he was man, but here like a giant refreshed and coming out of a great chaos of darkness he comes forth: "To this end I was born, and for this cause came I into the world" (Jn 18:37). It was his purpose to die for the world. Oh, brother, will it ever pass through your lips or your mind for a moment that you will not have a desire to serve Christ like that? Can you deign, under any circumstances, to take your cross full, to be in the place of any ridicule, any surrender, anything for the man who said he desired to eat the Passover with his disciples, knowing what it meant? It can only come out of the depths of love we have for him that we can say this morning, "Lord Jesus, I will follow." Oh, brother, there is something very wonderful in the decision in your heart! God knows the heart. You do not always have to be on the housetop to shout to indicate the condition of your heart. He knows your inward heart. You say, "I would be ashamed not to be willing to suffer for a man who desired to suffer to save me." "*With desire,*" he says.

I know what it is to have the kingdom of heaven within you. He said that even the least in the kingdom of heaven is greater than John the Baptist, meaning those who are under the blood, those who have seen the Lord by faith, those who know by redemption they are made sons of God. I say to you, he will never taste again until we are there with him. The kingdom will never be complete—it could not be—until we are all there at that great Supper of the Lamb where there will be millions and trillions of redeemed, which no man can number. We shall be there when that Supper is taking place. I like to think of that.

Shelter Under the Blood

I hope you will take one step into definite lines with God and believe it. It is an act of faith God wants to bring you into: a perfecting of that love that cannot fail to avail. It is a fact that he has opened the kingdom of heaven to all believers, and that he gives eternal life to them that believe. The Lord, the Omnipotent God, it is he that knoweth the end from the beginning, and has arranged by the blood of the Lamb to cover the guilty and make intercession for all believers. Oh, it is a wonderful inheritance of faith to find shelter under the blood of Jesus!

I want you to see that he says, "Do this in remembrance of me." He took the cup. He took the bread, and he gave thanks. The very attitude of giving thanks for his shed blood, giving thanks for his broken body, overwhelms the heart. To think that my Lord could give thanks for his shed blood! To think that my Lord could give thanks for his broken body! Only divinity can reveal this sublime act unto the heart! The natural man cannot receive it, but the spiritual man, the man who has been created anew by faith in Christ, he is open to it. The man who believes God comes in is inborn with the eternal seed of truth and righteousness and faith, and from the moment he sees the truth on the lines of faith, he is made a new creation. The flesh ceases, the spiritual man begins. One passes off, the other passes on, until a man is in the existence of God. I say the Lord brings a child of faith into a place of rest, causes him to sit with him in heavenly places, gives him a language in the Spirit and makes him know he belongs no longer to the law of creation.

The Bread Represents His Body

You see this bread which represents his broken body? The Lord knew he could not bring us any nearer to his broken body. Our bodies are made of bread. The body of Jesus was made of that bread, and he knew he could bring us no nearer. He took the natural elements and said, "This is my body which is given for you" (Lk 22:19). Now will it ever become that body of Christ? No, never. You cannot make it so. It is foolishness to believe it, but I take it as an emblem and when I eat it, the natural leads me into the supernatural, and instantly I begin to feed on the supernatural by faith. One leads me into the other.

Jesus said, "Take, eat: this is my body" (Mk 14:22). I have a real knowledge of Christ through this emblem. May we take from the table of the riches of his promises. The riches of heaven are before us. Fear not, only believe, for God has opened the treasure of his Holy Word.

(COMMUNION SERVICE)

The Betrayer Revealed

As they were all gathered together, he looked on them and said right into their ears, "One of you shall betray me" (Jn 13:21). Jesus knew who would betray him. He had known it for many, many months. They whispered to one another, "Who is it?" None of them had real confidence that it would not be he. That is the serious part about it; they had so little confidence in their ability to face the opposition that was before them, and they had no confidence it would not be one of them. Jesus knew. He had talked to Judas many times, rebuking him, and telling him that his course would surely bring him to a bad end. He never had told any of his disciples, not even John, who leaned on his breast. Now if that same spirit was in any church, it would purify the church. But I fear sometimes Satan gets the advantage and things are told before they are true. I believe God wants to so sanctify us, so separate us, that we will have that perfection of love that will not speak ill or slander a brother or sister.

True Servanthood Demonstrated

There was strife among them who should be the greatest, but he said, "He that is chief let him be as he that doth serve," and then he, the Master, said, "I am among you as he that serveth" (Lk 22:27). He, the noblest, the purest, he was the servant of all! Exercising lordship over another is not of God. We must learn in our hearts that fellowship, true righteousness, loving one another, and preferring one another must come into the church. Pentecost must outreach everything that ever has been, and we know it will if we are willing. But it cannot be if we will not. We can never be filled with the Holy Ghost so long as there is any human, craving desire for our own will. Selfishness must be destroyed. Jesus was perfect, the end of everything, and God will bring us all there. It is *giving* that pays; it is *helping* that pays; it is *loving* that pays; it is *putting yourself out of the way for another* that pays. "I am among you as he that serveth. Ye are they which have continued with me in my temptations. And I appoint unto you a kingdom, as my Father hath appointed unto me" (Lk 22:27-29).

I believe there is a day coming greater than anything any of us have any conception of. This is the testing road. This is the place where your whole body has to be covered with the wings of God that your nakedness shall not be seen. This is the thing that God is getting you ready for, the most wonderful thing your heart can conceive. How can you get into it? First of all, "Ye have continued with me in my temptations." He had been in trials, he had been in temptation. There is not one of us that is tempted beyond what he was. If a young man can be so pure that he cannot be tempted, he will never be fit to be made a judge, but God intends us to be so purified during these evil days that he can make us judges in the world to come. If we can be tried, if we can be tempted on any line, Jesus said, "Ye are they which have continued with me in my temptations." Have faith and God will keep you pure in the temptation. How shall we reach it? In Matthew 19:28, Jesus said, "Ye which have followed me, in the regeneration when the Son of man shall sit in the throne of his glory, ye also shall sit upon twelve thrones, judging the twelve tribes of Israel." "Follow in regeneration"—every day is a regeneration; every day is a day of advancement; every day is a place of

choice. Every day you find yourself in need of fresh consecration. If you are in a place to yield, God moves you in the place of
regeneration.

Wigglesworth's Spiritual Journey

For years and years God has been making me appear to hundreds and thousands of people as a fool. I remember the day
when he saved me and when he called me out. If there is a thing
God wants to do today, he wants to be as real to you and me as he
was to Abraham. After I was saved, I joined myself up to a very
lively lot of people who were full of a revival spirit, and it was
marvelous how God blessed. And then there came a lukewarm-
ness and an indifference, and God said to me as clearly as anything, "Come out." I obeyed and came out. The people said, "We
cannot understand you. We need you now and you are leaving
us." The Plymouth Brethren at that time were in conference.
The Word of God was with them in power, the love of God was
with them unveiled. Baptism by immersion was revealed to me,
and when my friends saw me go into the water, they said I was
altogether wrong. But God had called me and I obeyed. The day
came when I saw that the Brethren had dropped down to the
letter, all letter, dry and barren.

At that time the Salvation Army was filled with love, filled with
power, filled with zeal, every place a revival, and I joined up with
them. For about six years the glory of God was there, and then
the Lord said again, "Come out," and I am glad I came. It
dropped right into a social movement, and God has no place for
a social movement. We are saved by regeneration, and the man
who is going on with God has no time for social reforms.
[*Perhaps Wigglesworth made this statement after perceiving an imbal-
ance between the spiritual and social. The editors see a need, as shown
from the Gospels, a social concern for those in need.*]*

God moved on, and at that time there were many people who were receiving the baptism of the Holy Ghost without signs. Those days were "days of heaven on earth." God unfolded the truth, showed the way of sanctification by the power of the blood of Christ, and I saw in that the great inflow of the life of God. I thank God for that, but God came along again and said, "Come out." I obeyed God and went with what they called the "tongues" folks; they got the credit for having further light. I saw God advancing every movement I made, and I can see even in this pentecostal work, except we see there is a real death, God will say to us, "Come out." Unless Pentecost wakes up to shake herself free from all worldly things and comes into a place of the divine likeness with God, we will hear the voice of God say, "Come out." And he will have something far better than this. I ask every one of you, will you hear the voice of God and come out? You ask, "What do you mean?" Every one of you knows without exception, there is no word for Pentecost except being on fire. If you are not on fire, you are not in the place of regeneration. It is only the fire of God that burns up the entanglements of the world.

A Surrender and Cleansing

When we came into this new work, God spoke to us by the Spirit and we knew we had to reach the place of absolute surrender and cleansing, so that there would be nothing left. We were swept and garnished. Brother, that was only the beginning, and if you have not made tremendous progress in that holy zeal and power and compassion of God, we can truly say you have backslid in heart. The backslider in heart is dead. He is not having the open vision. The backslider in heart is not seeing the Word

*Note added by *The Latter Rain Evangel* editor in the original publication.

of God more fresh every day. You can put it down that a man is a backslider in heart if he is not hated by the world. *If you have the applause of the world you do not have the approval of God.* I do not know whether you will receive it or not, but my heart burns with this message, "changing in the regeneration"; for in this changing you will get a place in the kingdom to come where you shall be in authority, that place which God has prepared for us, that place which is beyond all human conception. We can catch a glimpse of that glory when we see how John worshiped the angel, and the angel said to him, "See thou do it not: for I am thy fellowservant, and of thy brethren the prophets" (Rv 22:9). This angel is showing John the wonders of the glorious kingdom and in his glorified state, John thought he was the Lord. I wonder if we dare believe for it.

The Image of the Heavenly

Let me close with these words: As sure as we have borne the image of the earthly, we shall have the image of the heavenly. It means to us that everything of an earthly type has to cease, for the heavenly type is so wonderful in all its purity. God, full of love, full of purity, full of power! No power except on the lines of purity! No open door into heaven except on the lines of the conscience void of sin between man and God, the heavens open only where the Spirit of the Lord is so leading, so that flesh has no power, but we will live in the Spirit. God bless you and prepare you for greater days.

Originally "The Appointed Hour—Life Out of Death," in *The Latter Rain Evangel* (Chicago), June 1923, pp. 2–6. Preached at a Communion service in the Stone Church, Chicago, November 5, 1922.

8

Great Grace Upon the Church

Just as the early church received great grace, so will we when we magnify the Lord: "And great grace was upon them all" (Acts 4:33). If ever you want to see what God means when he gets a chance at his people, have a peep at the fourth chapter of Acts, and see what God did.

Because all the people shouted aloud to him, he imparted to them such blessing that every person was filled with the Holy Ghost, and I believe what God wants to do in these days is to give an inward manifestation of his divine presence within the body until the body is moved by the power of the Spirit. Beloved, we are accustomed to earthly things; but when God sends the heavenly, it is beyond our understanding. Oh, to have the revelation of the mind of God! It fills my soul, the thought of it! Oh, for the kind of loosening of the body that we will never be bound again! Just filled with God!

I believe God wants us to understand something of the words of this life. What life? The manifestation of the power of Jesus in the human body, a divine life, a divine power, a quickening, thrilling energy given to you. I was baptized with the Holy Ghost in 1907. If anyone had said to me: "Now, Wigglesworth, you will see such and such things," it would have been beyond my human comprehension, but the tide has risen for fifteen years, and it is still rising. Thank God, there has never been a black day, nor a blank day.

Looking at the Early Church

When I think about the first church, I see how God favored her, how he burst through her, how he definitely spoke, how he transformed Christians and made them move with the power of the apostles. Wherever they went they transformed lives— God did such wonderful things, and when I think of it, I think that we should have something far in advance, and say: "Look up; your redemption draweth nigh!" I want to take a perspective of what they were, and what we must become. I am inwardly convinced of the power that awaits us, the installation of God's movement right in our hearts.

I notice in the first church it wasn't possible for a lie to live, and I want you to keep in mind that there is a time coming when nothing of uncleanness will be able to remain in his little flock. The first church was so pure God overshadowed it; he nursed it, brought it through, and he has his hand upon us at this time. How do we know? The Lord hath laid the foundation which is an immovable foundation. It is built upon the prophets; it is built upon the apostles; it is built upon the Word of God, and the church will yet come into the fullness of the manifestation of the body of Christ.

God will keep his Word. The church will be ready like a bride adorned for her husband; the gifts will be a ministry clothed upon; the graces will adorn the believer, and will be far beyond anything we have seen.

Now, Ananias and Sapphira were, I believe, baptized believers. I have a firm conviction in my heart that God in the first outpouring of the Spirit did his work so beautifully that those three thousand who were pricked in their hearts met the condition of the Bible pattern. Peter said unto them: "Repent, and be baptized, ... and ye shall receive the gift of the Holy Ghost" (Acts 2:38). They obeyed and we have reason to believe they received the Holy Ghost. I cannot conceive of anything else but that the early church all received the outpouring of the Holy Ghost. And I believe today that we should press home to every soul the necessity of meeting the conditions and being filled with the Holy Ghost.

Then I notice in the fifth chapter of Acts that God had the particular oversight of the church. I love to think of this. They gave of their substance willingly; they laid it down at the apostles' feet, and they were so eager to give that they began selling their property, and brought the proceeds to the apostles. But there were two people who had sold the land who began to talk over the thing at home, and this was the sense of their argument: "This thing may go down; it may leak out. If we give it all, we shall lose it all and have nothing left," and so they reserved for themselves a portion, but they missed it. Listen: God never wants anything from you but a spontaneous heart gift, and anyone who gives spontaneously to God will always get a big cup full. God is never in any man's debt.

I notice the moment God visited this people in showing up this sin and bringing death to Ananias and Sapphira, it instantly brought a tremendous fear over all the church, a fear that brought an answer. There is a fear that brings an answer. Were they afraid of God? No, it was something better than that. When they saw that God was there in judgment upon them, they turned with a holy fear, with a reverence. It sobered things, and the people began to see that God was zealous for them. There are two kinds of fear, one that is afraid of God, and another fear that loves God, and that was the fear that came over them, the fear of grieving God, which the Lord wants us to have. Oh, to fear him in such a way that you would rather be shot than to grieve him! That is it. This came over the people, and when it came, another thing happened. "No one durst join themselves to them." That was a wonderful time. May God so sanctify his church that no one durst come near without he means business. Brother, did God have a hand in your plan? Did you join this people because you felt they were a choice people, or did you have the constraining power of God upon you?

I see more and more in this glorious life of God, that there is a pure whiteness to be achieved; there is a pure sonship without fear, and the saints of God shall rise in such confidence until they will remove what people think are mountains, till they will subdue what you call kingdoms.

Ministering in Ireland

I have had some wonderful times in Belfast, and in fact all over Ireland. I was in Belfast one day and a young man came to me and said: "Brother Wigglesworth, I am very much distressed," and he told me why. They had an old lady in their assembly who used to pray heaven down upon them. She had an accident. Her thigh was broken and they took her away to the infirmary. They put her in a plaster of Paris cast and she was in that condition for five months. Then they broke the cast and lifted her onto her feet and asked her to walk. She fell again and broke her leg in another place. And they found out that the first break had never knit together. They brought her home and laid her on the couch and the young man asked me to go and pray for her. When I got into the house I asked, "Do you believe that God can heal you?" She said, "Yes. When I heard you had come to the city, I thought, 'This is my chance to be healed.'" An old man, her husband, was sitting in a chair, had been sitting there for four years, helpless. And he said, "I do not believe. I will not believe. She was the only help I had. She has been taken away with a broken leg, and they have brought her back with her leg broken twice. How can I believe God?"

I turned to her and said, "Now is it all right?" "Yes," she said, "it is all right." The right leg was broken in two parts. Physicians can join up bones beautifully, and make them fit together, but if God doesn't come in with his healing power, no physician can heal them. As soon as the oil was placed upon her head and hands laid on, instantly down the right limb there was a stream of life, and she knew it. She said, "I am healed." I said, "If you are healed, you do not need anybody to help you." I went out. She took hold of the mantle shelf above her head and pulled herself up and walked all around the room. She was perfectly healed.

The old man said, "Make me walk." I said, "You old sinner, repent." Then he began, "You know, Lord, I didn't mean it." I really believe he was in earnest, and to show you the mercy and compassion of God, the moment I laid hands upon him, the power of God went through him and he rose up after four years' being stiff and walked around the room. That day both he and his wife were made whole.

Having One Heart and One Mind

Do you not believe now that God has a plan in all these things? I want you to realize that what God wants to do in us and through us in these days is to blend us together, give us one heart and one mind. They were all of one heart and one mind, and they had such faith that the shadow of Peter worked a transformation in their bodies. Of course, it was God that did the healing. But as Peter came along I can see the people moved by his presence. Beloved, we have one in the meeting tonight who is a million times mightier than Peter. His touch will set you free. It is the living virtue! "Go ... speak ... to the people all the words of this life" (Acts 5:20), the life of the Son of God, the quickener by the Word.

The first outpouring was of the Spirit, and the latter is to be the fullness of the Spirit. When God's mighty power shakes the foundation and purifies, there is a transformation. The Lord is the life, and where the life of the Spirit and the Word are together; they bring forth an issue of transforming and quickening until the man is made like Jesus. Jesus is the firstfruits. It is lovely to think that God sent him in the likeness of sinful flesh, and for sin condemned sin in the flesh. Then we are here tonight with a clear conception of this thing, that the life of Jesus has come into our flesh and delivered us from the power of darkness and disease; from bitterness and covetousness, idolatry and lust; from the corruption of the present evil world, by the same Spirit, the same life.

In God's Perfect Timing

I believe the Lord would have me take you to a moment in my life. I was having some meetings in Belfast, and this is the rising tide of what I believe was the move of the Spirit in a certain direction, to show the greatness of that which was to follow. Night after night the Lord had led me on certain lines of truth. There was so much in it that one felt they could not give up, and every night until ten o'clock we were opening up the Word of God. They came to me and said, "Brother, we have been feasting and are so full we are ready for a burst of some kind. Don't you think it is time to call an altar service?" I said I knew that God was working and the time would come when the altar service would be called, but we would have to get the mind of the Lord upon it. There was nothing more said. They began early in the afternoon to bring the sick people. We never had a thing said about it. The meeting came and every seat was taken up, the windowsills were filled, and every nook and corner.

The glory of God filled the place. It was the easiest thing in the world to preach; it came forth like a river, and the power of God rested mightily. There were a lot of people who had been seeking the baptism for years. Sinners were in the meeting, and a number of sick people. What happened? God hears me say this: There was a certain moment in that meeting when every sick person was healed, every lame person was healed, and every sinner saved, and it all took place in five minutes. There comes into a meeting sometimes something we cannot understand, and it is amazing how things happen.

When I was on the ship there was a man who had trained all his life, as it were, to be a physician. He became eminent and was looked up to as one of the leading physicians, an Indian. He had been to England to lecture, and was going back on the ship on which I was traveling. When a Christian Science woman was healed (see p. 25-26), she saw the captain and told him what God had done.

The captain arranged a meeting, and I had a fine chance to preach to all on the ship. The Indian doctor was there and he was struck with what happened. At the close of the meeting, people decided for Christ; some people followed me into my stateroom, where God healed them. This Indian doctor came to me. "I am done," he said. "I have no spirit left. You must talk to me." For two hours we talked and God dealt with him. He stood before me. "I will never have any more medicine," he said. "God has saved me." That physician saw the power of God and recognized it. You ask, what is that? That is where God plans a life in a moment, through one act. God wants the way into our lives. He wants to transform you by his grace. He wants to make you know that you are only here to be filled with his power and his presence for his glory. The "seed of the woman" must "bruise the serpent's head."

The Continuity of the Acts of the Apostles

Now, beloved, the Acts of the Apostles were written to prove to us that the power and manifestation of God were to be continuous. Have you read about the scattering of these people at Jerusalem, how God was with them? Do not be afraid of persecution. I am never at my best until I am in a conflict, and until I have a fight with the enemy. They think I am rather unmerciful in my dealing with the sick, but I have no mercy for the devil and get him out at any cost. I resist him with all the power that is within me. God wrought mightily through the persecution which came upon the church, and he could do the same today under similar circumstances.

From *The Latter Rain Evangel* (Chicago), August 1923, pp. 18–20. Preached in Chicago, October 31, 1922.

Preparing for an International Ministry

A Revival Hits Shropshire

My wife and I went to a small place in Shropshire where we held a meeting in a Primitive Methodist Chapel. As my wife preached, the fire fell and people were baptized in the Holy Spirit all over that chapel. There was a good deal of opposition and plenty of persecution. It was a small country village and everyone round about seemed to be greatly moved. They all knew about the revival in that church.

The next morning after the "fire had fallen," I went walking around the village and entered a grocery shop. A deep conviction fell on three people who were in that shop and before I left the store, all three were saved. After I came out, I went up the road a little and saw two women in a field who were carrying buckets. I shouted out to them, "Are you saved?" Here again a tremendous conviction seized them. They dropped their pails and began to pray; and right in that field the Lord saved those two women.

Wherever I went conviction seemed to be upon people. I went into a stone quarry where a lot of men were employed, and I preached to them as they were dressing the big stones, and again conviction fell and many were saved.

There were many people healed and baptized at that time and the glory of the Lord constantly fell. Twenty years later I visited that same village and the people recounted the story of that wonderful visitation from God.

Smith Wigglesworth, in Stanley H. Frodsham, *Smith Wigglesworth, Apostle of Faith* (Springfield, Mo.: Gospel Publishing House, 1948), pp. 48–49. Used by permission.

9
Be Not Afraid, Only Believe

I believe that it is in the purpose and will of God that I read to you some verses out of the fifth chapter of Mark's Gospel from the twenty-second verse, and will speak from the words, "Be not afraid, only believe."

This is one of those marvelous, glorious truths of the Scripture that is written to help us, that we may believe as we see the almightiness of God and also our possibility not only to enter in by faith, but to become partakers of the blessing he wants to give us. My message is on the lines of faith. Because some do not hear in faith, it profits them nothing. There is a hearing of faith and a hearing which means nothing more than listening to words. I beseech you tonight that you shall see to it that everything that is done may bring not only blessing to you but strength and character, and that you may be able to see the wonderfulness and goodness of God in this meeting. I want to impress upon you the importance of believing what the Scripture says, and I may have many things to relate about people who dared to believe God until it came to pass.

This is a wonderful Word. In fact, all of the Word of God is wonderful. It is an everlasting Word, a Word of power, a Word of health, a Word of substance, a Word of life. It gives life into the very nature, if we believe, to everyone that lays hold of it. I want you to understand tonight that there is a need for the Word of God. But it is a need many times that brings us the blessing.

Wigglesworth's Healing Testimony

Why am I here tonight? Because God delivered me when no other hand could do it. I stand before you as one who was given up by everybody, when no one could help. I was earnest and zealous for the salvation of souls. If you were in Bradford you would know. We had police protection for nearly twenty years in the best thoroughfare in the city, and in my humble way with my dear wife, who was all on fire for God, we were ministering in the open air. Full of zeal? Yes. But one night, thirty years ago, I was carried home helpless. We knew very little about divine healing, but we prayed through. It is thirty years and more since God healed me. I am sixty-five years old and fresher, in better health, and more fit for work than I was at that time. It is a most wonderful experience when the life of God becomes the life of man. The divine power that sweeps through the organism, cleansing the blood, makes the man fresh every day. The life of God is resurrection power.

When they brought me home helpless, we prayed all night. We did all we knew. At ten o'clock the next morning, I said to my wife, "This must be my last roll call." We had five children around us. I tell you it was not an easy thing to face our circumstances. I told my wife to do as she thought best, but the poor thing didn't know what to do. She called a physician, who examined me, shook his head, and said, "It is impossible for anything to be done for your husband; I am absolutely helpless. He has appendicitis and you have waited too long. His system will not stand an operation. A few hours, at best, will finish him."

It was true what the doctor said. He left her and said he would come back again, but he couldn't give her any hope. When he was out of the house, an old lady and a young man came in who knew how to pray. The young man put his knees on the bed and said: "Come out, you devil, in the name of

Jesus." It was a good job, we had no time for argument, and instantly I was free. Oh, hallelujah! I was as free as I am now. I never believed that any person ought to be in bed in the daytime, and I jumped up and went downstairs. My wife said: "Oh, are you up?" "I am all right, wife; it is all right now," I said. I had some men working for me, and she said none of them had turned up that morning, so I picked up my tools and went to work.

Then the doctor came. He walked up the stairs, and my wife called, "Doctor, doctor, he is out!" "What?" he said. "Yes," she said, "he is out at work." "Oh," he said, "you will never see him alive again. They will bring him in a corpse."

Am I a corpse?

Oh, when God does anything, it is done forever! And God wants you to know that he wants to do something in you forever. There are people in this place who have been delivered from appendicitis in these meetings. I have laid my hands on people with appendicitis when the doctors were in the place, and God has healed them.

Power Over the Enemy

I will tell you one incident before I pass on. It will stir up your faith. I am not here to be on exhibition. I am here to impart divine truth to you concerning the Word of God, that after I leave, you can do the same thing.

I went to Switzerland, and after I had been there for some weeks, a brother said, "Will you not go to meeting tonight?" "No," I said, "I have been at it all this time; you can take charge tonight." "What shall we do?" he asked. "Do?" I said, "Paul the apostle left people to do the work and passed on to another place—I have been here long enough. Now, you do the work." So he went to the meeting.

When he came back he said, "We have had a wonderful time." "What happened?" He said, "I invited them all out, took off my coat and rolled up my sleeves and prayed, and they were all healed. I did just like you did."

Jesus says, "I give you power over all the power of the enemy." They entered into the houses and healed the sick that were therein. The ministry of divine operation in us is wonderful, but who would take upon himself to say, "I can do this or that?" If it is God, it is all right, but if it is yourself, it is all wrong. When you are weak, then you are strong. When you are strong in your own strength, you are weak. You must realize this and live only in the place where the power of God rests upon you, and where the Spirit moves within you. Then God will mightily manifest his power and you will know as Jesus said, "The Spirit of the Lord is upon me."

A remarkable, glorious fact God brings to our minds tonight, the healing of a little, helpless girl. The physicians had failed. The mother said to the father, "There is only one hope—if you can see Jesus! As sure as you can meet Jesus our daughter will live." Do you think it is possible for anybody in Washington to go looking for Jesus without seeing him? Is it possible to think about Jesus without Jesus drawing near? No. This man knew the power there was in the name of Jesus: "In my name shall they cast out devils" (Mk 16:17). But we must be sure we know that name, for in Acts 19, the seven sons of Sceva said to the man possessed with devils, "We adjure you by Jesus whom Paul preacheth" (Acts 19:13). The evil spirit said, "Jesus I know, and Paul I know; but who are ye?" (Acts 19:15). Yes, the devil knows every believer—and the seven sons of Sceva nearly lost their lives. The evil powers came upon them and they barely escaped. It is more than repeating the name; it is the nature of the name in you; it is more than that; it is the divine personality within the human life which has come to take up his abode in you; and when he becomes all in all then God works through you. It is the life, the power of God. God works through the life.

The Lord is that life, and the ministry of it, and the power in the ministry, but the Holy Spirit brings everybody in such a place of divine relationship that he mightily lives in us and enables us to overcome the powers of the enemy. The Lord healed that child as they got a vision of Jesus. The word of the Lord came not with observation but with divine, mighty power, working in them until as an oracle by the power of the Spirit. Men and women were created anew by this new life divine. We have to see that when this divine word comes to us by the power of the Holy Ghost, it is according to the will of God that we speak; not with men's wisdom, but with divine minds operated by the Word of God; not channels only, but as oracles of the Spirit.

Seeking Jesus
As the ruler of the synagogue sought Jesus, he worshiped him. How they gathered around him! How everybody listened to what he had to say! He spoke not as a scribe, but with authority and power, decked with divine glory. (A young man was once preaching in a marketplace. At the close of the address, some atheist came and said, "There have been five Jesuses. Tell me which one it is that you preach." He answered, *"Him that rose from the dead."* There is only one that rose from the dead. There is only one Jesus that lives. And as he lives, we live also. Glory to God! We are risen with him, are living with him, and will reign with him.)

This ruler, as he drew near the crowd, went up to Jesus and said, "My little daughter lieth at the point of death.… Come and lay thy hands on her, that she may be healed" (Mk 5:23). "I will come," Jesus said. What a beautiful assurance. But as they were coming along the road, a woman met them who had an issue of blood for twelve years. When she began with this trouble she sought many physicians. She had some money, but the physicians took it all and left her worse than they found her. Have you any that do the same thing around here?

(When I was a plumber, I had to finish my work before I got the money, and I didn't always get it then. I think that if there was an arrangement whereby no doctor got his fee until he cured the patient, there wouldn't be so many people dying.)

Twelve years of sickness this woman had. She needed someone now who could heal without money, for she was bankrupt and helpless. Jesus comes to people that are withered up, diseased, lame, crippled in all kinds of ways. And when he comes, there is liberty to the captive, opening of eyes to the blind, and the opening of ears to the deaf. Many had said to this woman, "If you had only been with us today. We saw the most marvelous things, the crooked made straight, the lame to walk, the blind to see"—and the woman twelve years sick said, "Oh, you make me feel that if I could only see him I should be healed." It strengthened her faith and it became firm. She had a purpose within her. Faith is a mighty power. Faith will reach at everything. When real faith comes into operation, you will not say, "I don't feel much better"; faith says, "I am whole." Faith doesn't say, "It's a lame leg"; faith says, "My leg is all right." Faith never sees a goiter.

A young woman with a goiter came to be prayed for. In a testimony meeting she said, "I do praise the Lord for healing my goiter." She went home and said to her mother, "Oh, Mother, when the man prayed for me, God healed my goiter." For twelve months she went about telling everybody how God healed her goiter. Twelve months afterward I was in the same place and people said, "How big that lady's goiter is!" There came a time for testimony. She jumped up and said, "I was here twelve months ago and God healed me of my goiter. Such a marvelous twelve months!" When she went home, her folks said, "You should have seen the people today when you testified that God had healed your goiter. They think there is something amiss with you. If you go upstairs and look in the glass you will see the goiter is bigger than ever it was." She went upstairs, but she didn't look in the glass. She got down on her knees and said, "Oh, Lord, let all the people know just as you have let me know, how wonderfully you have healed me." The next morning her neck was as perfect as any neck you ever saw. Faith never looks. Faith praises God—it is done!

This poor, helpless woman with the issue of blood, who had been growing weaker and weaker for twelve years, pushed into the crowded thoroughfare when she knew Jesus was in the midst. She was stirred to the depths, and she pushed through and touched him. If you will believe God and touch him, you will go out of this place as well as possible. Jesus is the Healer!

Now listen! Some people in this place tonight put the touch of the Lord in the place of faith. The Lord would not have that woman believe that the touch had done it. She felt as soon as she touched him that virtue had gone through her, which is true. When the people were bitten by fiery serpents in the wilderness, God's Word said through Moses, "Every one that is bitten, when he looketh upon it, shall live" (Nm 21:8). The look made it possible for God to do it. Did the touch heal the woman? No, the touch meant something more—it was a living faith. Jesus said, "Thy faith hath made thee whole" (Mk 5:34). If God would just move on us to believe, there wouldn't a sick person leave this place tonight. As soon as this woman in the street, with all the crowd about her, began to testify, the devil came. The devil is always in a testimony meeting. When the sons of God gathered together in the time of Job, he was there.

Only Believe

While this was happening in the street, three persons came rushing from the house of Jairus and said, "There is no use now, your daughter is dead. This Jesus can do nothing for a dead daughter. Your wife needs you at home." But Jesus said, "Be not afraid, only believe" (Mk 5:36). He speaks the word just in time! Jesus is never behind time. When the tumult is the worst, the pain most severe, the cancer gripping the body, then the word comes, "Only believe." When everything seems as though it will fail, and is practically hopeless, the word of God comes to us: "Only believe."

When Jesus came to that house, there were a lot of people weeping and wailing. I have taken the last wreath to the cemetery. To be absent from the body is to be present with the Lord, and if you believe that, you will never take another wreath to the cemetery. It is unbelief that mourns. If you have faith that they are with the Lord, you will never take another flower to the grave. They are not there. Hallelujah!

These people were round about, weeping, wailing, and howling. He says, "Why make ye this ado, and weep? The damsel is not dead, but sleepeth" (Mk 5:39). There is a wonderful word that God wants you to hear. Jesus said, "I am the resurrection, and the life" (Jn 11:25). The believer may fall asleep, but the believer doesn't die. Oh, that people would understand the deep things of God—it would change the whole situation. It makes you look out with a glorious hope to the day when the Lord shall come. What does it say? "Them also which sleep in Jesus will God bring with him" (1 Thes 4:14). Jesus knew that. "The damsel is not dead, but sleepeth. And they laughed him to scorn" (Mk

5:39-40). To show the insincerity of these wailers, they could turn from wailing to laughing. Jesus took the father and mother of the maid and, going into the room where she was, took her hand and said, "Daughter, arise." And the child sat up. Praise the Lord! And he said, "Give her something to eat."

Jesus Is in Our Midst

Oh, the remarkableness of our Lord Jesus! I want to impress upon you tonight the importance of realizing that he is in the midst of us. No person need go away without knowing that they are not only saved but that God can live in these bodies! You are begotten the moment you believe, unto a lively hope. I wonder if anyone in this place is a stranger to this new birth into life? "He that believeth on the son hath everlasting life" (Jn 3:36). You have eternal life the moment you believe. The first life is temporal, natural, material, but in the new birth you exist as long as God—forever. We are begotten by an incorruptible power, by the Word of God. The new birth is unto righteousness, begotten by God the moment that you believe. We are on divine lines tonight. Oh, the wonderful adaptability of God coming right into this place! You people who have not been satisfied, who have come out for salvation, had good impressions, perhaps, but never knew the reality and joy of the new birth, let me enlist you. The Word of God says, "Before they call, I will answer" (Is 65:24). The raising of your hand is a signification of your heart's desire. God always saves through the heart. He that believeth in the heart and confesseth with his mouth shall be saved.

Jesus is here tonight to loose them that are bound. If you are suffering in your body, he will heal you now as we pray. He is saying to every sin-sick soul, to every disease-smitten one, "Be not afraid, only believe."

From *The Latter Rain Evangel* (Chicago), November 1924, pp. 5–8. Preached in Convention Hall, Washington, D.C., September 28, 1924. Reported by M.B.D.

10
Clothed With the Spirit

God has a plan for us in this life of the Spirit, this abundant life. Jesus came that we might have life. Satan comes to steal and kill and destroy, but God has for us abundance, a full measure, pressed down, shaken together, an overflowing, abundant measure. It is God filling us with his own personality and presence, making us salt and light and giving us revelation of himself; God with us in all circumstances and afflictions, persecutions, in every trial, girding us with truth. It is Christ the initiative, the Triune God in control; our every thought, word, and action must be in line with him, with no weakness or failure. Our God is a God of might, light, and revelation, preparing us for heaven. Our life is hid with Christ in God; when he who is our life shall be manifested, we also shall appear with him in glory (see Col 3:3-4).

The Earnest of the Spirit
"For we know that if our earthly house of this tabernacle were dissolved, we have a building of God, an house not made with hands, eternal in the heavens.... For we that are in this tabernacle do groan, being burdened: not for that we would be unclothed, but clothed upon, that mortality might be swallowed up of life. Now he that hath wrought us for the selfsame thing is God, who also hath given unto us the earnest of the Spirit" (2 Cor 5:1, 4-5).

God's Word is tremendous, a productive word, producing what it is—power. Producing God-likeness. We get to heaven through the Word of God; we have peace through the blood of his cross. Redemption is ours through the knowledge of the Word. I am saved because God's Word says so: "If thou shalt confess with thy mouth the Lord Jesus, and shalt believe in thine heart that God hath raised him from the dead, thou shalt be saved" (Rom 10:9). If I am baptized with the Holy Spirit it is because Jesus said, "Ye shall receive power, after that the Holy Ghost is come upon you" (Acts 1:8). We must all have one idea—to be filled with the Holy Ghost, to be filled with God.

Message in tongues with interpretation: *God hath sent his Word to free us from the law of sin and death. Except we die we cannot live; except we cease to be, God cannot be.*

The Holy Ghost has a royal plan, a heavenly plan. He came to unveil the King, to show the character of God, to unveil the precious blood. As I have the Holy Spirit within me, I see Jesus clothed for humanity; he was moved by the Spirit, led by the Spirit. We read of some who heard the Word of God but were not profited, because faith was lacking in them. We must have a living faith in God's Word, quickened by the Spirit. A man may be saved and still have a human spirit. When many hear about the baptism of the Holy Ghost, the human spirit at once arises against the truth. The human spirit is not subject to the law of God, neither can it be. The disciples at one time wanted to call down fire from heaven. Jesus said, "Ye know not what spirit ye are of."

Look at the fifth verse of our text: "Now he that hath wrought us for the selfsame thing is God, who also hath given unto us the earnest of the Spirit" (2 Cor 5:5). The clothing upon of the Spirit, human depravity covered, all that is contrary to the mind of God destroyed. God must have bodies for himself, perfectly prepared by the Holy Ghost, for the day of the Lord. "For in this we groan, earnestly desiring to be clothed upon with our house which is from heaven" (2 Cor 5:2). Is Paul speaking here of the coming of the Lord? No; yet it is in conjunction with this condition of preparedness. The Holy Ghost is coming to take out a church and a perfect bride; he must find in us perfect yieldedness, every desire subjected to him. He has come to reveal Christ in us, that the glorious flow of the life of God may outflow, rivers of living water to the thirsty land. "If Christ be in you, the body is dead because of sin; but the Spirit is life because of righteousness" (Rom 8:10).

Message in tongues with interpretation: *This is that which God hath declared, freedom from the law. "If any man love the world, the love of the Father is not in him. For all that is in the world, the lust of the flesh, and the lust of the eyes, and the pride of life, is not of the Father, but is of the world" (1 Jn 2:15-16).*

The Plan of the Spirit

The Spirit has to breathe in a new tenancy, a new order. He came to give the vision of a life in which Jesus is perfected. "Who hath saved us, and called us with an holy calling, not according to our works, but according to his own purpose and grace, which was given us in Christ Jesus before the world began, But is now made manifest by the appearing of our Saviour Jesus Christ, who hath abolished death, and hath brought life and immortality to light through the gospel" (2 Tm 1:9-10).

Saved, called to be saints, called with a holy calling, holy, pure, godlike, sons with power. It is a long time now since it was settled and death abolished. Death has no more power; mortality is a hindrance; sin has no more dominion; you reign in Christ, you appropriate his finished work. Don't groan and travail for a week if you are in need, *only believe*. Don't fight to get some special thing, *only believe*. It is according to your faith. God blesses you with faith. Have faith in God. If you are free in God, *believe*, and it shall be.

"If ye then be risen with Christ, seek those things which are above, where Christ sitteth on the right hand of God" (Col 3:1). Stir yourselves up, beloved—where are you? I am risen with Christ, planted. It was a beautiful planting. Seated. God gives me credit and I believe him; why should I doubt?

Message in tongues with interpretation: *Wherefore do you doubt? Faith reigns. God makes it possible. How many receive the Holy Ghost and Satan get a doubt in? Don't doubt; believe. There is power and strength in him; who dares believe God?*

Move off of Doubting Street; live in faith, Victory Street. Jesus sent seventy away, and they came back in victory. It takes God to make it real. Dare to believe till there is not a sick person, no sickness, everything withered, and the life of Jesus implanted within.

The devil makes you remember the day you failed; you would give the world to forget. God has forgotten; when he forgives, he forgets. God wants to make us pillars, honorable, strong, holy; God will take us on. I am enamored with inspiration of the great fact of the possibility. God wants you to know that you are saved, cleansed, delivered, and marching on to victory. Set your affections on things above; get into the heavenly places with Christ; be transformed by the renewing of your mind. What a privilege to kneel and get right into heaven the moment we pray! That's where the glory descends and the fire burns and faith is active and the light dispels the darkness. Mortality hinders, but the life of Jesus eats up mortality.

Have You Received?

The Acts of the Apostles deals with receiving the Holy Ghost, and the Epistles are written to believers baptized in the Holy Ghost. When I was in New Zealand, some brethren came questioning about this baptism. They quoted the Epistles, but before we are in the experience of the Epistles we must go through the Acts. I asked them, "When did you speak in mysteries?" (see 1 Cor 14:2). But they had not yet come into the baptism of the Holy Ghost.

Jesus is the life and light of men; no man has this light and walketh in darkness. When Christ who is our life shall appear, we also shall appear with him in glory. Where his life is, disease cannot remain; where his life is full, the rudiments cannot remain. Is not he that indwells us greater than all? Yes, when he has full control. If one thing is permitted outside the will of God, it hinders in our standing against the powers of Satan. We must allow the Word of God to judge us, lest we stand condemned with the world when he who is our life shall appear. Have I any life apart from him?—any joy, any fellowship? Jesus said, "The prince of this world cometh and findeth nothing in me." All that is contrary in us is withered by the indwelling life of the Son of God.

"We that are in this tabernacle do groan, being burdened: not for that we would be unclothed, but clothed upon, that mortality might be swallowed up of life" (2 Cor 5:4). Are we ready, clothed upon? Mortality swallowed up of life? If he came who is our life, we should go. It's heaven on earth; heaven has begun with me; I am happy now and free, since the Comforter has come, the great revealer of the kingdom. He came to give us the more abundant life. God has designed the plan. Nothing really matters if the Lord loves us. God sets great store by us. The pure in heart see God. There are no stiff knees, nor cough, nor pain, in the Spirit; nothing ails us if we are filled with the Spirit. "If the Spirit of him that raised up Jesus from the dead dwell in you, he that raised up Christ from the dead shall also quicken your mortal bodies by his Spirit that dwelleth in you" (Rom 8:11).

Free from the law of sin and death, the perfect law destroying the natural law, spiritual activity taking in every passing ray, days of heaven upon earth, no sickness, not knowing we have a body, the life of God changing us, bringing us into the heavenly realm, where we reign over principalities and all evil, limitless, powerful, supernatural. If the natural body decays, the Spirit renews. Our spiritual power should increase until with one mind and one heart the glory is brought down over all the earth, right on into divine life, keeping the evidence, the whole life filled.

This is Pentecost! The life of the Lord manifest wherever we are, in bus and train, so filled with the life of Jesus unto perfection, rejoicing in hope of the glory of God, always looking for his coming. The life of the Lord in us acts as a magnet, drawing people to him. And his life eats up all nonessentials. I must have the overflowing life of the Spirit; God is not pleased with less. It is a disgrace to be on an ordinary plane after we are filled with the Holy Ghost. We are to be salt in the earth; not lukewarm, *hot;* which means seeing God with largeness, liberty, movement, and power. Believe! Believe! Amen.

From *Redemption Tidings* (England), June 1926, pp. 2–3.

11
The Pentecostal Power

Our passage from the Word of God is a wonderful reading. It has many things in it which indicate to us that there was something more marvelous about it than human power; and when I think about Pentecost, I am astonished from day to day because of how mighty and wonderful it is, and how the glory overshadows it. I think sometimes about these things and they make me feel we have only just touched it. Truly it is so, but we must thank God that we have touched it. We must not give in because we have only touched. Whatever God has done in the past, his name is still the same. When hearts are burdened and they come face to face with the need of the day, they look into God's Word and it brings in a propeller of power or an anointing that makes you know he has truly visited.

It was a wonderful day when Jesus left the glory. I can imagine all the angels and God the Father and all heaven so wonderfully stirred that day when the angels were sent to tell that wonderful story: Peace on earth and good will to men (see Lk 2:14). It was a glorious day when they beheld the Babe for the first time and God was looking on. What happened after that day and until he was thirty years old, I suppose, would take a big book to contain it. It was a working up to a great climax.

Touches of His Power

I know that Pentecost in my life is a working up to a climax, it is not all done in a day. There are many waters and all kinds of times until we get to the real summit of everything. The power of God is here to prevail. God is with us. The mother of Jesus hid a lot of things in her heart. The time came when it was made manifest at Jordan that Jesus was the Son of God. Oh, how beautifully it was made known! It had to be made known first to one that was full of the vision of God. The vision comes to those who are full. Did it ever strike you we cannot be too full for a vision, we cannot have too much of God? The more of God, then the visions begin. When God has you in his own plan, what a change, how things operate. You wonder, you see things in a new light. And how God is being glorified as you yield from day to day, and the Spirit seems to lay hold of you and bring you on. Yes, it is pressing on, and then he gives us touches of his wonderful power, manifestations of the glory of these things and indications of greater things to follow, and these days which we are living in now speak of better days. How wonderful!

Where should we have been today if we had stopped short, if we had not fulfilled the vision which God gave us? I am thinking about that time when Christ sent the Spirit; and Paul did not know much about that: his heart was stirred, his eyes were dim, he was going to put the whole thing to an end in a short time—and Jesus was looking on. We can scarcely understand the whole process only as God seems to show us, when he gets us into his plan and works with us little by little. We are all amazed that we are amongst the "tongues people"; it is altogether out of order according to the natural. Some of us would have never been in this pentecostal movement had we not been drawn, but God has a wonderful way of drawing us. Paul never intended to be among the disciples, Paul never intended to have anything to do with this man called Jesus, but God was working. God has been working with us and has brought us to this place. It is marvelous! Oh, the vision of God, the wonderful manifestation which God has for Israel!

Ministering in God's Way

I have one purpose in my heart, and it is surely God's plan for me, that I want you to see that Jesus Christ is the greatest manifestation in all the world, and his power is unequaled, but there is only one way to minister it. I want you to notice that these people, after they had seen Paul working wonders by this power, began on a natural line. I see it is necessary for me if I want to do anything for God, I must get the knowledge of God, I must get the vision of God, I cannot work on my own. It must be a divine revelation of the Son of God. It must be that. I can see as clearly as anything that Paul in his mad pursuit had to be stopped in the way, and after he was stopped in the way and had the vision from heaven and that light from heaven, instantly he realized that he had been working the wrong way. And as soon as the power of the Holy Ghost fell upon him, he began in the way in which God wanted him to go. And it was wonderful how he had to suffer to come into the way. It is broken spirits, it is tried lives, and it is being driven into a corner as if some strange thing had happened; that is surely the way to get to know the way of God.

Paul had not any power to use the name of Jesus as he did use it, only as he had to go through the privations and the difficulties; and even when all things seemed as though shipwrecked, God stood by him and made him know that there was something behind all the time that was with him, and able to carry him through, and bring out that for which his heart was all the time longing. Unconsciously he seemed to be so filled with the Holy Ghost that all that was needed was just the bringing of the aprons and the handkerchiefs and sending them forth. I can imagine these people looking on and seeing him and saying, "But it is all in the name, don't you notice that when he sends the handkerchiefs and the aprons he says, 'In the name of the Lord Jesus I command that evil to come out'?"

These people had been looking round and watching, and they thought, "It is only the name, that is all that is needed," and so these men said, "We will do the same." These vagabond Jews, those seven sons of Sceva, were determined to make this thing answer, and they came to the place where that man had been for years possessed with an evil power, and as they entered in they said, "We adjure you by Jesus whom Paul preacheth." The demon said, "Jesus I know, and Paul I know; but who are ye?" (see Acts 19:13-15). And this evil power leaped upon them and tore their things off their backs and they went out naked and wounded. It was the name, only they did not understand it. Oh, that God should help us to understand the name! It is the name! Oh, it is still the name, but you must understand there is the ministry of the name; there is something in the name that makes the whole world charmed. It is the Holy Spirit back of the ministry, it is the knowledge of him, it is the ministry of the knowledge of him, and I can understand it is only that.

Ministry of the Knowledge

I want to speak about the ministry of the knowledge; it is important. God help us to see. I am satisfied with two things: (1) I am satisfied it is the knowledge of the blood of Jesus Christ today, and (2) the knowledge of his perfect holiness. I am perfectly cleansed from all sin and made holy in the knowledge of his holiness. I am satisfied today that as I know him, and the knowledge of his power, and the Christ that is manifested, and the power that worketh in me to minister as I am ministering only in the knowledge of it, it is effective, so that it brings out the very thing which the Word of God says it will do, in the ministry of which, as I know it, it has power over all evil powers by its effectual working in that way. I minister today in the power of the knowledge of the ministry of it, and beyond that there is a certain sense that I overcome the world according to my faith in him, and I am more than conqueror over everything just in the knowledge that I have of him being over everything, as crowned by the Father to bring everything into subjection.

Shouting won't do it, but there is a lubrication about it which is gloriously felt within and brings it into perfect harmony with the will of God. It is not in the shout, and yet we cannot help but shout. It is in the ministry of the knowledge that he is Lord over all demons, all powers of wickedness.

Message in tongues with interpretation: *The Holy One which anointed Jesus is so abiding by the Spirit in the one that is clothed upon to use the name till the glory is manifested and the demons flee; they cannot stand the glory of the manifestation of the Spirit which is manifest.*

So I am realizing that Paul went about clothed in the Spirit. This was wonderful. His body was full of virtue? No! Virtue in Jesus, by the ministry of faith in the name of Jesus through the power of the unction of the Holy Ghost in Paul.

Message in tongues with interpretation: *The liberty of the Spirit bringeth the office.*

It is an office, it is a position, it is a place of rest, of faith. Sometimes the demon powers are dealt with very differently, not all the same way; but the ministry of the Spirit by which it is ministered by the power of the word "Jesus" never fails to accomplish the purpose for which the one in charge has wisdom or discernment to see because along with the Spirit of ministry there comes the revelation of the need of the needy one that is bound.

So differently the Spirit ministers the name of Jesus. I see it continually happening. I see those things answer and all the time the Lord is building up a structure of his own power by a living faith in the knowledge of the sovereignty of the name of Jesus. If I turn to John's Gospel, I get the whole thing practically in a nutshell. To know Thee, O God, and Jesus Christ whom Thou has sent, is eternal life. We must have the knowledge and power of God and the knowledge of Jesus Christ, the embodiment of God, to be clothed upon with God—God in human flesh. I see those who have come into line who are possessed with the blessed Christ, and the power of the baptism—which is the revelation of the Christ of God within. And it is so evident in the person who is baptized, and Christ is so plainly abiding that the moment he is confronted with evil, instantly he is sensitive to the position of this confronting, and he is able to deal accordingly.

The Word of God and Real Faith
The difference between the sons of Sceva and Paul is this: They said "It is only using the word." How many people only use the word? How many times are people defeated because they think it is just the word? How many people have been brokenhearted because it did not answer when they used the word? I can read into my text this afternoon, "He that believeth shall speak in

tongues, he that believeth shall cast out devils, he that believeth shall lay hands on the sick." On the surface it seems easy, but you must understand that there are volumes to be applied to the word "believe." To believe is to believe in the need of the majesty of the glory of the power, which is all power, which brings all other powers into subjection.

And what is belief? Sum it up in a few sentences. To believe is to have the knowledge of him in whom you believe. It is not to believe in the word "Jesus," but to believe in the nature, to believe in the vision, for all power is given unto him. Greater is he that is within thee in the revelation of faith than he that is in the world. And so I say to you, do not be discouraged if every demon has not gone out. The very moment you have gone, do not think there is an end of it. We have to see that if it had only been using the name, those evil powers would have gone out in that name by the sons of Sceva. It is not that. It is the virtue of the power of the Holy Ghost, with the revelation of the deity of our Christ of glory, where all power is given unto him. And in the knowledge of Christ, in the faith of what he is, demons must surrender, demons must go out. I say it reverently, these bodies of ours are so constructed by God that we may be filled with that divine revelation of the Son of God till it is manifest to the devils you confront, and they have to go. The Master is in, they see the Master. Jesus I know, and Paul I know. The ministry of the Master! How we need to get to know him till within us we are full of the manifestation of the King over all demons.

Christ Must Be Manifested

Brothers and sisters, my heart is full. The depths of my yearnings are for the pentecostal people. My cry is that we will not miss the opportunity of the baptism of the Holy Ghost, that Christ may be manifested in the human till every power of evil will be subject to him. The devils know. Two important things are before me. To master the situation of myself. You are not going to meet devils if you cannot master yourself, because you soon find the devil bigger than yourself, and it is only when you are subdued that Christ is enthroned and the embodiment of the Spirit is so gloriously covering the human life. It is then that Jesus is glorified to the full. So first it is the losing of ourselves and then it is the incoming of another; it is the glorifying of him which is to fulfill all things and when he gets us, he can do it. When we yield ourselves to God, he will be delighted to allow the Christ to be so manifested in you that it will be no difficulty for the devil to know who you are.

I am satisfied that Pentecost is to reestablish God in human flesh. Do I need to say it again? The power of the Holy Ghost has to come to be enthroned in the human life, so it does not matter what state we are in. Christ is manifested in the place where devils are, the place where religious devils are, the place where a false religion and unbelief is, the place where a formal religion has taken the place of holiness and righteousness. You have need to have holiness, the righteousness and the Spirit of the Master, so that in every walk of life everything that is not like our Lord Jesus will have to depart. And that is what is needed today.

I ask you in the Holy Ghost to seek the place where he is in power. "Jesus I know, and Paul I know; but who are ye?" May God stamp it upon us if the devil is not afraid of you. May the Holy Ghost make us today terrors of evildoers, for the Holy Ghost came into us to judge the world of sin, of unbelief, of righteousness, and that is the purpose of the Holy Ghost. The devils will know us, and Jesus will know us.

From *The Pentecostal Evangel* (Springfield, Mo.), November 12, 1927, pp. 6–7

12
Paul's Vision and the Baptism of the Holy Ghost

We need to kindle in one another a holier zeal than we have ever possessed before. No man can meet the need of today but the man filled with God. God has promised to fill us. You may be filled with the mighty power of God and yet in a way not realize it, be used by a power apart from yourself, a power that keeps you from self-exhibition. Just as the sun by its mighty power brings certain resources to nature, so I believe the power of God in the human soul is capable, as we exercise living faith, of bringing about things which otherwise could never be accomplished.

"Whereupon, O king Agrippa, I was not disobedient unto the heavenly vision" (Acts 26:19).

I want to speak of Pentecost and the fullness of the Spirit, and of what God is able to do with any man who is yielded to him. Paul is our example of one yielded to God: "Whereupon, O king Agrippa, I was not disobedient unto the heavenly vision" (Acts 26:19).

Paul's Conversion

If you will read the twenty-sixth chapter of Acts you will see Paul testifying to his conversion, to the commission given him to go to the Gentiles to turn them from darkness to light, from the power of Satan to God, and to the fact that he "was not disobedient unto the heavenly vision." In Acts 9, we read that for three days after this vision Paul was blind. I believe that in those days he was brought to a state of brokenheartedness. And then God had him. It is a wonderful thing when God gets you. You are not much good for anything until God gets you. When God gets you, you are loosened, you are free, but you act only as he wills for you to act. And when you act only for him and are living in the Spirit, some things that are worthwhile will be accomplished all the time.

I believe that in those three days Paul was brought to a place of weeping, contrition, heart-meltedness, yieldedness. It is when we are brought to a place of real repentance, of brokenhearted-ness, of contrition, that it is possible for God's likeness to be stamped on us. It is then that the water of life begins to fill us, and as we are open to the floods of the Spirit which come in the baptism in the Holy Ghost, we will find that the Holy Ghost will not only fertilize our own life but rivers of life will flow from us, rivers that will touch many others. No one can tell what a river can do when it is set flowing by God. The ever deepening river that Ezekiel speaks of brought abundance of life everywhere it flowed. So it is with the life in the Holy Ghost.

Many Opportunities

A life in the Holy Ghost is one of selflessness. You will remember that our Lord Jesus after he was filled with the Spirit refused to make bread for himself at the suggestion of Satan, but we find that he reached a place where he could make bread for thousands. And when I come to the place where I refuse to live for my own selfish interests, then God will do something for me; and by his grace, I will gladly do anything for him that he may desire me to do.

In his helplessness and brokenness, Paul cried: "Lord, what

wilt thou have me to do?" (Acts 9:6). That cry reached to heaven, and as a result there came to him a holy man touched with the same fire and zeal that filled his Master, and he laid his hands upon Paul and told him that he was to receive his sight and be filled with the Holy Ghost. And with that word of power a celestial glory came into the life of Paul. That was for Paul the beginning of a life in the Holy Ghost. It is evident from Paul's testimony that God gave him a vision, a vision to which he was not disobedient. There should always be a vision in the baptism in the Spirit. Be sure to get the vision of God's plan and purpose for your life. But visions are no good except we make them real, except we claim them as they come and make them our own, and the purpose of our life is to carry out what the Spirit reveals by vision.

Many people lack the power because they do not keep the vision, because they do not allow the fire which has come to continue to burn. There must be a continuous burning on the altar. Holy Ghost power in a man is meant to be an increasing force, an enlargement. When Ezekiel saw the vision of the river that came out from the threshold under the altar, that river did not grow smaller and smaller, but larger and larger. That is God's plan always. God has never anything of a diminishing type.

Changed Into Another Man
The Lord took particular care of Paul and did not rush him through the business. He gave him time to study the Word. He gave him time to get a revelation of his wonderful grace. There are some people who think that everything ought to be done in a tremendous hurry. With God it is not so. God takes plenty of time, and he has a wonderful way of developing things as he goes along. Trust him as he takes time to work in you to will and to do his own pleasure.

A man baptized in the Holy Ghost is no longer a natural man; he is transformed by the Spirit and changed into another man. Joshua and Caleb, as they were filled with faith, were different from all the men around them, and so they encouraged all the others by saying, "If the Lord delight in us, then he will bring us into this land, and give it us" (Nm 14:8). They had got the vision of God's plan and purpose and they were true to the vision. Is God the Holy Ghost arranging things for you, or are you arranging things according to your own plan? Catch the heavenly vision and enter into a place of rest where you can stand still and see the salvation of the Lord.

Reliance on God

A man who is dependent upon the Holy Ghost ceases from confidence in his own ability. He will rely only upon the omnipotent power of the Most High. The man who lives in the Spirit will always keep in touch with his Master, in the passing crowds or wherever he may be. He should have no room for anything that steps lower than the unction that was on his Master, or for anything that hinders him from being about his Master's business. If you are filled with the Holy Ghost, you will long for the spiritual food that you find in the Word of God, and you will have no resources but those that are heavenly. You have been "planted" with Christ and have "risen with him," and you are "seated with him in heavenly places" (see Eph 2:6); your language is the heavenly language, your source of inspiration is the will of the Lord; God is enthroned in your whole life and you see things from above and not from below.

The revelation of Jesus to my soul by the Holy Ghost brings me to the place where I am willing, if need be, to die on what the Word says. The three Hebrew children said to the king, "We are not careful to answer thee in this matter" (Dn 3:16);

and when a man of God is quickened by the Spirit, he does not fear the threatenings of men. The furnace seven times heated is of no consequence to the man who has heard the voice of God; the lions' den has no terrors for the man who opens his windows and talks to the Father. The people who live in the unction of the Spirit are taken out of the world in the sense that they are kept in the world without being defiled by the evil of the world.

A Life of Revelation

The Lord said to Paul, "I have appeared unto thee ... to make thee a minister and a witness both of these things which thou hast seen, and of those things in the which I will appear unto thee" (Acts 26:16). Paul was given the vision as far as he could take it in; then the Lord said, "There are other things in which I shall again appear unto thee." Did he ever appear unto Paul after that? Certainly he did.

At a later date Paul said, "When it pleased God, who separated me from my mother's womb, and called me by his grace, to reveal his Son in me, that I might preach him among the heathen; immediately I conferred not with flesh and blood" (Gal 1:15-16). There is no man who can be clothed with the Spirit and catch the fire and zeal of the Master every day and many times a day, without ceasing in every way to be connected with the "arm of flesh" which would draw him aside from the power of God. Many men have lost the glory because they have been taken up with the natural. If we are going to accomplish in the Spirit the things that God has purposed for us, we must never turn again to the flesh. If we are Spirit-filled, God has brought us into relationship with himself, and now he is all in all to us. Nehemiah stood before the king, and when the king, seeing his countenance sad, said to him, "For what dost thou make request?" (Neh 2:4), he immediately communed with the God of heaven. If we keep in continuous communion with the Lord of heaven we should be ready for every emergency.

Eager for the Vision

When Paul was preaching to the saints in Troas (Acts 20) the holy, radiant glory that was filling his soul was so great that the people became eager for it, so that until midnight they drank in at the fountain of life. And as the rivers of water were pouring forth from him a young man fell down from the third loft. Paul went down and embraced him, and the life of the Lord given to Paul was imparted to the young man, and he was brought back to life. There was always equipment for every emergency: blessed, holy equipment given by God. It is wonderful to think that we too can be partakers of the divine nature just as Paul was and can enter into the fellowship of the Lord Jesus Christ even as he did, for the same Holy Ghost that was imparted to Paul, our Lord is willing to impart to us.

Fellowship With Jesus

It was a necessity that Jesus live with his disciples for three years and walk in and out among them and show forth his glory from day to day. The Lord had continually day by day to bring himself into their vision, into their mind, into their very nature. He had to press himself into their life, to make them a success after he had ascended to heaven. He had to show them how wonderfully and gracefully and peacefully he could move the crowds. He had to bring himself so into the minds and hearts of the disciples as to convince them that he was really and truly the Son of God. They could never accomplish what they had to accomplish until he had proved that to them. They could only manifest him to others when he had imparted his life into the very core of their nature. He told them that it was expedient that he go away. After his death and resurrection, the Holy Spirit would come and he himself would come unto them and manifest his life and power through them. Just as he was clothed with the Spirit himself, he wanted them to be clothed with the Spirit. And there was a wonderful continuance of his ministry through these yielded men when they were filled with the Spirit. And today there will be a mighty continuance of the glorious ministry of our risen Lord through men and women filled with the Spirit who refuse to live for their own purposes and plans, but who are eager to fulfill the vision given them by our ascended Lord.

What is the Baptism?

Some people have a wrong notion concerning the baptism in the Holy Ghost. The baptism is nothing less than the Third Person of the Blessed Trinity coming down from the glory, the executive Spirit of the Triune God indwelling your body, revealing the truth to you, causing your bowels to yearn with compassion for the lost, just as Jesus yearned, to travail as he travailed, to mourn as he mourned, to groan as he groaned. Oh, that God might bring from our hearts the cry for a deluge of the Spirit so that we may be prepared for him to fulfill all his purposes in us and for us. What a blessing it is when you are at wits'-end corner to be able to throw yourself on the omnipotent power of God, and what a wonderful transformation he can bring in a moment.

Last week I went into a house where they were very much distressed. A young woman was there who, they told me, had not been able to drink for six years. Her body had gone down, but the Lord had inspired her with faith and she said to her father, "Oh, Father, I ought to have relief today. Somehow I feel this whole trouble ought to go today." I knew what it was. It was a demon in the throat. I believe that the devil is at the bottom of practically every evil in human lives. It was a serious thing to see that beautiful young woman, who, because of this one thing in her life, was so disorganized in her mind and body. I knew it was the power of Satan. How did I know? Because it attacked her at a vital point, and the thing had preyed on her mind and she was filled with fear so that she said, "I dare not drink, for if I do I shall choke."

Deliverance to the Captives

I asked the father and mother to go out of the room and then I said to the young woman, "You will be free and drink as much as you want when I have done with you if you will only believe. As sure as you are there you will drink as much as you want." I said further, "Our brethren are going out in the streets to preach tonight and I shall be among them, and in our preaching we will say definitely, 'Every one that will believe on the Lord Jesus Christ can be saved.' We will also tell them that everyone that believes can be healed. The Word of God shows us plainly that the Son of God bore our sins and our sicknesses at Calvary. They will emphasize it over and over again. It is just as true to say, 'Himself took our infirmities, and bare our sicknesses' (Mt 8:17) as it is to say, 'He was wounded for our transgressions, he was bruised for our iniquities'" (Is 53:5). So I said to her, "Now do you believe?" She said, "Yes, I believe that in the name of Jesus you can cast the evil power out." I then laid my hands on her in the name of Jesus. "It is done; you drink."

She went out laughingly and drew the first glass of water and drank. She cried out, "Mother! Father! Brother! I have drunk one glass!" There was joy in the house. What did it? It was the living faith of the Son of God. Oh, if we only knew how rich we are, and how near we are to the Fountain of Life. "All things are possible to him that believeth." Aeneas, who had kept his bed for eight years, was told by Peter, "Jesus Christ maketh thee whole: arise, and make thy bed" (Acts 9:34), and he arose immediately. What did it? A life clothed with the Spirit.

An Enlarged Ministry

When I was baptized in the Holy Ghost, there was the unfolding of a new era of my life and I passed into that and rejoiced in the fact of it, and others with me. But the moment I reached that, God had been ready with another ministry for me. Jesus said, in substance, "If you honor me here, I will honor you yonder." Whatever it may be that you are working at for God here, he is working out a far greater and a divine glory for you. You have no need to be constantly talking of what you are going to appear like in glory. The chief thing is that you realize in yourself a deeper manifestation of the power of God today than yesterday, and that you have something more clear today of the mind of the Spirit than you had the day before; that nothing comes between you and God to cloud your mind. You are to have more of a vision of the glory of God today than yesterday, and to be living in such a state of bliss that it is heavenly to live. Paul got to the place where the Holy Ghost could enlarge him more and more. I find that if I continually keep my mind upon God he unfolds things to me; and if I obediently walk before God and keep my heart pure and clean and holy and right, he will always be lifting me higher than I have ever expected to be.

Present Your Bodies

In Romans 12:1, Paul speaks about a certain place being reached. He speaks about an altar upon which he has laid himself. When he had experienced the mercies of the Lord he could do no other than make a presentation of his body on the altar. It was to be always on the altar, never to be taken off. And he beseeches us to be in this place of continual sacrifice. It is at this place the Holy Ghost will bring forth things new and old for us. Paul so lived in the Spirit that he could write and speak as the oracle of the Holy Ghost, things that portrayed the mind of God. As we read these things today, they come to us as the river flowing from the throne of God himself.

God wants us, also, to be oracles through whom he can cause the water of life to flow. How does it come? It comes when we are in a place low enough for God to pour in, pour in, pour in. God wants to do the same for us as he did for Paul. Shall we stop short of what he says we ought to be? Shall we cease to come into line with the Mind that is always thinking for our best? Shall we cease to humble ourselves before him, who took the way of the cross for us? Shall we withhold ourselves from him, who could weep over the doomed city, from the Lord Jesus Christ, who "trod the winepress alone"? Shall we cease to give him our all? To what profit will it be if we hold back anything from him who gives us a thousand times more than ever he asks from us? In Hebrews 2, he says he is going to bring many sons to glory. It means that he is going to clothe them with his glory. Let that be your vision. If you have lost the vision, he is tender to those who cry to him. He never turns away from the broken heart, and those that seek him with a whole heart will always find him.

Great Grace

The people in the days of the apostles took joyfully the spoiling of their goods, and I know there is a like measure of grace given to the man who says, "I will go all the way with Jesus."

What is that measure of grace? It is the grace which enables us to press forward to the goal that God will have us reach. We should heed those words, "Let no man take thy crown." We have only touched the very fringe of this outpouring of the Spirit. We must go in for all that God has for us. If we do not fall into line with the will of God, there will be somebody else who will. God is able to raise up men who will carry out his behests. At the triumphal entry when the multitude cried out in praise, and the Pharisees objected, Jesus said, "If these should hold their peace, the stones would immediately cry out" (Lk 19:40).

I have a Jesus like that, who can speak the word and the thing is done. I have a Jesus indwelling me and vitalizing me with a faith that believes that all his promises are true; I have a Jesus within me who has never let me get fainthearted. Let us press on in faith along the line of God's will, and the outpouring which we have longed to see will come. Cheer up, hold on, never let go of the vision. Be sure it is as much for you as for anybody else, and God will surely bring it to pass. All blessings come from above; therefore, keep your eyes on Jesus. Never weary. He will be with you to strengthen you in the way. Hallelujah!

From *The Pentecostal Evangel* (Springfield, Mo.), April 21, 1928, pp. 1, 6–7.

Preparing for an International Ministry

Executioner's Life Transformed

James Berry was the Crown's Public Executioner from 1884 to 1892. He was so vile and his language so filthy that even the most ungodly men of the city would avoid meeting him. He was responsible for all the executions in the area, and he later told Wigglesworth that he believed that the demon power in the murderers he hanged entered into him at their death. He was possessed with a legion of demons.

Although he had retired from the post of hangman some years earlier, the thoughts of the men he had executed haunted him day and night. In the end he determined to kill himself; he intended boarding a train in Bradford and hurling himself from it into the path of an oncoming train as a quick way of ending his miserable life. But God had other plans for him.

There was a young man at the railway depot who had been converted at the Wigglesworths' Mission the previous evening. He was filled with newfound enthusiasm to witness to others about his Savior; seeing Berry standing alone at the station, he decided to witness to him.

Eventually the young man persuaded the hangman to accompany him to the Mission for the evening service. There Berry experienced great conviction of sin. "For two and a half hours," said Smith, "he was literally sweating under conviction and you could see a vapor rising up from him." Then he surrendered his life to God.

Wigglesworth sent up a silent prayer. "Lord, tell me what to do." He heard God tell him, "Don't leave him. Go home with him." Both men made their way to the new convert's home, where he said to his wife, "God has saved me." She was overwhelmed and wept many tears. Then she too gave her life to Christ. "I tell you there was a difference in that home," recalled Wigglesworth. "Even the cat knew the difference."

The sequel to the story is that James Berry, following his conversion, became a prominent campaigner for the abolition of the death penalty.

Jack Hywel-Davies, *The Life of Smith Wigglesworth* (Ann Arbor, Mich.: Servant, 1987), pp. 47–48. Used by permission. See also Justin Atholl, *The Reluctant Hangman, The Story of James Berry, Executioner 1884–1892*, pp. 180–82, pamphlet: "Conversion of James Berry at Bowland Street Mission Bradford," n.d.

13
About the Gifts of the Spirit

"Forasmuch as ye are zealous of spiritual gifts, seek that ye may excel to the edifying of the church" (1 Cor 14:12).

This is the Word of God, and it is most important that when we read it we do so with purpose of heart to obey its every precept. We have no right to open the Word of God carelessly or indifferently. I have no right to come to you with any message unless it is absolutely in the perfect order of God. I believe we are in order to consider further this subject in these days when so many people are receiving the baptism of the Holy Ghost, and then do not know which way to go.

We have a great need today. It is that we may be supplied with revelation according to the mind of the Lord, that we may be instructed by the mind of the Spirit, that we may be able rightly to divide the Word of Truth, that we may not be novices, seeing that the Spirit of the Lord has come to us in revelation. We ought to be alert to every touch of divine, spiritual illumination.

We should carefully consider what the apostle said to us: "Grieve not the Holy Spirit of God, whereby ye are sealed unto the day of redemption" (Eph 4:30). The sealing of the Spirit is very remarkable and I pray God that not one person may lose the divine inheritance that God has chosen for you, greater than you could choose if you had your mind ten times more largely exercised. God's mind is greater than yours. His thought is higher than the heavens over you, so that you need not be afraid.

I have great love for my boys in England, great love for my daughter here; but it is nothing in comparison to God's love toward us. God's love is desirous that we should walk up and down the earth as his son, clothed, filled, radiant, with fire beaming forth from the countenance, setting forth the power of the Spirit, so that the people jump into liberty.

Purpose of the Gifts

But there is deplorable ignorance among those who have gifts. It is not right for you to think that because you have a gift you are to wave it before the people and try to get their minds upon that, because if you do you will be out of the will of God. Gifts and callings may be in the body without repentance, but remember that God calls you to account for the gift's being properly administered in a spiritual way after you have received it. It is not given to adorn *you*, but to sustain, build, edify, and bless the church. When the church receives this edification and God ministers through that member, then all the members will rejoice together. God moves upon us as his offspring, as his choice and fruit of the earth. He wants us to be decked in wonderful raiment, even as our Master.

His operations upon us may be painful but the wise saint will remember that among those whom God chastens it is he who is exercised by that chastening to whom "it yieldeth the peaceable fruit of righteousness" (Heb 12:11). Therefore let him do with you what seemeth good to him, for he has his hand upon you and he will not willingly take it off till he has performed the thing he knows you need. So if he comes with a fan, be ready for the fan. If he comes with chastisement, be ready for chastisement. If he comes with correction, be ready for correction. Whatever he wills to do, let him do it and he will bring you to the land of plenty. *Oh, it is worth the world to be under the power of the Holy Ghost!*

If he chastens you not, if you sail placidly along without incident, without crosses, without persecutions, without trials, remember that "if ye be without chastisement, whereof all are partakers, then are ye bastards, and not sons" (Heb 12:8). Therefore, "Examine yourselves, whether ye be in the faith" (2 Cor 13:5). Never forget that Jesus said this word: "My sheep hear my voice, and ... they follow me" (Jn 10:27). Jesus wants you all to follow, wants you to have a clear ring in your testimony.

You are eternally saved by the power of God. Do not be led astray by anything, do not take your feelings for your salvation, do not take anybody's word for your salvation. Believe that God's Word is true. What does it say? "He that hath the Son hath life; and he that hath not the Son of God hath not life" (1 Jn 5:12).

When your will becomes entirely the will of God, then you are clearly in the place where the Holy Ghost can make Jesus lord in your life, lord over your purchases, lord over your selling, lord over your eating and your drinking, your clothing, and your choice of companionship.

"Now there are diversities of gifts, but the same Spirit. And there are differences of administrations, but the same Lord. And there are diversities of operations, but it is the same God which worketh all in all. But the manifestation of the Spirit is given to every man to profit withal" (1 Cor 12:4-7).

Variety of Gifts Available

The variation of humanity is tremendous. Faces are different, so is physique. Your whole body may be so tempered that one particular gift would not suit you at all while it would suit another person.

So the Word of God deals here with varieties of gifts, meaning that these gifts perfectly meet the condition of people in this place. That is God's plan. Not one person, it may be, would be led out to claim all gifts. Nevertheless, do not be afraid; the Scriptures are definite. Paul said that you need not come behind in any gift. God has for you wonderful things beyond what you have ever known. The Holy Ghost is so full of prophetic operation of divine power, that it is marvelous what may happen after the Holy Ghost comes.

How he loosed me! I am no good without the Holy Ghost. The power of the Holy Ghost loosed my language. I was like my mother. She had no language. If she began to tell a story, she couldn't go through. My father would say, "Mother, you will have to begin again." I was like that. I couldn't tell a story, I was bound. Plenty of thought, but no language. But oh, after the Holy Ghost came!

When he came I had a great desire after gifts. So the Lord caused me to see that it is possible for every believer to live in such holy unction, such divine communion, such pressed-in measure by the power of the Spirit that every gift can be his.

But is there not a vast and appalling unconcern about possessing the gifts? Ask of a score of saints chosen at random from almost any assembly, "Have you any of the gifts of the Spirit?" and the answer will be, "No," and given in a tone and with a manner that conveys the thought that the saint is not surprised at not having the gifts, that he doesn't expect to have any of them, and does not expect to seek from them. Isn't this terrible when this living Word exhorts us specifically to "Covet earnestly the best gifts"? (1 Cor 12:31).

Working With God

So that the gift might be everything and in evidence, we have to see that we cease to live excepting for his glory. He works with us, we work with him, cooperative, working together. This is divine. Surely this is God's plan.

God has brought you to the banquet and he wants to send you away full. We are in a place where God wants to give us visions. We are in a place where his great love is being bent over us with kisses. Oh, how lovely the kiss of Jesus, the expression of his love!

Oh come, let us seek him for the best gifts, and let us strive to be wise and rightly divine the Word of Truth, giving it forth in power that the church may be edified and sinners may be saved.

From *The Pentecostal Evangel* (Springfield, Mo.), October 27, 1928, pp. 1, 5.

14
Full of the Holy Ghost

Jesus saith, "Be not afraid, only believe" (Mk 5:36). The people in whom God delights are the ones who rest upon his Word without wavering. God has nothing for the man who wavers, for let him that wavereth expect nothing from God (see Jas 1:6-7). Therefore I would like us to get this verse deep down into our hearts, until it penetrates every fiber of our being:

> *Only believe! Only believe!*
> *All things are possible—*
> *Only believe.*

God has a plan for this meeting, beyond anything that we have ever known before. He has a plan for every individual life, and if we have any other plan in view, *we miss the grandest plan of all!* Nothing of the past is equal to the present, and nothing of the present can equal the things of tomorrow, for tomorrow should be so filled with holy expectations that we will be living flames for him. God never intended his people to be ordinary or commonplace; his intentions were that they should be on fire for him, conscious of his divine power, realizing the glory of the cross that foreshadows the crown.

Seven Deacons Chosen
God has given us a very special scripture for this service: Acts 6:1-5.

During the time of the inauguration of the church the disciples were hard pressed on all lines; the things of natural order could not be attended to, and many were complaining concerning the neglect of their widows. The disciples therefore decided upon a plan, which was to choose seven men to do the work—men who were full of the Holy Ghost. What a divine thought! No matter what kind of work was to be done, however menial it may have been, the person chosen must be filled with the Holy Ghost. The plan of the church was that everything, even of natural order, must be sanctified unto God, for the church had to be a Holy Ghost church. Beloved, God has never ordained anything less! There is one thing that I want to stress in these meetings; that is, no matter what else may happen, first and foremost I would emphasize a question: "Have you received the Holy Ghost since you believed?" Are you filled with divine power?

This is the heritage of the church, to be so endued with power that God can lay his hand upon any member at any time to do his perfect will. There is no stop in the Spirit-filled life; we begin at the cross, the place of ignominy, shame, and death, and that very death brings the power of resurrection life. And, being filled with the Holy Spirit, we go on "from glory to glory." Let us not forget that possessing the baptism in the Holy Spirit means there must be an "ever-increasing" holiness. How the church needs divine unction—God's presence and power so manifest that the world will know it. The people know when the tide is flowing; they also know when it is ebbing.

The necessity that seven men be chosen for the position of "serving tables" was very evident. The disciples knew that these seven men were men ready for active service, and so they chose them. In the fifth verse we read: "And the saying pleased the whole multitude: and they chose Stephen, a man full of faith, and of the Holy Ghost, and Philip." There were others, of course, but Stephen and Philip stand out most prominently in the Scriptures. Philip was a man so filled with the Holy Ghost that a revival always followed wherever he went. Stephen was a man so filled with divine power that, although serving tables might have been all right in the minds of the other disciples, yet God had a greater vision for him—a baptism of fire, of power and divine unction. This took him on and on to the climax of his life, until he saw right into the open heavens.

Stephen, the Godly Example

Had we been there with the disciples at that time, I believe we should have heard them saying to each other, "Look here! Neither Stephen nor Philip are doing the work we called them to. If they do not attend to business, we shall have to get someone else!" That was the *natural* way of thinking, but divine order is far above our finite planning. When we please God in our daily ministration, we shall always find in operation the fact "that everyone who is faithful in little, God will make faithful in much." We have such an example right here—a man chosen to "serve tables." Stephen had such a revelation of the mind of Christ and of the depth and height of God that there was no stop in his experience, but he went forward with leaps and bounds. Beloved, there is a race to be run, there is a crown to be won; we cannot stand still! I say unto you, Be vigilant! Be vigilant! "Let no man take thy crown!"

God has privileged us in Christ Jesus to live above the ordinary human plane of life. Those who want to be ordinary and live on a lower place can do so; but as for me, *I will not!* For the same unction, the same zeal, the same Holy Ghost power is at our command as was at the command of Stephen and the apostles. We have the same God that Abraham had, that Elijah had, and we need not come behind in any gift or grace. We may not possess the gifts, as abiding gifts, but as we are full of the Holy Ghost and divine unction, it is possible, when there is need, for God to *manifest every gift of the Spirit* through us. As I have already said, I do not mean by this that we should necessarily possess the gifts permanently, but there should be a *manifestation of the gifts* as God may choose to use us.

This *ordinary* man, Stephen, became mighty under the Holy Ghost anointing, until he stands supreme, in many ways, among the apostles—"And Stephen, full of faith and power, did great wonders and miracles among the people" (Acts 6:8). As we go deeper in God, he enlarges our conception and places before us a wide-open door; and I am not surprised that this man chosen to "serve tables" was afterwards called to a higher plane. "What do you mean?" you may ask. "Did he quit this service?" No! But he was *lost* in the power of God. He lost sight of everything in the natural, and steadfastly fixed his gaze upon Jesus, "the author and finisher of our faith" (Heb 12:2), until he was transformed into a shining light in the kingdom of God. Oh, that we might be awakened to believe his Word, to understand the mind of the Spirit, for there is an *inner* place of whiteness and purity where we can "see God." Stephen was just as ordinary a man as you and I, but he was in the place where God could so move upon him that he, in turn, could move all before him. He began in a most humble place, and ended in a blaze of glory. Beloved, *dare to believe Christ!*

Resisting God's Servant

As you go on in this life of the Spirit, you will find that the devil will begin to get restless and there will be a stir in the synagogue;

it was so with Stephen. Any number of people may be found in the "synagogue," who are very proper in a worldly sense—always correctly dressed, the elite of the land, welcoming into the church everything but the power of God. Let us read what God says about them:

"Then there arose certain of the synagogue, which is called the synagogue of the Libertines, and Cyrenians, and Alexandrians ... disputing with Stephen. And they were not able to resist the wisdom and the spirit by which he spake" (Acts 6:9-10).

The Libertines could not stand the truth of God. With these opponents, Stephen found himself in the same predicament as the blind man whom Jesus healed. As soon as the blind man's eyes were opened they shut him out of the synagogue. They will not have anybody in the "synagogue" with their eyes open; as soon as you receive spiritual eyesight, out you go! These Libertines, Cyrenians, and Alexandrians, rose up full of wrath in the very place where they should have been full of the power of God, full of love divine, and reverence for the Holy Ghost; they rose up against Stephen, this man "full of the Holy Ghost." Beloved, if there is anything in your life that in any way *resists* the power of the Holy Ghost and the entrance of his Word into your heart and life, drop on your knees and *cry aloud* for mercy! When the Spirit of God is brooding over your heart's door, do not resist him but open your heart to the touch of God. There is a resisting "unto blood" striving *against sin*, and there is a resisting of the Holy Ghost that will drive you *into sin*.

Stephen spoke with marked wisdom; where he was, things began to move. You will find that there is always a moving when the Holy Spirit has control. These people were brought under conviction by the message of Stephen, but they resisted; they did anything and everything to stifle that conviction. Not only did they lie, but they got others to lie against this man, who would have laid down his life for any one of them. Stephen was used to heal the sick, perform miracles, and yet they brought false accusations against him. What effect did it have on Stephen? "And all that sat in the council, looking stedfastly on him, saw his face as it had been the face of an angel" (Acts 6:15).

Something had happened in the life of this man, chosen for menial service, and he became *mighty for God.* How was it accomplished in him? It was because *his aim was high;* faithful in little, God brought him to full fruition. Under the inspiration of divine power by which he spoke, they could not but listen—even the angels listened, as with holy prophetic utterance he spoke before that council. Beginning with Abraham and Moses, he continued unfolding the truth. What a marvelous exhortation! Take your Bibles and read it, "listen in" (as the angels listened in). As light upon light, truth upon truth, revelation upon revelation, found its way into their callused hearts, they gazed at him in astonishment; their hearts perhaps became warm at times, and they may have said, "Truly, this man is sent of God." But then he hurled at them this truth: "Ye stiffnecked and uncircumcised in heart and ears, ye do always resist the Holy Ghost: as your fathers did, so do ye. Which of the prophets have not your fathers persecuted? and they have slain them which shewed before of the coming of the Just One; of whom ye have been now the betrayers and murderers: Who have received the law by the disposition of angels, and have not kept it" (Acts 7:51-53). Then what happened? These men were *moved;* "they were cut to the heart, and they gnashed on him with their teeth" (Acts 7:54).

There are two marvelous occasions in the Scriptures where the people were "pricked to the heart." In the second chapter of the Acts of the Apostles, thirty-seventh verse, after Peter had delivered that inspired sermon on the Day of Pentecost, the people were "pricked in their heart" with conviction, and there were added to the church three thousand souls. Here is Stephen, speaking under the inspiration of the Holy Ghost, and the men of this council being "pricked to the heart" rise up as one man to slay him. As you go down through this chapter, from the fifty-fifth verse, what a picture you have before you. As I close my eyes, I can get a vision of this scene in every detail— the howling mob with their vengeful, murderous spirit, ready to devour this holy man, and he "being full of the Holy Ghost," "looked stedfastly into heaven." What did he see there? From his place of helplessness, he looked up and said: "Behold, I see the heavens opened, and the Son of man *standing* on the right hand of God" (Acts 7:56, emphasis added).

Is that the position that Jesus went to take? No! He went to "sit" at the right hand of the Father; but in behalf of the first martyr, in behalf of the man with that burning flame of Holy Ghost power, God's Son *stood up* in honorary testimony of him who, called to serve tables, was faithful unto death. But is that all? No! I am so glad that it is not all. As the stones came flying at him, pounding his body, crashing into his bones, striking his temple, mangling his beautiful face, what happened? How did this scene end? With that sublime, upward look, this man chosen for an ordinary task but filled with the Holy Ghost, was so moved upon by God that he finished his earthly work in a blaze of glory, magnifying God with his last breath. Looking up into the face of the Master, he said, "'Lord Jesus, receive my spirit.... Lay not this sin to their charge.' And when he had said this, he fell asleep" (Acts 7:59-60).

Friends, it is worth dying a thousand deaths to gain that spirit. My God! What a divine ending to the life and testimony of a man that was "chosen to serve tables."

From *The Pentecostal Evangel* (Springfield, Mo.), May 28, 1932, pp. 1, 8–9.

Preparing for an International Ministry

The Bowland Street Mission

The Bowland Street Mission [Smith and Polly Wigglesworth's church in Bradford] was never a Pentecostal church though a number of the members were. Wigglesworth had a constant battle with some of the leadership over this. After his wife Polly died in January 1913, his situation became more difficult. In fact, it was during a period when he was absent on a preaching tour that some of the leaders took action that resulted in Wigglesworth and his supporters being deprived of the use of Bowland Street. The building in the Manningham district began life as a school and subsequently the Parish Hall attached to St. Jude's Anglican Church. Built in 1867, it went through many different hands. Polly and Smith Wigglesworth were associated with this hall when they were linked with the work of Reader Harris and his Pentecostal League. The League's paper *Tongues of Fire* carried notices of the Bowland Street meetings in its pages several years before Wigglesworth visited Sunderland [where he was baptized in the Spirit, 1907]. It was in this same Bowland Street Mission also that the former public executioner of England, James Berry, found peace through believing. (See "Executioner's Life Transformed," p. 144)

Bowland Street Mission changed hands on a number of occasions. For a time it was an educational institution. Later it was a Holiness Mission. In 1919 it was purchased

as a War Memorial Hall in memory of the former members of St. Jude's parish who lost their lives in the First World War when so many of those known as the "Bradford Pals" perished on the battlefields of Flanders....
In 1932 it became a Catholic club, and it remains the same today.

Desmond W. Cartwright, "The Real Wigglesworth," unpublished paper, n.d. Used by permission.

15
How to Be Transformed

Jacob was on his way to the land of his fathers, but he was very troubled at the thought of meeting his brother Esau. Years before, Jacob and his mother had formed a plan to secure the blessing that Isaac was going to give Esau. How inglorious was the fulfilling of this carnal plan! It resulted in Esau's hating Jacob and saying in his heart, "When my father is dead, then will I slay my brother Jacob." Our own plans lead us frequently into disaster.

Jacob had to flee from the land, but how good the Lord was to the fleeing fugitive. He gave him a vision of a ladder, and angels ascending and descending. How gracious is our God! He refused to have his plans of grace frustrated by the carnal workings of Jacob's mind, and that night he revealed himself to Jacob, saying, "I am with thee, and will keep thee in all places whither thou goest, and will bring thee again into this land; for I will not leave thee, until I have done that which I have spoken to thee of" (Gn 28:15). It is the goodness of the Lord that leads to repentance. I believe that Jacob really did some repenting that night as he was made conscious of his own meanness.

Many things may happen in our lives to show us how depraved we are by nature, but when the veil is lifted we see how merciful and tender God is. His tender compassion is over us all the time.

Since the time when Jacob had had the revelation of the

ladder and the angels, he had had twenty-one years of testing and trial. But God had been faithful to his promise all through these years. Jacob could say to his wives, "Your father hath deceived me, and changed my wages ten times; but God suffered him not to hurt me" (Gn 31:7). He said to his father-in-law, "Except the God of my father, the God of Abraham, and the fear of Isaac, had been with me, surely thou hadst sent me away now empty. God hath seen mine affliction and the labour of my hands" (Gn 31:42).

Getting Alone With God

Now that Jacob was returning to the land of his birth, his heart was filled with fear. If he ever needed the Lord, it was just at this time. And he wanted to be alone with God. His wives, his children, his sheep, his cattle, his camels, and his asses, gone on, "And Jacob was left alone; and there wrestled a man with him until the breaking of the day" (Gn 32:24). The Lord saw Jacob's need, and came down to meet him. It was he who wrestled with the supplanter, breaking him, changing him, transforming him.

Jacob knew that his brother Esau had power to take away all that he had, and to execute vengeance upon him. He knew that no one could deliver him but God. And there alone, lean in soul and impoverished in spirit, he met with God. Oh, how we need to get alone with God, to be broken, to be changed, to be transformed! And when we do meet with him, he interposes, and all care and strife is at an end. Get alone with God and receive the revelation of his infinite grace, and of his wonderful purposes and plans for your life.

This picture of Jacob left alone is so real to me, I can imagine his thoughts that night. He would think about the ladder and the angels. I somehow think that as he would begin to pray, his tongue would cleave to the roof of his mouth. He knew he had to get rid of a lot of things. In days gone by, it had all been Jacob! Jacob! When you get alone with God, what a place of revelation it is. What a revelation of self we receive. And then what a revelation of the provision made for us at Calvary. It is here that we get a revelation of a life crucified with Christ, buried with him, raised with him, transformed by Christ and empowered by the Spirit.

Hour after hour passed. Oh, that we might spend all nights alone with God! We are occupied too much with the things of time and sense. We need to spend time alone in the presence of God. We need to give God much time in order to receive new revelations from him. We need to get past all the thoughts of earthly matters that crowd in so rapidly. It takes God time to deal with us. If he would only deal with us as he dealt with Jacob, then we should have power with him, and prevail.

Jacob was not dry-eyed that night. Hosea tells us, "He wept, and made supplication" (Hos 12:4). He knew that he had been a disappointment to the Lord, that he had been a groveler, but in the revelation he received that night he saw the possibility of being transformed from a supplanter to a prince with God. The testing hour came when, at the break of day, the angel, who was none other than the Lord and Master, said, "Let me go, for the day breaketh" (Gn 32:26). This is where we so often fail. Jacob knew that if God went without blessing him, Esau could not be met. You cannot meet the terrible things that await you in the world unless you secure the blessing of God.

How to Gain the Victory

You must never let go. Whatever you are seeking—a fresh revelation, light on the path, some particular thing—*never let go.*

Victory is yours if you are earnest enough. If you are in darkness, if you need a fresh revelation, if your mind needs relief, if there are problems you cannot solve, lay hold of God and declare, "I will not let thee go, except thou bless me" (Gn 32:26).

In wrestling, the strength is in the neck, the breast, and the thigh, but the greatest strength is in the thigh. The Lord touched Jacob's thigh. With his human strength gone, surely defeat was certain. What did Jacob do? He hung on. God means to have people who are broken. The divine power can only come when there is an end of our own self-sufficiency. But when we are broken, we must hold fast. If we let go, then we shall fall short.

Jacob cried, "I will not let thee go, except thou bless me." And God blessed him, saying, "Thy name shall be called no more Jacob, but Israel: for as a prince hast thou power with God and with men, and hast prevailed" (Gn 32:28). Now a new order begins. The old supplanter has passed away; there is a new creation: Jacob the supplanter has been transformed into Israel the prince.

When God comes into your life, you will find him enough for every situation. As Israel came forth, the sun rose upon him, and he had power over all the things of the world, and power over Esau. Esau met him, but there was no fight now; there was reconciliation. They kissed each other. How true it is, "When a man's ways please the Lord, he maketh even his enemies to be at peace with him" (Prv 16:7). Esau inquired, "What about all these cattle, Jacob?" "Oh, that's a present." "Oh, I have plenty; I don't want your cattle. What a joy to see your face again!" What a wonderful change! The material things did not count for much after the night of revelation. Who wrought this change? God.

Can you hold on to God as did Jacob? You certainly can if

you are sincere, if you are dependent, if you are broken, if you are weak. It is when you are weak that you are strong (see 2 Cor 12:10). But if you are self-righteous, if you are proud, if you are high-minded, if you are puffed up in your own imagination, you can receive nothing from him. If you become lukewarm instead of being at white heat, you can become a disappointment to God. And he says, "I will spue thee out of my mouth" (Rv 3:16).

But there is a place of holiness, a place of meekness, a place of faith, where you can cry to God, "I will not let thee go, except thou bless me." And in response he will bless you exceeding abundantly above all you ask or think.

Sometimes we are tempted to think that he has left us. Oh, no. He has promised never to leave us, nor forsake us. He had promised not to leave Jacob, and he did not break his promise. He has promised not to leave us, and he will not fail. Jacob held on until the blessing came. We can do the same.

If God does not help us, we are no good for this world's need; we are no longer salt, we lose our savor. But as we spend time alone with God, and cry to him to bless us, he resalts us, he reempowers us; but he brings us to brokenness and moves us into the orbit of his own perfect will.

Dependence Upon the Holy Spirit

The next morning as the sun rose, Jacob "halted upon his thigh" (v. 31). You may ask, "what is the use of a lame man?" It is those who have seen the face of God and have been broken by him, who can meet the forces of the enemy and break down the bulwarks of Satan's kingdom. The Word declares, "The *lame* take the prey" (Is 33:23, emphasis added). On that day Jacob was brought to a place of dependence upon God.

Oh, the blessedness of being brought into a life of dependence upon the power of the Holy Spirit. Henceforth we know that we are nothing without him; we are absolutely dependent upon him. I am absolutely nothing without the power and unction of the Holy Ghost. Oh, for a life of absolute dependence! It is through a life of dependence there is a life of power. If you are not there, get alone with God. If need be, spend a whole night alone with God, and let him change and transform you. Never let him go until he blesses you, until he makes you an Israel, a prince with God.

From *The Pentecostal Evangel* (Springfield, Mo.), July 14, 1945, pp. 2–3.

16
Supernatural Power

G od wants us to travel in the place where Jesus and his disciples traveled. He has left this place open. "Greater works than these shall he do; because I go unto my Father" (Jn 14:12). Jesus left nothing less than this, a power which was for them and to which more was to be added if we believe.

We have recently had seven years of earthly power, and are feeling the effects of it today. How it has broken hearts, homes, and in fact the whole world, and filled it with such distressing effects and made it an awful place, that we never want it again. [Smith was referring to World War I.]

God's power is so much different. It restores the fallen, it heals the brokenhearted, it lifts, it lives, it brings life into existence in your own hearts. All the time there is something that is round about you, something that you know is lasting and will be forever until the Lord will receive us unto himself.

God, help me to speak tonight. I came not to speak only, but to stir us up to our privilege, to make men feel they are responsible for the state of things round about.

Power and Progress
It thrills my soul and makes me think that I must step into line where God has called me. Some of you know what a tragedy it is to see baptized souls making no progress. If this is your situation, you are a backslider in the sight of God. It's because you

have had the privilege of the revelation of the Spirit within you, the privilege and more power of entering into more light. It is a wonderful thing to get into touch with the living God. It is a glorious thing, a blessed condescension of God to fill us with the Holy Ghost.

"Ye shall receive power" (Acts 1:8). Brothers, it is so real. His life for me, the life of the Son of God within, characteristics to make the whole body a flame of fire—"after that ye shall receive power." I am clearly coming to understand this in my ministry. God has given me a gracious ministry, and I thank him for it. God has given me a ministry which I prize because it helps me to stir people, especially leaders. I am here tonight to stir you. I could not think that God would have me leave you as I found you. He has not entrusted me to speak for half an hour and leave you as I found you. So my desire is that this half hour shall be so full of divine purpose, that everyone shall come into line with the plan of God tonight.

Power and Purity

I am as satisfied as anything that if I wait further, I will have misrepresented the position; on this line I so want to say things to prove the situation. There is a great deal too much said about wanting to "only feel the power." Our young brother said distinctly that the Holy Ghost came to abide. What are we waiting for? What is God waiting for? For you to get into the place. What do I mean? I mean this, that Jesus was a perfect activity, a life in activity. The Scripture declares it. He began to do, and then to teach, it is as clear as possible in a realm of divine appointment.

So I am truly on the Word of God tonight. If we have received the power, the power is there. I am not going to say that there has not to be an unbroken fellowship with him. He never separates power from holiness. The pure in heart shall see God. But I believe that if he has come to reveal him unto us, you cannot lack it because he that believes that Jesus is the Christ, overcomes the world.

He is the purifier. He is the abiding presence, the one great source of righteousness. Then all the fullness of the Godhead bodily dwells in him. There is the situation.

And you know that after the Spirit gave the revelation of the purity of Christ by the Word of the Lord, he made you see things as you never saw them before.

I would like to speak for a few moments on the breath of the Spirit, because I see the Holy Spirit came as a breath or as the moving of a mighty wind. I see so much divine appointment in this for humanity. The Holy Spirit fills the life by the breath. This prophetic position is wonderful. "Whom did you hear speak?" "Yes, I heard Mr. Wigglesworth and Mr. Carter." Yes, that is the term; behind it all you will find that language is breath.

When you are filled with the breath of the Spirit, the breath of God, the holy fire and the Word, it is Christ within you.

Life is given: "He that heareth my word, and believeth on him that sent me, hath everlasting life" (Jn 5:24). We need the Spirit in order to be filled with prophetic power and to bring forth life to the needs of the people. This is life. I am perceiving that I must be so in this order. Let me give you one or two positions.

Power in Action

God wants everybody, without exception, to begin on the Word of God; and to "act" it will be the most surprising thing that ever came. As you stand on the Word, it will be an amazing thing.

One day as I was going down the streets of San Francisco in a car, I looked out the window and saw a great crowd of people at the corner of the street. "Stop," I said, "there is something wrong." So I rushed as fast as possible to the edge of the crowd. I was so eager, I pressed myself into the crowd, and I saw a boy laid on the ground who was held in a deathlike grip.

"The word is nigh thee, even in thy mouth" (Rom 10:8). I put my ear to his mouth as the boy lay there struggling. "Tell me, boy, what it is"; and the boy said, "It is cramp." So I put my hands around him and said, "Come out in the name of Jesus." The boy immediately jumped up, ran off, and had no time to say thank you. It is for everyone. After that you have received, you are in the place. I am not saying that glibly. My thoughts are too serious for that. Spiritually, I cannot be any more behind tonight than I was today, and tomorrow is mightier than today. This is the reason the tide is changing with God. This is the reality.

It is no little thing to be baptized [in the Spirit]. It is the promise of the Father. Jesus must be there, and the Holy Ghost also, bringing us to the place where we can be baptized. Are you going to treat it as a great thing? What do you really believe it is? I believe when the Holy Ghost comes, that he comes to crown the King.

And the King from that day gets his rightful place, and we don't have to claim anything, and he becomes King of all the situations.

I only say this to help you. It is a need that I cannot get away from, because everywhere I look I see growth. I see you people, I see the growth. I have been away from England three years, and I see changes, and even though we see there is growth, life, and blessing, there is much more ground to be possessed, and we shall have to dare before God can work.

God has given me an open door. Nothing moves me, only this, except I see men and women coming into line with this.

I want the people of Pentecost to rise as the heart of one man. God has us for a purpose in these last days, and in the meeting God helps me.

At a certain meeting, I said, "There is a man in this meeting suffering, and shall I preach before I help this man, or would you like to see this person free before I commence?" This man was a stranger and did not know who I was speaking about. There he was, with cancer on the face and full of pain, and I asked whether it was right to preach, or to heal this man?

I saw the right thing, and I went down off the platform and placed my hand on him in the name of Jesus.

This was because of what the Word said; that man knew nothing of healing, but in a moment he was able to stand up, and said, "I have been twelve years in pain. Something has happened to me." And that night he gave himself to God and testified night after night that he was completely cured. What was it? God ministered through me when I dared to believe his Word. There are cases round about you, and what a story you would have to tell next year, if only people took a stand on the Word of God from tonight.

A woman brought her husband to me and said, "I want you to help my husband." I said, "Well, I will." She said, "He has too many complaints to tell you of."

I said, "There is a man here so full of pains and weakness that I am going to pray for him on the authority of God's Word, and tomorrow night I am going to ask him to come back and tell you what God has done for him." And I placed my hand on him in the name of Jesus. The next night this man came walking straight, and he said, "Will you let me speak to these people tonight?

"For forty years I have had ulcers and running sores, and today is the first day that my clothes have been dry. And now I am a new man." Brothers and sisters, this is declared in the Word, and wonderful things happen.

I had been speaking about divine healing, and six seats from the rear was a man with a boy, and he lifted him up when I had finished. The boy was held together with irons, and his head, loins, and shoulders were bandaged. The father handed him over to me.

There he put the irons down with the boy standing in them. I have never known what there is in the laying on of hands. Let me give you a description of it. This boy was about nine years of age, and during my laying hands on him in the name of Jesus, there was perfect silence, when suddenly this boy cried out. "Dad, it is going all over me." And I said, "Take the irons off." You say that is our power. No, it is his power. No, it is the Father you have received. Dare we be still and be quiet? The stones would cry out if we did.

Sometimes I go in for what they call wholesale healings. My son and daughter are here, and they can declare that they have seen one hundred healed without the touch of a hand. I believe there are to be wholesale baptisms of the Holy Ghost. One day God told me something at a place called Staranga in Norway.

I said to my interpreter, "We are both very tired; we will rest today until 4 P.M." I can never forget the sight; this memory has just come to me. May God bend your ears down. There is a hearing of faith, a much higher faith. May the Lord bend our ears.

We had been out for a short time, and coming back into the street I shall never forget the sight. The street was filled with all kinds of wheelchairs. We went along the street, and the house was filled with people, and the woman asked, "What can we do?"

So I pulled off my coat and got down to business. My brothers, you ought to have been there, for the power of God came like a cloud, and people were healed on every side.

God healed all the people. This is what I have to tell you. We were sat down for a little refresher before the meeting, and the telephone rang. The pastor went to the phone and said, "What can we do? The great town hall is packed. Come down as soon as you can."

And this is what I mean by the hearing of faith. I declare that the people could not have fallen down if they had wanted to. I never saw a place so packed, and I began to preach. When I was preaching, the voice of the Lord came. "Ask and I will give thee every soul." The voice came again, "Ask and I will give you every soul." I dared to ask, "Give me every soul," and there was a breath that came like a mighty wind, and it shook everybody and fell on everyone. I have never seen anything like it.

I am hoping to see this experience repeated in London. Is there anything too hard for God? Cannot God begin to do these things? Will we let him?

Is it not possible to have a consecration service tonight? Who is there who will begin tonight to act in the power of the Holy Ghost?

Originally published as "Power," in *Redemption Tidings* (England), October 1925, pp. 2–3. An address given at the Second annual convention of the Assemblies of God in Kingsway Hall, Monday, June 9, 1925.

Preparing for an International Ministry

The Effects of the Baptism in the Holy Spirit

Wigglesworth was always a blunt Yorkshireman who said what he thought without fear of the consequences. Many thought him uncouth and resented his brusqueness. Nevertheless he was sincere and honest and always avoided sham and hypocrisy. Immediately after his baptism [in the Holy Spirit, in 1907] he returned to the meeting which was then in progress and interrupted the vicar, who was on his feet, speaking. Smith asked if he could speak. Alexander Boddy agreed to this unusual request, promptly took his seat, and allowed Wigglesworth to address the meeting.

The effect was dramatic. Though previously he had never been able to hold the attention of any congregation for the briefest periods, now those in the meeting gave him rapt attention as he spoke with great conviction. When he had finished, a man stood to his feet and said, "We have been rebuking this man because he was so intensely hungry, but he has come to us for a few days and has received the baptism. And some of us have been waiting here for weeks and have not received."

This stirred the congregation to the extent that within a short time fifty of those present were filled with the Holy Spirit and spoke in tongues.

Jack Hywel-Davies, *The Life of Smith Wigglesworth* (Ann Arbor, Mich.: Servant, 1987), p. 69. Used by permission.

17
Christ Manifest Through Man

For a short time I want especially to speak to those in this meeting who are saved. God wants them to be holy. He wants them to be filled with the power that will keep them holy. He wants us to have a revelation of what sin and death are, and what the Spirit and the life of the Spirit are. Look at these two verses: It is full of matter. "There is therefore now no condemnation to them which are in Christ Jesus, who walk not after the flesh, but after the Spirit. For the law of the Spirit of life in Christ Jesus hath made me free from the law of sin and death" (Rom 8:1-2). "No condemnation!"

This is the primary word for me tonight, because it means so much. It has everything within it. If you are without condemnation, you are in a place where you can pray through, where you have a revelation of Christ; for, for him to be in you brings you to a place where you cannot, if you follow the definite leadings of the Spirit of Christ, have any fellowship with the world. And I want you to see that the Spirit of the Lord would reveal unto us this fact tonight. If you love the world, you cannot love God, and the love of God cannot be in you. So God wants a straight cut tonight because if you are in Christ Jesus, you are of a new creation order; you are *in him* and, therefore, you walk in the Spirit and are free from condemnation.

Message in tongues with interpretation: *It is the Spirit alone that by revelation brings the whole truth, visiting Christ in your hearts and revealing unto you the capabilities of sonship that are in you after you are created after the image of him.*

No Condemnation

So the Spirit of the Lord tonight would bring you into revelation. He wants you without condemnation. What will that mean? Much every way, because God wants all his people to be targets. More than that. He wants them to be salted; to be lights; to be like cities set on a hill which cannot be hid; so "in God for the world's redemption" that the world may know that ye belong to God. That is the law of the Spirit. What will it do? The law of the Spirit of life in Christ Jesus will make you free from the law of sin. Sin will have no dominion over you. You will have no desire to sin, and it will be as true of you as it was of Jesus when he said, "Satan cometh, but findeth nothing in me." He cannot condemn; he cannot draw; he has no power. His power is destroyed in the tenth verse: "the body is dead because of sin" (judged): "but the Spirit is life because of righteousness" (abounding). To be filled with God means that you are free! Filled with joy, peace, blessing, enduement, strength of character in God, and transformed by his mighty power.

Notice there are two laws: the law of the Spirit of life in Christ Jesus making you free from the law of sin and death. The same law is in you as was in you before, but it is dead; the same flesh, only it is dead; you are just the same, only quickened into spiritual life; you are in a new creation, a new creature, created in God afresh after the image of Christ.

Now, beloved, some people who come into line with this

do not understand their inheritance, and they go down; and instead of making you weak, and inclined to go under, you have to rise triumphantly over it. You say, "Show us this law!" I will, God helping me.

Reigning in Life

Romans 7:25 reads: "I thank God through Jesus Christ our Lord. So then with the mind I myself serve the law of God; but with the flesh the law of sin." God wants to show you that there is a place where we can live in the Spirit and not be subject to the flesh. Live in the Spirit till sin has no dominion; till we reign in life and see the clothing of God over us in the Spirit. Sin reigned unto death, but Christ reigned over sin and death, and so we reign with him in life.

There is not a sick person here who could be said to be reigning in life: satanic power reigns there, and God wants you to know that *you* have to reign. God made you like himself, and Jesus bought back for you in the Garden of Gethsemane everything that was lost in the Garden of Eden, through that agony which he suffered. He bought that blessed redemption.

When I think of *redemption!* People say, "Could anything be greater than the fellowship which prevailed in the Garden of Eden, when God walked and talked and had fellowship with men?" Yes, redemption is greater. Nothing but that which was local was in the garden, but the moment a man is born again he is free from the world and lives in heavenly places. He has no destination, except "in the glory."

Redemption is, therefore, greater than the Garden, and God wants you to know that you may come into this glorious redemption not for salvation only, but also for your bodies;

to know they are redeemed from the curse of law, to know you have been made free, and to know that all praise and glory are due to the Son of God. Hallelujah! No more Egypt places! No more sandy deserts! Praise the Lord! Free from the law of sin and death.

How was it accomplished? The third verse tells us. It is the master verse: "For what the law could not do, in that it was weak through the flesh, God sending his own Son in the likeness of sinful flesh, and for sin, condemned sin in the flesh: That the righteousness of the law might be fulfilled in us, who walk not after the flesh, but after the Spirit" (Rom 8:3-4). *Righteousness was fulfilled in us!* Brother, sister, I tell you there is a redemption, there is an atonement in Christ, a personality of Christ to dwell in you; there is a God-likeness for you to attain unto, a blessed resemblance of Christ, of "God in you" that shall not fail *if you believe the Word of God.*

Message in tongues with interpretation: *The living Word is sufficient for thee. Eat it. Devour it. It is the Word of God.*

Filled With God

Jesus was manifested to destroy the works of the devil. God was manifested *in him;* the fullness of God came into Jesus, and he walked about, filled with God. Is it to be mine? May I be filled with God? Yes. How can I be so filled with God that all my movements, all my desires, my mind and will are so moved upon by a new power that "I am not," for God has taken me? Praise the Lord! *Certainly it can be so.* Did you ever examine the condition of your new birth unto righteousness? Did you ever investigate it? Did you ever try to see what there was in it? Were you ever able to fathom the fullness of that redemption plan that came to you through believing in Jesus?

You have to see that before the foundation of the world this redemption was all completed and set in order before the Fall; and then notice that this redemption had to be so mighty and had to redeem us all so perfectly, that there should be no lack in the whole of redemption! Let us see how it comes about. He became flesh! Then, he was filled with the Holy Ghost. Then, he became the "operation" or "voice" and the operation of the Word, by the power of God through the Holy Ghost, became "the Authority." Now, let me go further with you.

You are born of an incorruptible power of God; born of the Word, who has the personality, the nature of God. You were begotten of God, and you are not your own. You have passed from death unto life, and have become an heir of God and a joint-heir of Christ in the measure in which you believe his Word. The natural flesh, the first order, has been changed into a new order for the first order was Adam, the natural, and the last order was Christ, the heavenly; and now you become changed by a heavenly power existing in an earthly body. I want you to see that you are born of a power, and have existing in you a power, of which God took and made the world that you are in. It is the law of the Spirit of life in Christ Jesus that makes you free from the law of sin and death.

Now, let us look at the law without the Spirit; the law of sin and death. Here is a man who has never come into the new law. He is still in the law of Adam, never having been regenerated, never having been born again. He is led captive by the devil at his will. There is no power that can convert a man except the power of the blood of Jesus. Brother, the carnal life is not subject to the will of God, neither, indeed, can be. Carnality is selfishness and uncleanness. It cannot be subject to God; it interferes with you; it binds, and keeps you in bondage; but, beloved, God destroys carnality by a new life, which is so much better, and fills you with joy unspeakable and full of glory. The half can never be told. Everything that God does is too big to tell: his grace, his love, his mercy, his salvation, are all too big to understand.

Do you not know that ours is an abundant God who is able to do for us far exceeding and abundantly above all that we can ask or think? We are illuminated and quickened by the Spirit, looking forward to a day of rapture when we will be caught up and lifted into the presence of God. God's lines are magnitude—wonderful and glorious!

Now, let me touch another important point. Can you think about Jesus being dead in the grave? (v. 11). Do you think that God could do anything for us if Jesus were still there? After his crucifixion and until he was laid in the grave, everything had to be done for him, and I want you to see that a dead Christ can do nothing for you. He carried the cross—so don't you carry it. The cross covered everything, and the resurrection brought everything to life. When he was in the grave, the Word of God says that he was raised from thc grave by the operation of God through the Spirit, and this Jesus was quickened by the Spirit in the grave, and this same Spirit dwells in your mortal bodies. Jesus rose by the quickening power of the Holy Ghost. "But if the Spirit of him that raised up Jesus from the dead dwell in you, he that raised up Christ from the dead shall also quicken your mortal bodies" (Rom 8:11).

If you will allow Jesus to have charge of your bodies, you will find that this Spirit will quicken you, will loose you. Talk about divine healing! You cannot get it out of the Scriptures. They are full of it. You will find, also, that all who are healed by the power of God—especially believers—will find their healing an incentive to make them purer and holier. If divine healing were merely to make the body whole, it would be worth very little. Divine healing is the divine act of the providence of God coming into your mortal bodies.

And after being touched by almightiness, can you ever remain the same? No, you will come out to worship and serve God.

From *Redemption Tidings* (England), January 1926, pp. 2–3.

18
A Divine Vocation in a New Epoch

F aith is an act, a changing. If we dare believe God's Word, he moves and changes the situation. Our purpose is to let the Holy Ghost glorify God through us. Only believe! It shall be to you as you believe.

Hebrews 11 is a bundle of treasure of divine purpose. Here God unfolds his truth to us and through us to others. Dare to believe God; he will not fail. Faith is the greatest subject—power to lay hold of the Word of God.

God Brings the Victory Through Jesus

It is God who bringeth us into victory through the blood of the slain Lamb. Faith quickens into a divine order, a living new source, a holy nature, having divine rights through Jesus. A new epoch, a new vocation, white hot! "Eye hath not seen, nor ear heard, neither have entered into the heart of man, the things which God hath prepared for them that love him. But God hath revealed them unto us by his Spirit" (1 Cor 2:9-10).

We must be ablaze with passion for souls that someone may catch a new ray to bring in a new day, for the end is not yet. Praise the Lord! Glory!

Faith is the substance, bigger than we know, the power to express the new creation and bring forth the glory of God. Faith is always at peace, undisturbed whatever happens. The waves may be terrible, the wind contrary. When he was asleep, his disciples asked, "Carest Thou not that we perish?" (Mk 4:38). He spoke! There was a great calm. Jesus Christ, the author and finisher of faith, the divine authority with inspiration. This is the word of faith which we preach to bring forth to the world the touch of heaven.

The Lord is in this place. He is here to revive, to fill, to change, to express, to give power over all the power of the enemy. "There is therefore now no condemnation to them which are *in* Christ Jesus, who walk not after the flesh, but after the Spirit. For the law of the Spirit of life in Christ Jesus hath made me free from the law of sin and death" (Rom 8:1-2, emphasis added). Life came out of death because of the cross, then resurrection, a manifestation of the operation of God. I was dead in trespasses and sins and now I am alive unto God. Eternal life.

He openeth the prison doors to all who believe; by faith we enter in. He is made unto us righteousness, we are one with him forever. Heirship and joint-heirship made possible unto us by his death and ascension.

There is no condemnation to them that are in Christ Jesus— no cloud—nothing between. Oh, the thrill of it. Hidden with Christ in God—immersed, covered—nothing can break through. It is the grace of God to be here, and as sure as we are here we shall be there, receiving a kingdom which cannot be moved, for our God is a consuming fire. There is something very beautiful about being in Christ in God, ready for everything—ready!

He hath begotten us unto a lively hope—to make us like unto himself. The radiance of the divine to break through makes a new creation. The law of the Spirit of Life making us free from the law of sin and death.

The quickening Spirit, fellow-heirs, a divine flow—white heat. Full! Holy! Inflammable! It causes others to catch fire—quickening—no condemnation. Do you know it? Glory! A large conception, this of our eternal relationship—catching the rays of divine glory—a changing all the time. Ready because of the intensity of the fire within! Jesus manifested in the flesh, ruling—reigning—until the rivers flow and flood-tide is here. Bringing life, life to all.

Becoming Extraordinary People

Filled with the Holy Ghost,
Has he come?
Does he abide?

I know the Lord laid his hand on me,
He fills me with the Holy Ghost,
I know the Lord laid his hand on me.

Filled! A flowing, quickening, moving flame of God. Not drunk with wine, but filled with the Spirit, more and more filled with this life, this great expansiveness of God's gifts, graces, and beatitudes—changing us all the time—moving us on to greater enlargement in the Spirit.

God is with thee. The Spirit of the Lord is upon thee. Count on him. Be a chosen vessel in fellowship with God for this day. If you in any way fail to be filled, some need will be unmet. God makes the opportunity for the man that is ready. The Bible is our all. There God reveals his plan and feeds us. Those who trust in him shall never be confounded.

We cannot be ordinary people; God must be glorified in us. Some say: "If I could only feel the power!" Do not mind what you feel if in the needy place you are moved to an act, the authority of the power. God makes the occasion when we are in the place—hidden in God—with Christ in God. The law of the Spirit of life is opposed to death, disease, opposed to that which is earthly; for within us is a heavenly production. Fresh desire for God's glory makes us ready for the place of opportunity. Our God is a consuming fire. The cross is empty, and Jesus is glorified through us. The risen rivers are in white heat!

Multitudes, multitudes in the valley of determination, the day of the Lord is near in the valley of determination.

Decide and the floods appear.

Faith is the victory—for faith is substance and evidence.

Originally published as "A New Epoch—A Divine Vocation," in *Redemption Tidings* (England), March 1926, p. 2. Smith Wigglesworth's farewell message at Mrs. Margaret Cantell's London Faith Home.

Preparing for an International Ministry

Speaking in Tongues

One of the clear proofs that Pentecost with tongues is of God is that all the scribes and Pharisees of the present day condemn it. I have seen many receive the gift of tongues and the baptism of power, but never among them were there any critics or a fleshly or proud man or woman. The clean and impure cannot dwell together. Ye cannot have God and mammon. Pentecost with tongues is a holy work, and comes upon holy people for a holy purpose, being the beginning of greater days of manifestations.

I hold much fellowship with those that speak and sing with new tongues. All have one story to tell, namely, that the blessing and joy is beyond describing. Why stop at the barren field of justification, when there are waters of God's love to swim in? Why live in the experience of Romans 7 when there is Romans 8, full of life in the Spirit without condemnation?

My soul is filled with boundless love
Whilst gazing on the precious blood,
I catch the rays of Jesus' face
Transfixed in me, the Throne of Grace.
Wonders beyond the human mind
Rushing into me, a Life Divine;
I feel the Power of the Holy Dove,
And speak in "Tongues" of things above.
—AUTHOR UNKNOWN

Smith Wigglesworth, "Report from Yorkshire," *Confidence*, April 1908, p. 7.

19
Greater Works Shall We Do

Praise the Lord! Well, if I could say all that my heart would like to say, I am sure we should never go away today. What a joy it is for the Lord to bring us together in this way, where we hear the words that are so precious and convincing of all that Jesus said. For there was never one who came to the world with such a loving compassion, and who entered into all the needs of the people as Jesus did.

Now we see Jesus at the right hand of the Father today, interceding with God for the needs of the people, and there is something about his last message to the world which is so wonderful. Because he was going to the Father, the Father cooperates with him for the redemption of the world, and because of this, the Father will grant us all that we need. Jesus said, "If I depart, I will send him [the Comforter] unto you" (Jn 16:7). And he kept his word, and the Father kept his word, and that promise was made real on the day of Pentecost! He had ascended with the purpose of giving new power, new blessing, new vision, and a living faith to all those that should follow, that the great work should be carried on.

We have today and for many days been drinking at this measureless measure, that makes our hearts swell over with such rapture and delight, and we know we are living and moving in the power of the Holy Ghost! What wonderful things are held out to us. Now the vision is clear.

Belief in Divine Healing Growing

Many of you know as far back as twelve or fourteen years ago, how we used to gather with small companies of people, and divine healing was a small thing in those days, but as we lived and moved among the people they were healed and they are healed today. God meant to work out his purpose, that we should loose people who were bound with graveclothes, and that they should be set free by the power of God. We should be so filled with the power of God, that we should not know what it is to have a body. Hallelujah!

All over the world I tell the people that since the Lord healed me over thirty years ago, I don't know what it is to have a body. Hallelujah! It is redemption in all its fullness, no neuralgia, no stomach trouble, no kidney disease, no dyspepsia, no rheumatism. Hallelujah! No lumbago, no corns, absolutely and entirely a new order of things. This is the inheritance of all that seek him, this is the inheritance there is in Jesus. Jesus said to the woman, "It is not meet to take the children's bread, and cast it to dogs" (Mt 15:26). But hallelujah! There is bread, there is life, there is perfect healing from the Son of God. There was power in him that moved every evil thing. It changes our circumstances, and makes you know that the new creation is a living, vital thing. My word to you this afternoon is a special word, because it is the word of the Master.

Jesus is moved with compassion as he sees us here today. Many people are around us that want a new vision of Jesus, that they may go away from this convention to carry on the work, for we are here to make disciples for the Nazarene. It is God's will that we should do the works that Jesus declared we should do.

There are two things in faith. There is a faith which acts; there is a faith which needs to be accompanied with works. And we believe today that Jesus meant all he said. Now let us look at what he said. There are three very important verses, and I trust you will not forget them, whatever else you forget. What is the word? It is in the fourteenth chapter of John, verses 12, 13, and 14. Looking at them we are filled with joy. How I love, how I cherish the words of Jesus; truly they are lovely. When I think of the infinite wisdom of God in this measure, why did not God come to us and make himself openly manifested to us? Why not? Because our finite beings could not stand his glory. You remember that as Saul went into Damascus, the light of the Son just flashed on the road, and those with him fell to the earth, and he was turned blind at the same time. We could not stand God's glory because we are only finite beings. But God did the very best for us. When he could not present himself to us, he gave us his Word. His Word has a quickening power. David knew it. He said, "Thy word hath quickened me" (Ps 119:50). This Word is the divine revelation. It is the Word of life, of healing, of power. God has given us his own Word. I would that all who can hear me would give themselves carefully over to reading more of the Word of God. If you only knew how I love it. There is something about the Word which is so wonderful. It brings new life into you, until you realize you are a new creature. Hallelujah!

God Is Greater Than All

Listen to this word today. "Verily, verily, I say unto you, He that believeth on me, the works that I do shall he do also; and greater works than these shall he do, because I go unto my Father" (Jn 14:12). Oh, glory to God! "There hath not failed one word of all his good promise" (1 Kgs 8:56). Sometimes we fail, but God never does. Hallelujah. What do I mean? Well, I am here today to get you to a place of resting upon the Word of God. If I can get you there, you can say in faith, "It is done." If I can speak to you today by the grace of God, it can be finished in your seat. The Word of God cannot fail because it is the living Word. Listen to the words of Jesus as he says, "Greater works than these shall he do" (Jn 14:12). I know as truly as I stand upon this platform that we shall see the rising tide of blessing and divine healing go forth with greater power. But Satan will always try to hinder the real work of God. Whenever the power of God is being manifested, Satan will be there trying to upset it.

Satanic forces will be there, but God is greater. When we were baptized in the Holy Ghost, the spiritualist people got to know of it and they came to one of our meetings. They heard that we were speaking in tongues so they came and filled two seats. Then I began speaking in tongues (that was natural to me), and then these muttering devils began also. I went to these two seats and I said, "Go out, you devils, go out," and they came out like a flock of sheep! They went right outside, and when they got outside they cursed and cursed, but they were outside. So I know that the devil will have manifestations, but in the name of Jesus their power is gone.

What I want to impress upon you is that we must see these greater works that the Lord promised we should see. Listen, "Greater works than these shall he do; because I go unto my Father. And whatsoever ye shall ask in my name, that will I do, that the Father may be glorified in the Son" (Jn 14:12-13).

What is it that you want? "Whatsoever ye shall ask in my name, that will I do." Glory to God. Is there any purpose in it? Yes, "that the Father may be glorified in the Son." If you want God to be glorified in Jesus, you must live in the position where these things are being done.

Praise God, he has been delivering people in these meetings. Now you people that have been delivered this morning, put up your hands. Now we will have some testimonies of the deliverances. The power of God is here to deliver the people, but I am not satisfied. You think that I am satisfied? I have never seen anything yet to satisfy me. I am the hungriest person there is in this place!

Greater Power

There is something very remarkable and forceful in this verse. It says, "Verily, verily, I say unto you,… greater works than these shall he do." In the power of his name there is power against the devil, and all his hosts. It is a marvelous force against all these things. Glory to God.

I will give you an illustration of this. In the course of my travels I went to Sweden, and while going along one day I saw a man fall into a doorway. People came along and said he was dead. I could not speak Swedish but I could speak English, and the devil knew I could speak English (he knows all the languages), and I used the power and authority of the name of Jesus, and instantly he was delivered. The man had been troubled like this for years. The Lord told me to make him a public example, so I got him to come to the meeting, and he came and told us of his deliverance. He told us the most awful things that the devil had been telling him, and then he told us how the devil had gone right out of him. Praise God.

While I was in Ceylon, someone asked me to go to a certain place to pray for a sick person. I asked, "What is the case?" It was a woman dying of cancer. I said, "Take this handkerchief in the name of the Lord." But nothing happened. They said to me, "You must go this time." I went and looked at the woman. She was in a terrible condition with cancer in the womb, and nearly dead. The house was full of people, and I preached Jesus to them, and how precious he became to me as I did so. I said to them, "I know this woman will be healed, but I want you to know the power of my Lord. This case can be delivered, but I want you to know him that can deliver." Jesus said, "greater works"—what did he mean? Standing on the authority of the Word of God. Hallelujah! The deliverance was so marvelous, and had such an effect upon the home, that they went to the papers themselves and published it, and the woman herself came to the meeting and stood up and told the people what great things the Lord had done for her. Hallelujah! "Greater works than these shall he do."

You say how? Only believe. What is it to believe? It is to have such confidence in what the Lord said that we take him at his word, because he said it. Glory to God.

> *Yes, I know this book is true,*
> *Yes, I know this book is true,*
> *I'm acquainted with the Author,*
> *And I know this book is true.*

Whatsoever You Shall Ask

Let us look at the last part of this verse; it is very important. It says, "And whatsoever ye shall ask in my name, that will I do, that the Father may be glorified in the Son." Tell me, what does whatsoever mean? It means everything. You say there is a difference between everything and anything. Everything means the world, anything means you, so it is you that I am dealing with. I am not dealing with America today, but you. Redemption is so complete that the person who believes is made complete. Look at our Master as he calls the man who had the withered hand to stand before him. Jesus looked upon that withered hand, and at his command the hand was restored. He gave the living word, "Stretch forth thy hand" (Lk 6:10), and the arm was healed. People today are waiting for the manifestation of the sons of God. The world is crying out for something after the new creation order.

I remember one day a man came to see me about a woman that was dying and asked me to visit her. When I got into the room, I saw there was no hope, as far as human aid was concerned. The woman was suffering from a tumor, and it had sapped her life away. I looked at her, and I knew there was no possibility of help except a divine possibility. Thank God I knew he was able. I never say it cannot be. I find God is able to do everything. I said to her, "I know you are beyond everything now, but if you cannot lift your arm, or raise it at all, it might be possible that you could raise your finger as an indication that you desire to get better." Her hand lay upon the bed, but she lifted her finger just a little. I said to my friend, "We will pray with her, and anoint her." After anointing her, her chin dropped, death came on, and my friend said, "She is dead." He was scared. I have never seen a man so frightened in my life. He said, "What shall I do?"

You may think what I did was one of the most absurd things to do, but I did it. I reached over into the bed and pulled her out, and carried her across the room and stood her against the wall and held her up, as she was absolutely dead. I looked into her face and said, "In the name of Jesus I rebuke this death," and from the crown of her head to the sole of her foot her whole body began to tremble, and then her feet stood on the floor, and I said, "In the name of Jesus, I command you to walk," and she began to walk. I repeated, "In the name of Jesus, in the name of Jesus, walk," and she walked back to the wardrobe, and back into bed.

My friend went out and told the people that he had seen a woman raised from the dead! One of the elders of the mission where she attended said he was not going to have this kind of thing and tried to stop it. The doctor heard of it and went to see the woman. He said, "I have heard from Mr. Fisher, the elder, that you have been brought back to life, and I want you to tell me if it is so." She told him it was so. He said, "Dare you come and give your testimony at a certain hall, if I take you in my car?" She said, "I will go anywhere to give it."

She came to the hall looking so white, but there was a lovely brightness on her face. She was dressed in white, and I thought how beautiful she looked. This is what she said. "For many months I have been going down to death. Now I want to live for my children. I came to the place where it seemed there was no hope. I remember a man came to pray with me and said, 'If you cannot speak, or cannot lift your hands, if you want to live, move one of your fingers.' I remember moving my finger, but from that moment I knew nothing else until I was in the glory. I feel I must try and tell you what the glory is like. I saw countless numbers of people, and oh! the joy, and the singing. It was lovely, but the face of Jesus lit up everything. And just when I was having a beautiful time, the

Lord suddenly pointed to me, without speaking, and I knew I had to go, and the next moment I heard a man say, 'Walk, walk, in the name of Jesus!' If the doctor is here, I would like to hear what he has to say."

The doctor rose. He had a white beard, and I cannot forget the color of his waistcoat. It was a canary-colored pattern. When he stood up, he began to speak, but he could not at first. His lips quivered and then his eyes looked like a fountain of waters and I wondered what was about to happen. Then he said that for months he had been praying, and at last he felt there was no more hope, and he told them at the house that the woman would not live much longer; in fact, it was only a matter of days. Never live? Hallelujah, but this is where "the greater works" come in.

Thank God, if we believe all things are possible. It can be done now, this moment as you sit in your seat, if you believe it shall be done for the glory of God. I ask you while I preach today to believe God's Word, and it shall come to pass. Glory to God.

Now I want a wholesale healing this afternoon. I believe it may be possible for some to have that divine, inward, moving of living faith that will make you absolutely whole. If you deny yourself, and believe God's Word, you will be healed at the touch of the Lord. Now I want you to live in the sunshine.

I went to Dover to preach, and we had twenty people instantly healed at once. I have seen a hundred people healed in the meeting instantly, as they believed. People have been healed as they have risen from their seats. I want you to get to such a place of faith that you will not know you have a body. Mr. Stephen Jeffreys will be telling you tonight that there is perfect redemption for all our needs. We want everyone in this meeting to go away with the knowledge of a full redemption. If you believe on the authority of God's Word you are healed; you will have perfect health from your fingers' ends to your whole body. In closing, we will sing that chorus—

I do believe, I will believe that Jesus heals me now,
I do believe, I will believe that Jesus heals me now.
Amen.

Originally published as "Greater! Greater! Greater!" in *Redemption Tidings* **(England), July 1926, pp. 5–7. An address given at the convention held at Kingsway Hall, London, May 1926.**

20
The Pathway to Spiritual Floodtide

Wherever Jesus went, the multitudes followed him because he lived, moved, breathed, was penetrated, clothed, and filled with God. He was God and as Son of Man the Spirit of God rested upon him, the Spirit of creative holiness. It is lovely to be holy. Jesus came to impart to us the Spirit of holiness, a flame of holy, intense desire after Godlikeness.

Message in tongues with interpretation: *God, who quickeneth and bringeth into likemindedness the human by his power, divine sons with power, created after the image of the new man. The Spirit of holiness and truth. Jesus was the Truth.*

We are only at the edge of things. The almighty plan is marvelous for the future. God must do something to increase, a revival to revive within and without all we touch. And we'll see a floodtide with a cloudburst behind it.

Jesus left one hundred twenty men to turn the world upside down. The Spirit is upon us to change our situation. We must move on to let God increase in us for the deliverance of others. We must travail through until souls are born and quickened into new relationship with heaven. Jesus had divine authority with power, and he left it for us. We must preach truth, holiness, and purity in the inward parts. "Thou hast loved righteousness, and hated iniquity; therefore God, even thy God, hath anointed thee with the oil of gladness above thy fellows" (Heb 1:9). I am thirsty for more of God. He was not only holy, but he loved holiness.

Message in tongues with interpretation: *It is the depths that God gets into that we may reflect him and manifest a life having Christ enthroned in the heart, drinking into a new fullness, new intuition, for as he is, so are we in this world.*

Holiness and Revival

Jesus trod the winepress alone, and he despised the cross and the shame. He bore it all alone that we might be partakers of the divine nature, sharers in the divine plan of living, desiring holiness. That's a revival. Jesus manifested divine authority. He was without sin. They saw the Lamb of God in a new way. Hallelujah! Let us live holiness, and revival will come down. God will enable us to do the work to which we are appointed. All Jesus said came to pass. Signs, wonders. Amen. Only believe, and yield and yield, until all the vision is fulfilled.

God has a design, a purpose, a rest of faith. We are saved by faith, kept by faith. Faith is substance, it is also evidence. God is! He is! And he is a rewarder of them that diligently seek him. I am sure of this. We have to testify, to bear witness to what we know. To know that we know is a wonderful position.

Message in tongues with interpretation: *The Lord is the great promoter of divine possibility, pressing you into the attitude of daring to believe all the Word says. We are to be living words, epistles of*

Christ, known and read of all men. The revelation of Christ, past and future, in him all things consist. He is in us.

We are living in the inheritance of faith because of the grace of God, saved for eternity by the operation of the Spirit bringing forth purity unto God. A substance of divine proposition and attainment, bringing heaven to earth until God quickens all things into beauty, manifesting his power in living witnesses. God in us for a world, that the world may be blessed. Power to lay hold of omnipotence and impart to others the Word of Life. This is to be a new epoch, new vision, new power. Christ in us is a thousand times greater than we know. All things are possible if you dare believe. The treasure is in earthen vessels that Jesus may be glorified.

Let us go forth ringing glory to God. Faith is substance, a mightiness of reality, a deposit of divine nature, God creative within. The moment you believe you are mantled with a new power to lay hold of possibility and make it reality. They said, "Lord, evermore give us this bread" (Jn 6:34). Jesus said, "He that eateth me, even he shall live by me" (Jn 6:57). Have the faith of God. The man that comes into great association with God needs a heavenly measure. Faith is the greatest of all. Saved by a new life, the Word of God, an association with the living Christ. A new creation continually taking us into new revelation.

Personal Revival Preparation
"In the beginning was the Word, and the Word was with God, and the Word was God.... All things were made by him; and without him was not any thing made that was made" (Jn 1:1, 3). All was made by the Word. I am begotten by his Word; with-

in me there is a substance that has almighty power in it if I dare believe. Faith going on to be an act, a reality, a deposit of God, an almighty flame to move you to act, so that signs and wonders are done. A living faith in the earthen casket. Are you begotten? Is it an act within you? Some need a touch, liberty to captives. Faith takes you to the place where God reigns and imbibes God's bountiful store. Unbelief is sin, for Jesus went to death to bring us the light of life.

Jesus asked, "Are ye able to drink of the cup that I shall drink of, and to be baptized with the baptism that I am baptized with?" (Mt 20:22). The cup and the baptism, a joined position. You cannot live if you want to bring everything into life. His life is manifested power overflowing. The human must decrease if the life of God is to be manifested. There is not room for two kinds of life in one body. Death for life, the price to pay for the manifested power of God through you. As you die to human desire, there comes a fellowship within, perfected cooperation, you ceasing, God increasing, you decreasing. God in you a living substance, a spiritual nature, you live by another life, the faith of the Son of God.

Message in tongues with interpretation: *The Spirit he breatheth through and quickeneth until the body is a temple exhibiting Jesus, his life, his freshness, a new life divine. Paul said, "Christ liveth in me: and the life which I now live in the flesh I live by the faith of the Son of God" (Gal 2:20).*

As the Holy Ghost reveals Jesus, he is so real, the living Word, effective, acting, speaking, thinking, praying, singing. Oh, it is a wonderful life, this substance of the Word of God, including possibility and opportunity, and confronting you, bringing you to a place undaunted. Greater is he that is in you. Paul said, "When I am weak, then am I strong" (2 Cor 12:10).

Jesus walked in supremacy, he lived in the kingdom, and God will take us through because of Calvary. He has given us power over all the power of the enemy. He won it for us at Calvary, and all in us must be subject. What shall we do to work the works? This is the work of God that ye believe. Whatsoever he saith shall come to pass. That is God's Word.

A man, frail, weak, with eyes shrunk, and neck shriveled, said, "Can you help me?" Beloved, there is not one that cannot be helped. God has opened the doors for us to let him manifest signs and wonders. The authority is inside, not outside. Could I help him? He had been on liquid food three months, fed through a tube. I said, "Go home and eat a good supper." He did, and woke up to find the tube hole closed up. God knew he did not want two holes. We must keep in a strong, resolute resting on the authority of God's Word with one great desire and purpose to do what he saith.

Originally published as "The Christian Pathway for World Floodtide," in *Redemption Tidings* (England), December 1926, pp. 2–3.

An International Ministry

Wigglesworth's First Meetings in America

Among the Stone Church [Chicago] visitors during the month of June [1914] was a Mr. Smith Wigglesworth of Bradford, Yorkshire, England. Brother Wigglesworth is visiting conventions and campmeetings in the United States and Canada. He spent a few days in the home of *The Evangel* and told us many interesting things about the Lord's work in England. He lays no claim to learning. God took him out of one of the humbler walks of life, anointed him with a heart of love and compassion for the sick and the suffering, and put his Spirit upon him. He told us of some interesting cases of healing that occurred under his ministry.

A friend of his lay dying. They had been kindred spirits from their boyhood days; perfect love existed between them. When Mr. Wigglesworth reached home one evening he found his wife had gone to see his friend who was sick, and he immediately started down to see him also.

As he neared the house he knew something serious had happened, and as he passed up the stairway he found the wife of the sick man lying on the stairs, brokenhearted. Death had already taken place. As he entered the room where the man lay, the deep love he had always cherished overcame him and he lost control of himself and began crying out to God.

His wife who was present remonstrated with him, but

as his heart went out to God he was lost to all around and felt he was being drawn up by the Spirit into the heavenlies.

The deep cry of his heart was, "Father, Father, in Jesus' name bring him back." He opened his eyes to find out there was no altered condition, but with a living faith he cried out, "He lives! He lives! Look! Look!" The dead man opened his eyes and revived, and he is living today.

From "Miracles of Healing Wrought in England," *The Latter Rain Evangel* (Chicago), July 1914, pp. 6–7.

21
Jesus, the Author and Finisher of Our Faith

Praise the Lord! I remember coming to London for the first convention many years ago. At that time I was in a very strange place, but there were people who were very kind to me. The kindness of the people of God at that time was wonderful.

You probably don't know, but I have had a month or six weeks in Canaan. I have crossed the river of Jordan, been on the lake of Galilee, bathed in the Dead Sea, drunk at Jacob's well, had a drink at Elijah's fountain, preached on the top of Mount Olives, stood with tears running down my face just opposite Mount Calvary. With hands lifted up, I saw the place of sacrifice, passed by the spot where the holy inn stood at Bethlehem. And as I thought of all the holy associations connected with that land, my heart was melted. God has been very good to me.

Jesus Is Robed in His Majesty
One of my favorite texts tonight is in the twelfth chapter of Hebrews. I want to read a few verses there. What a wonderful revelation the Hebrews is to us. I will read the first verse: "Wherefore seeing we also are compassed about with so great a cloud of witnesses, let us lay aside every weight, and the sin which doth so easily beset us, and let us run with patience the race that is set before us, Looking unto Jesus the author

and finisher of our faith" (Heb 12:1-2).

The thought here is Jesus as the author and finisher of our faith. Glory to God. What a sight to see our Lord Jesus Christ come forth robed in his own majesty and glory, as no man was ever robed. He is clothed in majesty. What compassion he had when he saw the heaving multitude; when he saw the crowds in need, his heart yearned with compassion (see Jn 6:1-14). How he handled the bread. Never any man handled bread like Jesus. I can almost look into his face, and see his eyes glisten as he sees the multitude. He said to Philip, "I would like to feed these people, how much would it take to feed them?" Philip said, "Two hundred pennyworth of bread is not sufficient, and beside, this is a desert place."

If you had been to Palestine and seen the sights I have seen, you would understand what is meant by a desert place. I have looked for many things in the Scriptures as I was over there, and God has spoken to me through it. They have the early and the latter rain there, and the land is a beautiful land. Praise the Lord! It was lovely to be there and see these things; but, beloved, it made me cherish the Bible as I have never cherished it before. Why? Because God has given us the assurance that makes our hearts know it is true. If you never see the Holy Land, you can live in the Holy Land and see all the wonderful things, and read of them in your Bible.

The Author and Finisher of Our Faith

Beloved, I want to speak tonight on "The Author and the Finisher of Our Faith," and I want us to remember that Abraham and Daniel and all the prophets were men of faith. We must not look at the things that have been done in the past; we must look at Jesus, the author and the finisher of our

Smith Wigglesworth treasured the friendship of Stanley and Alice Frodsham, fellow English Pentecostals who moved to the U.S. in 1912. Frodsham edited the *Pentecostal Evangel* and wrote several books, including the best-selling *Smith Wigglesworth, Apostle of Faith* and *With Signs Following.* Here are the Frodshams in 1918 with their daughter Faith.

COMING!   COMING!

CITY WIDE REVIVAL AND HEALING CAMPAIGN

SMITH WIGGLESWORTH

Internationally Known Evangelist of Bradford, England

WITH

Rev. & Mrs. JAMES SALTER

Missionaries from the CONGO, AFRICA

NOV. 27TH TO DEC. 2 INCLUSIVE

AT

OLD-FASHIONED
GOSPEL TABERNACLE

505 L STREET, N. E.   WASHINGTON, D. C.

J. A. McCAMBRIDGE, Pastor

Bring the sick - JESUS HEALS and is
the same Yesterday, Today and Forever

SCHEDULE OF MEETINGS

Tuesday Nov. 27,	8:00 P. M.
Wednesday	8:30 P. M.
Thursday Thanksgiving Day	11:00 A. M. 3:00 P. M. 7:30 P. M.
Friday	8:30 P. M.
Saturday	8:00 P. M.
Sunday last day	2:00 P. M. and 8:00 P. M.

Washington, D.C., was a 1934 stop for Wigglesworth on one of his frequent trips to the U.S.

James and Alice Wigglesworth Salter, Wigglesworth's daughter and son-in-law, who traveled with the evangelist on some of his around-the-world trips. The Salters were missionaries to the Belgian Congo (now Zaire).

Wigglesworth and his daughter Alice Salter in September 1924. Despite the fact that Alice was nearly deaf, she continued to minister with her father as he prayed for the sick.

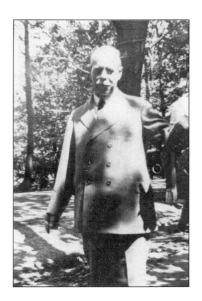

Teenager Linnie Haymaker asked Smith Wigglesworth to pose for this 1925 camp meeting photo at Eureka Springs, Arkansas.

LINNIE HAYMAKER BLAIR

A typical Wigglesworth preaching pose promotes 1920s meeting at Glad Tidings Temple, San Francisco.

FLOWER
PENTECOSTAL
HERITAGE CENTER

OLD TIME PENTECOSTAL REVIVAL

Evangelist
Smith
Wigglesworth
of England

Evangelist Smith Wigglesworth

December 8
to
December 22
Inclusive

WEEK DAYS—10:30 A. M. and 7:45 P. M.
SUNDAYS—11:00 A. M., 3:00 and 7:15 P. M.

All Are Invited to Attend These Special Meetings
The Sick Prayed for at Each Service

*Apply Early and We Will Arrange Accommodation
for You*

The Australian Evangel

Vol. 1.   FEB. 1, 1927   No. 8.

1 Kings. 7:21   Eph. 2:19-22

SPECIAL ISSUE

Wigglesworth Campaign

Reports of the

Melbourne Meetings

Sermon by SMITH WIGGLESWORTH
Testimonies of Healings

NEXT MEETING—

ADELAIDE

Central Picture Theatre, Wakefield Street

FEBRUARY 24 — to — MARCH 13

A Paper Publishing The Message of Pentecost

When Wigglesworth returned to Australia for a second campaign in 1927, *The Australian Evangel* gave valuable publicity with news and photos of meetings and reprinted his sermons. Several people who were healed in the 1922 campaign testified in this second meeting.

ASSEMBLIES OF GOD IN AUSTRALIA

This widely circulated portrait was probably taken in the 1920s when Wigglesworth became well-known as a salvation-healing evangelist.

During his years in the evangelistic field, Smith Wigglesworth marketed this anointing oil bottle, designed to be used in churches or while visiting the sick. Glad Tidings Temple, San Francisco, distributed the bottle in the U.S. during the 1930s.

Wigglesworth
Leak-Proof
Anointing
Bottle

A very neat, compact bottle of convenient size. Sure to please.

Guaranteed
Leak-Proof

Illustration actual size

Price $1.00
Postpaid

(We are the sole agents in this country)

The "Ideal Anointing Vial for Pastors and Evangelists!

Address all Mail Orders to Glad Tidings Book Room, 1441 Ellis Street, San Francisco, Calif.

YOU SIMPLY MUST HEAR

Evangelist
Smith Wigglesworth

OF ENGLAND

EVANGELISTIC AND
DIVINE HEALING CAMPAIGN

at the

First
Pentecostal
Church

31st Street, near Grove

January 2

—to—

January 15

Evangelist Smith Wigglesworth

WEEK DAYS—10:30 A. M. and 7:45 P. M. except Mondays and
Saturdays. Saturdays at 7:45 P. M.

SUNDAYS—11:00 A. M., 3:00 and 7:45 P. M.

THE SICK PRAYED FOR AT EACH SERVICE

A RARE OPPORTUNITY TO HEAR A WORLD EVANGELIST

A 1930s meeting advertisement in Oakland, California. Wigglesworth turned 70 in 1929 and ministered for another 17 years.

Smith Wigglesworth prided himself in being a man of the Word and challenged others to ever find him without a copy of the Bible.

Wigglesworth prays for a sick child at Aimee Semple McPherson's Angelus Temple, Los Angeles, about 1929. This photo was published in Sister McPherson's *Bridal Call* magazine.

This painting of Smith Wigglesworth, by artist Doug Latta, hung in the Barn Auditorium at PTL's Heritage U.S.A. during the 1980s.

faith. We must "run with patience the race that is set before us, looking unto Jesus." We must so look at the author and the finisher of our faith that the same glory and power shall be resting upon us as was upon him. We must have such grace, such holiness that we shall be landmarks showing his power is upon us. Praise the Lord.

Don't stumble at what I am going to say, but I praise God we not only have the abiding presence of the Spirit's power in our midst, but we have the living Word, the living Christ. He is the author and the finisher of our faith. He has given to us eternal life; that is, if we have his Word and believe.

My dear wife has now entered the glory, but during her lifetime, she was a great revivalist. She was the preacher. I have seen the mighty power of God fall upon her, and seen her face light up with a heavenly light as she preached, and many are the ministers of the gospel today through her preaching and her faithfulness, and others are missionaries and working for God. We shall never know the extent of her work, until the last day. You see, beloved, as we are faithful to God, and come into line with him and labor for him, our work will be rewarded. A great crowd is looking on. God is doing a work in these days, and these are

Days of Opportunity

God has been blessing in New Zealand (you must hear all about that land), and in Australia four hundred people were baptized in the Holy Ghost. Everywhere the Holy Ghost is being poured out, and the tide of blessing is rising. The power of the Holy Ghost is greater than we have ever conceived. The ring of the pentecostal testimony should be holiness. What is the strength of our position today? Holiness. I say to you and to everyone in this meeting tonight, if you fall a thousand times in a week, strive to be holy. It does not matter how many times you fall, do not give in because you fall.

I was staying in a house, and the lady of the house prepared a room and a bed for me to rest upon, as I had just got off the train and was very tired. When I awoke she said, "I want you to lie in my son's bed; I should like him to know you have lain in the bed." I slept in that bed for three nights, and two people slept in the same bed and both got baptized in the Spirit. Hallelujah! I would that everyone who is seeking would get baptized in the same way. That lady had such a sense of the presence of God that she said, "Lie in my son's bed." As soon as I opened my eyes, I looked across the room and saw these words, "A man does not fall because he makes a blunder, he falls because he makes a blunder the second time." But God does not want us to fall but to be kept by his grace from falling and to strive for holiness. I see the Word of God is the living Word, and Jesus is the author of that word. The Holy Ghost is the enlightener of the Word. If you look at the first chapter of Acts, you will see these words, "He through the Holy Ghost had given commandments" (v. 2). This is the Word we have tonight. We shall find as we go on that the Lord Jesus Christ is

The Author of Our Life
He is the source of our life, our spiritual life, and he is producing holiness.

I am going to stop soon, for I have such respect for my brother who is going to speak. I love him so. I want to leave this word with you. I had intended to speak about the vision, but as my time is short, I cannot speak about it now. I want you to see what David said in the sixty-third Psalm, "To see thy power and thy glory, so as I have seen thee in the sanctuary" (v. 2). Jesus said, "O Father, glorify thou me with thine own self with the glory which I had with thee before the world was" (Jn 17:5). The greatest glory that was ever seen was manifested on the cross. The glory was manifested when Jesus offered himself "through the eternal Spirit" (Heb 9:14) on the cross. He said to Judas, "That thou doest, do quickly," and "now is the Son of Man glorified" (Jn 13:27, 31). So we see that God was glorified in Jesus. He was reconciling the world unto himself.

Everyone who has desires tonight for God, believe the Word of God. Take Jesus as the author and the finisher of your faith. All the desires and purposes of your heart shall be accomplished, because God is faithful. God cannot fail. His Word is true. But what is real Pentecost? It is the manifestation of the power of God, the manifestation of the power of the Holy Ghost. Real Pentecost is the manifestation of the signs and wonders; real Pentecost is speaking the divine utterances; real Pentecost is manifested in those who are determined to know nothing among men, "save Jesus Christ, and him crucified" (1 Cor 2:2).

I say tonight, as I have said before, "Whom have I in heaven but thee? and there is none upon earth that I desire beside thee" (Ps 73:25). He is my all in all. Amen.

Originally published as "Author and Finisher of Faith," in *Redemption Tidings* **(England), February 1927, pp. 5–6. An address given at the convention, Kingsway Hall, London, May 1926.**

22
A True Prophet

The prophet's message is a word of the Lord that has become a burden upon the soul or a fire shut up in the bones, a burden, a pent-up fire, an anguish, and a travail. The Word of the Lord is a living flame—the symbol of Pentecost is a tongue of fire. Jeremiah had spoken his message; he felt that God had let him down and exposed him to ridicule and mockery. He would speak no more, but in the silence the fire burnt in his bones. He was full of the fury of the Lord until he was prostrate with holding himself in. The fire consumed him until he could no longer hold, until one day the fire suddenly leapt forth in forked lightning, or a flaming sword. The moment comes when the prophet is full of power by the Spirit of the Lord or to declare unto Jacob his transgression and Israel his sin. The fire constrains and consumes him, and his generation persecute and despise his word. The Lord came to bring fire. He was straightened in spirit but it was accomplished. So is every man that brings fire. There is a brooding—questioning, reasoning, excusing—hoping, foreboding. The whole being is consumed. The very marrow burns. Speech may not or must not or will not come. Then in a moment suddenly it flames out. He becomes a voice through which another speaks. Fire compels attention, it announces itself, and you don't have to advertise a fire. When the fire comes, the multitudes come.

From *Redemption Tidings* (England), March 1927, p. 2.

An International Ministry

Going After the Devil

From my ringside seat at Sion College, I once saw [Wigglesworth] push a frail crippled lady who had come to him for healing. After asking her to describe her trouble, he barked, "Do you believe God can heal you?" "Yes," was her somewhat faltering reply. He prayed, commanded the sickness to leave her body, then gave her the order, "Walk." Hesitatingly she began to walk. Then he pushed her. As she hobbled into a run, he followed her down the centre aisle shouting, "Run, woman, run." She managed to gain some strength to run and keep out of his reach. But Wigglesworth, with arms akimbo and legs apart, stood in the aisle thundering like Thor, "Run, woman, run." She eventually reached the exit and ran out into London's busy streets, apparently healed as well as frightened. I was told that the next man in the healing line quickly rediagnosed his sickness from a stomach ulcer to a mild headache.

Jack Hywel-Davies, *The Life of Smith Wigglesworth* (Ann Arbor, Mich.: Servant, 1987), p. 18. Used by permission.

23
A Transformed Life

We see from Mark 1 how Jesus was quickened by the power of God's Spirit, how he was driven by the Spirit into the wilderness. Also we see how John was filled with God's Spirit and had a cry within him, and with that cry all Israel was moved Godward, showing that when God gets hold of a man in the Spirit, he can have a new cry, a something that shall be in the order of God. A man may cry for fifty years without the Spirit of the Lord, and the more he cries, the less notice people will take of it. But if he was filled with the Holy Ghost and cried once, the people would feel the effects of it.

So there is a necessity for each one of us to be filled with God. It is not sufficient just to have a "touch," or to be filled with a desire. There is only one thing that can meet the needs of the people, and that is immersion in the life of God—God filling you with himself until you live in God, so that whether you eat or drink or whatever you do, all shall be for the glory of God. In that place you will find that all your strength and mind and soul are filled with a zeal not only for worship, but for proclamation: proclamation accompanied by the power of God, moving satanic power out and disturbing the world, making it feel upset. The reason the world is not seeing Jesus is because Christians are not filled with the power of God. They are satisfied with weekly meetings and occasionally reading the Bible and sometimes praying.

Beloved, if God lays hold of you by the Spirit, you will find that there is an end of you, and a beginning of God through you, so that your whole being becomes seasoned with a divine likeness to God, and God begins not only to use you, but to take you in hand, so that you may be a vessel unto honor, prepared unto every good work.

For if we live unto ourselves we shall die; but if we, through the Spirit, mortify the deeds of the body, we shall live. Thus we are subject to the power of God, living a life of freedom, service, blessing, and joy, bringing life to others.

Filled With the Spirit

We have two important factors. One is Jesus filled with the Holy Ghost, driven by the Spirit's power. The other is John the Baptist, so filled with the Holy Ghost that his aim was to preach. We find Jesus in the wilderness. It was natural, after he had served the multitude, to go for a time of fellowship with his Father. He wanted strength and power and association, keeping him in a place of submission.

When Jesus came down from the mountain after communion with his Father, being clothed with his holy presence and Spirit, when he met demon power, it had to go out. When he met sickness, it had to leave. He came to meet the needs of the people whatever they were. It is an awful thing to me to see Christians lifeless and powerless, so parallel with the world, that one with difficulty discriminates where they are. They are in the place where sin is in the ascendancy; but when the Holy Ghost comes, it is separation and annihilation of yourself, changing you from nature to grace. Christ in you mighty over the power of the enemy, causing you to know that there has begun in you a life of faith in the Son of God. "There remaineth therefore a rest to the people of God. For he that is entered into his rest, he also hath ceased from his own works" (Heb 4:9-10). God is in the life and you are in a new order, a flaming fire with a message from God, dethroning the powers of Satan, with an unlimited supply for every soul, so that just as John moved the whole of Israel with a cry, God by the power of the Holy Ghost will move the people.

Born Again

Ye must be born again. Amen. A new plan, new life, new creation, living in the world but not of the world, reigning in life, sin having no dominion. How shall we attain? Beloved, if we live in the Spirit, mortality shall be swallowed up of life and we shall live above disease, unbound from any power of the enemy, for the Son of God was manifested to destroy all the works of the devil. "All have sinned, and come short of the glory of God" (Rom 3:23). "The blood of Jesus Christ his Son cleanseth us from all sin" (1 Jn 1:7). Give no place to the devil, who brings evil, discord, and all things painful. God wants you to be free, having liberty. Sons of God, free in the Holy Ghost. Before the disciples received the baptism of the Holy Ghost they were so conscious of inability, that when the Master said, just before the crucifixion, "One of you shall betray me," they said one to another, "Is it I?" And they all forsook him.

Yet after they received the promise of Acts 1:8, the enduement of power, they could face the multitude and accuse them of crucifying the Lord of Glory. The Holy Ghost bore witness to these words and thousands were saved. Purity makes for boldness. God wants divine purity of heart and life, holy boldness. Brother, God can make you an overcomer. Oh, this life in the Spirit, making us free from the law of sin. There is an audacity about it, also a personality. It is the personality of deity, Christ in you, the hope of glory.

Transformation

God is able to transform, change, and bring you into his new order by the Spirit, no defeat. But without the cross, without the new birth, without Christ's righteousness, without the indwelling Christ, this divine incoming of God, we are bound to fail. But God the Holy Ghost can come and renew us in righteousness, making us sons of God. God has made man to be a son, to walk the earth with power, putting in him a capability and a capacity that brings all else into subjection to his will, a capacity of the power of Christ to dwell in you, bringing all evil under your feet, until within you nothing rises but that which will magnify and glorify the Lord. Filled with God, the rivers of living water flowing out, blessing other lives.

We see Peter after the Upper Room, filled with God, bold as a lion. And when he came to death, even to crucifixion, he counted himself unworthy of being crucified like his Lord, and asked to be put head downwards. There was a deep submissiveness. Peter had changed into the power of God, he had become identified with his Lord.

Know the truth and the truth will make you free. Jesus said, "I am the way, the truth, and the life" (Jn 14:6). "This spake he of the Spirit, which they that believe on him should receive" (Jn 7:39). I find nothing in the Bible but holiness, and nothing in the world but worldliness. Live in the Bible, become holy, let the power of God remodel you, causing you to hate sin and love righteousness. Pure in mind. Jesus is the best there is. God gave his Son to be the propitiation for our sins, and also for the sins of the whole world.

Jesus came to make us free from sin, free from disease and pain. When I see a person diseased or in pain I have great compassion for them, and I lay my hands upon them in Jesus' name.

I know God means men to be so filled with him that the power of sin shall have no effect upon them; and they will be so endued with power, helping the sick, the needy and afflicted, preaching the kingdom of God and his righteousness. The disciples began by preaching repentance towards God and faith in our Lord Jesus Christ. If you have been changed by God, there is a repentance in your heart not to be repented of.

Through the revelation of the Word of God we find that divine healing is solely for the glory of God. And salvation is to make you know you have to be inhabited by Another, even God, and to walk in newness of life, magnifying the name of our Lord Jesus Christ, endued with the power to bless others. Amen.

Originally published as "Life! Life!" in *Redemption Tidings* (England), April 1927, pp. 2–3.

24
Being Hid With Christ in God

The Lord wishes to bring before us a living fact which shall by faith bring into action a principle within us, so that Christ can destroy every power of Satan. We need to stir ourselves so that we understand the mighty power God has for us—not a dormant position, but a power, a revelation, a life—the possibility of man in the hands of God.

John the Baptist had a wonderful revelation and a mighty anointing. The power of God rested upon him, and God through John moved Israel to repentance. Now when John heard in prison of the works of Jesus, he sent two disciples, and they said unto him, "Art Thou he that should come, or do we look for another?" (Mt 11:3).

I come across men who might be giants in faith, leaders who might subdue kingdoms, but they go down because they allow Satan to dethrone their better knowledge of the power of God. Jesus sent these men back with a personal, effective knowledge that they had met him whom the prophets had spoken of. Jesus answered and said to them, "Go and shew John again those things which ye do hear and see: The blind receive their sight, and the lame walk, the lepers are cleansed, and the deaf hear, the dead are raised up, and the poor have the gospel preached to them" (Mt 11:4-5). And when they saw the miracles and wonders and heard the gracious words that he spoke as the power of God rested upon him, they were ready. You shall hear the truth, and the truth shall make you free.

"As they departed, Jesus began to say unto the multitudes concerning John, 'What went ye out into the wilderness to see? A reed shaken with the wind?'" (Mt 11:7). No, God wants to make men flames of fire; strong in the Lord and in the strength of his might powerful.

The Spirit of the Lord breathes upon the slain and upon dry bones, and upon the things that are not, and changes them in a moment of time and makes the weak strong. He is among us tonight to quicken the dead and make alive.

"From the days of John the Baptist until now the kingdom of heaven suffereth violence, and the violent take it by force" (Mt 11:12). Every believer has the life of the Lord in him. If Jesus were to come into our life, our life would go out to meet his life. "Your life is hid with Christ in God" (Col 3:3). The kingdom of heaven suffereth violence. Every suffering one, every needy one, every paralyzed condition, every weakness means that the kingdom of heaven is suffering violence at the hand of the adversary. Could the kingdom of heaven bring weaknesses? Beloved, the kingdom of heaven is within you. The kingdom of heaven is the life of Jesus, the power of the Highest—no disease, no imperfection. It is as holy as God is.

Satan comes to steal, to kill, and to destroy. Every ailment is of satanic origin. There may be some here still asleep concerning the deep things of God. I want God to give you a revelation, an awakening, an audacity, a flowing indignation against the power of Satan. Lot had a righteous indignation against Satan, but it was too late. He should have had it when he went into Sodom. There is something you must wake up to where you will never allow disease to have you, or a weak heart, or pain in the back. You will never allow anything but perfect life. The power of God brings glory.

If some were as sorry for their sickness as their sin, they would be out of it tonight. Satan has tremendous power over certain functions of the body. Satan will make the pain and weakness so distracting that it will always bring down your mind to where the pain is. Anything that takes me from an attitude of worship is of Satan; if only a finger or a toothache, the kingdom of heaven suffereth violence, and blessed is he who shall not be offended in me.

Oh, again the blind receive their sight, the lame walk, the lepers are cleansed, and the poor have the gospel preached unto them.

> *Just the same, just the same,*
> *he is just the same today.*

Praise the Lord. Amen.

Originally published as "Not Offended!" in *Redemption Tidings* (England), April 1928.

An International Ministry

The Unexpected Happens in Melbourne

The platform in the Olympia was about eight feet high, and one evening Smith was more "mobile" than ever. As his sermon unfolded, so he got closer and closer to the edge of the platform. At the height of his fervor the inevitable happened. He went perilously close to the edge, swayed to and fro for a few seconds trying to regain his balance. His arms flailing, Wigglesworth fell to the floor, and, still swaying somewhat, he surprisingly managed to land on his feet, whereupon he staggered up the aisle, his arms swinging like windmill sails, in a last-ditch effort to maintain his balance.

All the while, he managed to keep preaching without so much as a pause. In a last desperate attempt to remain upright, he placed his hand on the shoulder of a man seated on one side of the aisle. At the close of the meeting the man came forward, excitedly explaining that the pain in his body for which he was going to ask for prayer had left him immediately [when] Smith Wigglesworth's hand rested on his shoulder.

It was estimated that altogether one thousand people professed conversions during this series of meetings [in Melbourne, Australia].

Jack Hywel-Davies, *The Life of Smith Wigglesworth* (Ann Arbor, Mich.: Servant, 1987) p. 126. Used by permission.

25
Staying Wide Awake

Faith brings into action a principle within our hearts so that Christ can dethrone every power of Satan. God's accomplishment for us can be proved in our experience, not a dormant position, but a power, a revelation, a life. Oh, the greatness of it. The possibilities of man in the hand of God are brought out in revelation and force.

John the Baptist had a wonderful revelation, a mighty anointing; how the power of God rested upon him. All Israel was moved. Jesus said: "There hath not risen a greater than John the Baptist: notwithstanding he that is least in the kingdom of heaven is greater than he" (Mt 11:11). We see how satanic power can blind the mind unless we are filled or insulated by the power of God. Satan suggests to John: "Don't you think you have made a mistake?" I find men who might be used by God to subdue kingdoms, but they fall by allowing Satan to dethrone their better knowledge of the power of God.

So John sent two of his disciples to Jesus: "Art Thou he that should come or do we look for another?" (Mt 11:3). Jesus said, "Go and shew John again those things which ye do hear and see" (Mt 11:4). And when they saw the miracles and wonders they were ready. Jesus said, "What went ye out ... to see? A reed shaken with the wind?" (Mt 11:7). No, God wants men to be flames of fire, strong in the Lord and the power of his might. Let us live as those that have seen the King, having a resurrection touch. We know we are sons of God as we believe his Word and stand in the truth of it.

Message in tongues with interpretation: *The Spirit of the Lord breathes upon the bones and upon the things that are not and changes them in a moment, making the weak strong, quickening that which is dead into life.*

The kingdom of heaven is within us, the Christ, the Word of God. The kingdom of heaven suffereth violence. How? Every suffering one, every paralyzed condition, if you feel distress in any way, it means that the kingdom is suffering violence at the hands of the adversary. Could the kingdom of heaven bring weakness, disease, consumption, cancers, tumors? The kingdom of God is within you; it is the life of Jesus, the power of the Highest, pure, holy; it has no disease or imperfection. But Satan cometh to steal and kill and destroy.

I have in my mind a beautiful girl, nine years old. An evil spirit possessed her, and she screamed and moaned for years. The neighbors complained.

The father said, "These hands shall work, but my child shall never go to an asylum." One day I went to this home; the Spirit of the Lord came upon me; I took hold of the child, looked right into her eyes and said, "You evil spirit, come out in the name of Jesus." She went to a couch and fell asleep, and from that day she was perfect. I know deliverance came, but I want you to see the wiles of Satan and his dethronement in the name of Jesus, the almightiness of God against the might of Satan.

Oh, be not asleep concerning the deep things of God! Have a flaming indignation against the power of Satan. Lot had a righteous indignation, but too late; he should have had it when he went into Sodom. Be thankful you are alive to hear and that God can change the situation. We all have a greater audacity of faith and fact to reach. Many because of their iniquity are afflicted; they draw near to death, then they cry to the Lord in their trouble and he healeth them out of their distresses. Catch faith by the grace of God and be delivered. Anything that takes me from an attitude of worship, peace, and joy, of consciousness of God's presence, has a satanic source. Greater is he that is in you.

Is there anyone here suffering? [A young man steps out.] "Are you saved?"

"I am."

"Do you believe that the kingdom of God is within you?"

"I do."

"Now, young man, say in Jesus' name, 'Come out of my leg, thou evil power.' Are you free?"

"Yes."

Oh, people, put the Bible into practice and claim your blood-bought rights! Every step of my way since I received the baptism of the Holy Ghost, I have paid the price for others, letting God take me through that I might show people how to get free. Some say, "I am seeking the baptism; I am having such a struggle, is it not strange?" No, God is preparing you to help somebody else.

The reason I am so rigid on the necessity of receiving the baptism of the Spirit is, I fought it out myself. I could have asked anybody, but God was preparing me to help others. The power of God fell on me. I could not satisfy or express the joy within as the Spirit spoke through me in tongues. I had anointings before; but when the fullness came with a high tide, I knew it was the baptism, but God had to show me.

There is a difference between having the gift of tongues and speaking as the Spirit giveth utterance; the Holy Ghost uses the gift. If I could make every person who has a bad leg so vexed with the devil that he would kick the other leg, we should get through with something. I only use extreme statements to wake you up. Many times I have been shut up with insane people, praying for their deliverance; the demon power would come and bite, but I never gave in. It would dethrone a higher principle if I gave in. It is the inward presence of God that suffereth violence at the hands of Satan, and the violent take it by force.

By the grace of God we are to see tonight that we are to keep authority over the body, making the body subject to the higher power—God's mighty provision for sinful humanity.

> *Jesus paid it all,*
> *All to him I owe;*
> *Sin had left a crimson stain,*
> *He washed it white as snow.*

Originally published as "Be Wide Awake," in *Redemption Tidings* **(England), September 1928, p. 4. An address given at Adelaide, Australia.**

An International Ministry

Signs and Wonders in Switzerland

There was strong opposition by the authorities in several places [in Switzerland]. Wigglesworth was imprisoned twice during ... visits to the country. In the first town where he had been arrested because of complaints by doctors about his healing meetings, a woman well known to the police for her drunkenness had been healed. The minister of the church presented the woman to the police and said, "This woman came to one of our meetings in a state of drunkenness. While she was there in this condition Mr. Wigglesworth laid his hands on her and asked God to deliver her. Her body was broken out in terrible sores. But God healed her. And she was also delivered from her drunkenness." Then the woman spoke. "God saved my soul," she told the officers. "I am no longer a slave to drink." Impressed by the obvious change in this notorious character, the senior officer said, "I refuse to stop this kind of work. Somebody else will have to arrest this man."

On the second occasion a police officer came to his cell in the middle of the night and, without any explanation, told him to collect his belongings and leave. "No," he said. "I'll only go on one condition: That every officer in this place gets down on his knees and I'll pray for you."

Jack Hywel-Davies, *The Life of Smith Wigglesworth* (Ann Arbor, Mich.: Servant, 1987), pp. 109–10. Used by permission.

26
Fishers of Men and Women

Every time I preach I am impressed with the fact that the Word of God is full of life and vitality. It is changing us. God's Word must come to pass in us. How can we get more faith? God's Word tells us, "Faith cometh by hearing, and hearing by the word of God" (Rom 10:17). Faith is a gift. We receive our inheritance by faith. A new order. Spiritual children. Sons—born a living fact. Sons of God without rebuke. May God manifest it in us by the power of his might.

The people of our Lord's day said, "Blessed is she that bare thee," but Jesus said, "Blessed are they that hear the Word of God, and keep it" (see Lk 11:27-28). "This blessed Christ of God," they said. "Never men spake like this man" (see Jn 7:46). We do not hear him like scribes; we hear him with authority. The living Son of God, the Son of his love, came to us with open understanding, ministering the breath of his Father. We knew a quickening spirit. The moment we believed we knew we had a new nature, a new life. He had a wonderful word, a sweet influence; men saw love in those beautiful eyes and were convicted of sin in his presence. The people pressed upon him—yet he said, "Foxes have holes, and the birds of the air have nests; but the Son of man hath not where to lay his head" (Mt 8:20). Jesus said to Peter, "Launch out into the deep, and let down your nets for a draught." Peter said, "We have toiled all the night and have taken nothing" (Lk 5:4-5). Lord, you know nothing about fishing—daytime is the wrong time to fish—nevertheless, at thy word I will let down the net. I believe every fish in the lake tried to get into that net; they wanted to see him: I must see Jesus.

There was a banquet for cripples, and in the middle of it a father brought a boy on his shoulder; the father lifted the boy up. I said, "In the name of Jesus." The boy said, "Papa! Papa! It is going all over me." Jesus healed him.

And that's what happened on the lake. Peter filled one ship—then another. Oh, what would happen if you put down all the nets? Believe God! He says, "Look unto *me* and be ye saved." He says, "Come unto me, all ye that labour and are heavy laden, and I will give you rest" (Mt 11:28). He says, "He that believeth on the Son hath everlasting life" (Jn 3:36). Believe! Oh, believe. It's the Word of God. There is a river that makes glad the City of God. Peter saw the ship sinking. He looked round and he saw him. He fell down at Jesus' feet, saying, "Depart from me; for I am a sinful man, O Lord" (Lk 5:8), for he was astonished and all that were with him at the draught of the fishes which they had taken. That spotless Lamb stood there. They looked unto him and were lightened, and their faces were not ashamed.

To see Jesus is to see a new way, to see all things differently: new life, new plans. As we gaze at him we are satisfied; there is none like him. Sin moves off. Jesus was the express image of the Father. The Father could not be in the midst, so he clothed Jesus with a body—with eternal resources. Let us gather together unto him. Oh, this moving unto him. He has all we need. He will fulfill the desire of our hearts, granting all our petitions.

There was a man who had a cancer in the rectum; night and day he had morphia every ten minutes. I went to see him. He said, "I do not know how to believe God! Oh, if I could believe. Oh, if I could, if God would work a miracle." I placed my hand upon him in Jesus' name. I said to the nurse, "You go to the other room. God will work a miracle." The Spirit of God came upon me; in the name of Jesus I laid hold of the evil power, with hatred in my heart against the power of Satan; while I was praying it burst. I said to the nurse, "Come in." She did not understand, but the man knew God had done it. Now, previously, this man had a hobby; it was yachting. He was very fond of his yacht; it was all he wanted to talk about. Did he want to talk about yachting now? No! He said, "Tell me about Jesus—the sin bearer—the Lamb of God." He who made things happen—will you let him in? One body. The bread and the wine is a presentation of Christ: his body broken for you—broken to meet every human need.

Hebrews 4:12: The Word is quick and powerful. How it works in spirit, soul, and body, separating the desires, heart, thought, word, deed, intent, stiff knees—the Word enters into the joints and the marrows. The Word of the living God, one body, one bread—so conductive. He says, "Begin to do if you want the furniture of God's place put in order." I kneel down; I begin to pray. You begin in the Spirit; the Spirit leads you to pray by the Spirit. You begin—God will come in. God will lift you as you begin. We are here to help you to a place of beginnings—you must begin; come in to an eternal person who has no end. It is Jesus by his Spirit; feed upon him, believe him. The day is a day of communion. One body with unbroken fellowship; look at him, reign with him, live in his presence.

> Peace—Peace—sweet peace;
> Sweet peace—the gift of God's love.

God could give us many gifts; but the lovely gift of him that suffered and died for us—God is satisfied with him. *Keep the vision* and bring your ships to land. Forsake all and follow him. "For he was astonished, and all that were with him, at the draught of the fishes which they had taken: … 'Fear not; from henceforth thou shalt catch men'" (Lk 5:9–10).

Originally published as "Men Catchers! Astonishment!" in *Redemption Tidings* **(England), April 1929, p. 6.**

An International Ministry

A 1922 Report of Victory in New Zealand

Smith Wigglesworth's 1922 appearance in New Zealand is considered the beginning of the pentecostal movement in that country. E. E. Pennington, who was chairman of the New Zealand Evangelical Mission, reported:

"Evangelist Wigglesworth came to Wellington, little known to any of us. There was no flourishing of trumpets to herald this event. A few small advertisements in the local press announced his meetings.... His message was truly wonderful. If ever it could be said of a preacher of righteousness since the days of Philip that he preached Christ unto them, it surely would apply to Brother Wigglesworth. Never has the writer witnessed such scenes that followed the presentation of the Word of God by this Spirit-filled man, although he has been associated with such mighty evangelical services as those of Drs. Torrey, Henry, Chapman and others in their New Zealand Campaign. In the Wigglesworth services sometimes four to five hundred responded in a meeting with whole families entering the kingdom of God."

"Here and There," *Pentecostal Evangel*, January 5, 1924, pp. 6–7.

27
A Ministry in the Spirit

Three things have been pressing through this morning: (1) the way of faith; (2) the manifestation of the power of the Spirit; and (3) the ministry of the Spirit. Now is entrusted to us the ministry of the Spirit. The word may be in letter or in power; we must be in the place of edifying the church. Law is not liberty; but if there is a moving of God within you, God has written his laws in our hearts that we may delight in him.

Delighting in God

God desires to set forth in us a perfect blending between his life and our life, that we may have abounding inward joy, a place of reigning over all things, not an endeavor society, but a delight to run in the will of God. There is a great difference between an endeavor and a delight. "Be ye holy for I am holy." Trying will never reach it, but there is an attitude where God puts you in faith in resting on his Word, a delighting inwardly over everything. I delight to do thy will. There is a place of great joy. We know there is something within that has been wrought by the power of God, something greater than there could be in the natural order of the flesh. We are the representatives of Jesus; he was eaten up with zeal. This intense zeal so changes us by the operation of the Word, we rest not in the letter, but allow the blessed Holy Spirit to lift us by his power. "Ye are our epistle" (2 Cor 3:2). Such a beautiful order prevailed in this church, a place of holiness and power in Christ, perfect love, the sweetness of association with Christ.

The disciples were with Jesus three years: He spoke out of the abundance of his heart towards them. John said, "We have handled him, our eyes have gazed into his eyes" (see 1 Jn 1:1). Did Jesus know about Judas? Yes. Did he ever tell? No. They said one to another, "Is it I?" And Peter said to John who was close to Jesus, "Get to know." The essence of divine order is to bring the church together, so that there is no schism in the body, but a perfect blending of heart to heart. The letter killeth. The sword cut off Malchus' ear, but the Spirit healed it again. Our ministry has to be in the Spirit, free from the law of sin and death. When we live in the ministry of the Spirit we are free; in the letter we are bound. If it is an eye for an eye we have lost the principle; if we are to come to a place of great liberty the law must be at an end. Yet we love the law of God; we love to do it and not put one thing aside.

Message in tongues with interpretation: *The way is made into the treasure house of the Most High as God unfolds the Word, hearts are blended, an incision being made by the Spirit of the living God, that we may move, live, act, think, and pray in the Holy Ghost. A new order, life in the Holy Ghost, ministry in the Spirit.*

Epistles of Christ
"Manifestly declared to be the epistle of Christ ministered by us ... with the Spirit of the living God in fleshy tables of the

heart" (2 Cor 3:3). It's heart worship when God has sent the Holy Spirit. There is something beautiful about a little child. Jesus said, "Whosoever therefore shall humble himself as this little child, the same is greatest in the kingdom of heaven" (Mt 18:4).

When I was in Rome, I saw thousands of pilgrims kissing the steps there. It made me sorrowful. How I thank God for his Word. There are many pentecostal assemblies in Italy, and I saw on the people there a great hunger and thirst after God. God moved mightily among them, and people were saved and baptized in the Holy Ghost in the same meeting. To be baptized in the Holy Ghost is to be in God's plan, the Spirit preeminent, revealing the Christ of God, making the Word of God alive, something divine, able to minister the Spirit.

"Our sufficiency is of God; Who also hath made us able ministers ... of the spirit [which] giveth life" (2 Cor 3:5-6). I knew a brother who carried out bags of coal; he had been in bed three weeks away from his work. I showed him a verse in Romans 7:25: "I thank God through Jesus Christ our Lord. So then with the mind I myself serve the law of God; but with the flesh the law of sin." I said, "Keep your mind on God and go to work; shout victory." He did, and the first day he was able to carry a hundred bags, his mind stayed on God and kept in peace. If your peace is disturbed there is something wrong. If you are not free in the Spirit, your mind is in the wrong place. Plead the blood of Jesus and keep your mind stayed upon Jehovah. There, hearts are fully blest, finding as he promised, perfect peace and rest. Keep the mind on God, gaining strength in him day by day.

The law came by Moses, but grace and truth came by

Jesus Christ. This new dispensation, this divine place, Christ in you, the hope and evidence of glory.

Message in tongues with interpretation: *Let thine eyes be stayed upon him, thy heart moved by the Spirit, thy whole being in a place of refining to come forth as gold. Behold, see the glory. God covereth thee with a mantle of power.*

For the Lord delighteth in thee, to serve him with all thy heart and strength. Take all the land, rest in faith. Ask largely of him.

May God so gird you with truth. I commend you to him in the name of Jesus. Amen.

Originally published as "Way—Manifestation—Ministry," in *Redemption Tidings* **(England), June 1929, p. 7.**

An International Ministry

God at Work in Copenhagen

Anna Lewini, a former Danish actress, wrote about meetings Smith Wigglesworth conducted in Copenhagen:

"For three weeks, thousands daily attended the meetings. Each morning 200 or 300 were ministered to for healing. Each evening the platform was surrounded. Again and again, as each throng retired, another company came forward seeking salvation. Many were baptized in the Holy Ghost. One brother was lost in intercession for the hundreds of sick waiting to be ministered to for healing."

Stanley H. Frodsham, *With Signs Following* (Springfield, Mo.: Gospel Publishing House, 1946), p. 74. Used by permission.

28
Realizing Your Ambition and Fulfilling Your Desire

What would happen to us and to the need of the world, if we would get to the place where we could believe God? May God give the desire. Faith is a tremendous power, an inward mover. We have not yet seen all that God has for us.

When I was a little boy, I remember asking my father for a pennyworth of something. He did not give it to me. So I sat down by his side and every now and then I touched him ever so gently, saying: "Father, father." My mother said to my father, "Why don't you answer the child?" My father replied, "I have done so." But still I sat on: "Father, father, father," ever so quietly. Then, if he went into the garden, I followed him. I would just touch his sleeve and say, "Father, father!" Did I ever go away without the accomplishment of my desire? No, not once. Let God have his way with us. Let God fulfill his great desire in us for heart purity, that Christ may dwell in our hearts by faith, that the might of God's Spirit may accompany our ministry. Filled with divine enthusiasm with rivers flowing.

Precious Faith
"To them that have obtained like precious faith" (2 Pt 1:1). When our foundation test comes during a time of strain, we

can have a faith of divine origin springing up in our hearts. But the outside must be as the inside. It is good to have the Holy Spirit, but the sun inside must give a brilliancy outside. Faith! "Like precious faith," greater than the mind or body or any activity. Faith, a living power revealed in you; the moment you believe, you have what you believe for. For faith is substance and evidence.

You were not saved by feelings or experiences. You were saved by the power of God the moment you believed the Word of God. God came in by his Word and laid the foundation. Faith. Bursting up the old life-nature by the power of God, the old life changed by the Word of God.

You must come to God's Book. His Word is our foundation. When we speak of the Word we speak of almighty power, a substance of rich dynamite diffusing through the human, displaying its might, and bringing all else into insignificance. The Word of God formed within the temple, a living principle laid down of rock, the Word of the living God formed in us. The Word is mighty in thought, language, activity, movement, and unction—a fire mightier than dynamite and also able to resist the mightiest pressure the devil can bring against it. In these eventful days we must have nothing ordinary but extraordinary, allowing God by his wonderful revelations to display his goods in your hearts for the deliverance of others. Peter said, "like precious faith," the same kind that Abraham had. Have the faith of God. Being born again, we are in the working of a supernatural power, the unique peace of God, working with a changed vision; we are more wonderful than we know. Peter and John said to the lame man, "Such as we have we give thee, in the name of Jesus," and there was operation and manifestation. Faith!

"Like precious faith," all of the same material: believe in God's Word. Noah had tried faith. Abraham had faith, and all the prophets had this one fact: working faith!

No Limitation

They had limitation, but God has come to us with no limitation, "exceeding abundantly above all we can ask or think." There have been memorable days when the Holy Ghost has come. At twenty-one years of age, God flooded my life with his power, and there has not been a day since without happenings wonderful. God by his divine power flooding human vessels. God manifest in flesh, in our flesh, Christ being made manifest by the power of God. God has chosen us in a new way. He has made us kings and priests himself, and the day is not far distant when we shall be with him forever. The Holy Ghost could not come without Jesus coming first. The Holy Ghost crowning him King and all the power of his power is to be manifested through us. How?

Message in tongues with interpretation: *Rivers of Living Water. This man divinely operating, discerning the mind of Christ without measure. To live, to drink, to sup, to walk, to talk with him.*

> *Oh, 'tis all right now,*
> *Oh, 'tis all right now,*
> *For Jesus is a friend of mine*
> *And 'tis all right now.*

But Jesus must come in first; all God's fullness is in him. All God's revelation is in him. The incoming life of God by faith. "Like precious faith," an eternal process of working, no end, but a beginning. Faith cometh by hearing and hearing by the Word of God. Faith is a forming in our human nature, things of eternal forces. Faith, God's embrace, the grip of almightiness.

What is faith? It is the eternal nature of God. It can never decay or fade away. It is with you all the way to end in eternal day. Faith has so many springs. "For ever, O Lord, thy word is settled in heaven" (Ps 119:89), a copy of things to come. Be a man of desire, hungry and thirsty. Don't be satisfied.

I cannot move on faith unless it is better than my mind, greater than me. None are made on trailing clouds of glory; we are made in hard places; at wits'-end corner, with no way out. A man is made in adversity. David said, "In distress, God brought me to a large place, and I was enlarged, and he helped me."

Eight years ago [1922], after a distressing voyage, I went straight from the ship to the meeting. As I entered the building, a man fell down across the doorway in a fit. The Spirit of the Lord was upon me, and I commanded the devil to leave. In my visit to the same place this year, I ventured to ask, "Does anyone remember the incident?" I spoke in English. The man [who was delivered] did not know a word of English; he stood up, and I told him to come to the platform. He said he knew the binding power of the name of Jesus, and he had not had a fit since the stranger [Wigglesworth] came.

I had to know Acts 2:15-16 and then I began to do: "These are not drunken, as ye suppose, seeing it is but the third hour of the day. But this is that which was spoken by the prophet Joel."

Oh, my God, keep me there! In Palestine at Damascus'

Gate and on the Mount of Olives, I saw men baptized with the Holy Ghost as in Acts 2. Begin to do, and then to preach. God is always waiting to manifest his divine power. God intends us to begin.

Communication
Be a communicator of divine life for others. "His divine power hath given unto us all things that pertain unto life and godliness, through the knowledge of him that hath called us to glory and virtue" (2 Pt 1:3). My wife used to say, "He giveth grace and glory too." Oh, beloved, receive virtue. Believe for the virtue of the Lord to be so manifested through your body that, as they touch they are healed. Then the illumination of the power of the life! Believe for the current to go through you to others. It is amazing in a necessity what can happen, and God can arrange for a necessity—no time to pray, only to act. The man that is filled with the Holy Ghost lives in an act. I come with the life of the risen Christ, my mouth enlarged, my mind operative to live and act in the power of the Holy Ghost. We must so live in God that we claim an enlarging in the wisdom of God.

At one place there were six thousand people outside the building—poor things in chairs. And as I went laying my hands on them, they were healed, as they touched they were whole. This faith means increase in the knowledge of God and the righteousness of Christ—life filled with God! His mantle upon you with grace multiplied. God did for Abraham and added blessing on blessing. "Blessed are they that hear the word of God, and keep it" (Lk 11:28). What shall we do to do the works of God? Believe on him whom he has sent and "greater works than these shall you do" (see

Jn 14:12). Faith sees the glory of another, and it is from faith to faith. You may increase wonderfully before I see you again.

When I was in Orebro, Sweden, eight years ago, I ministered to a blind girl twelve years old. Recently when I returned there, they told me she had perfect sight from that day. I never knew it; it is after I get away that testimonies come. "Whosoever shall say unto this mountain, Be thou removed, and be thou cast into the sea; and shall not doubt in his heart, but shall believe that those things which he saith shall come to pass; he shall have whatsoever he saith. Therefore I say unto you, What things soever ye desire, when ye pray, believe that ye receive them, and ye shall have them" (Mk 11:23-24). Have faith in God!

If I believe, what? What I wish as I begin to say; God brings it to pass—not a fig tree or a mountain—what you saith.

In one place a man said, "You have helped all but me." I said, "What is the trouble?" He said, "I cannot sleep. I am losing my reason!" So I began to say, "No need to go anywhere; believe!"

There are nine fruits of the Spirit and nine gifts of the Spirit. Wisdom is coupled with love—knowledge with joy—faith with peace.

Examine yourselves; are you in peace? God is delighted when we are in peace, so I said to the brother, "Go home and sleep; and I will believe God." He went home. His wife said, "Well, did you see him [Wigglesworth]?" He said, "He helped all but me." However, he fell asleep. His wife said, "I wonder if it is all right." Morning, noon, night he was still asleep. He awoke bright and happy, rested and restored.

What was it? Belief in God—then speaking. "He shall have whatsoever he says." Have you this "like precious faith"? Deal bountifully with the oppressed. "He that asketh receiveth." Ask—it is done. Live for God. Keep clean and holy. Live in unction, in God's desires and plans. Glorify him in the establishment of blessing for the people—seeing God's glory manifested in the midst. Amen.

Originally published as "Ambition Realized—Desire Fulfilled," in *Redemption Tidings* **(England), July 1930, pp. 6–7.**

29
Separated Unto God

"They that sow in tears shall reap in joy" (Ps 126:5). The Lord hath set apart him that is godly for himself. His enemies will be at peace with him, and God will send him prosperity in hard times. A life on the altar for service.

Paul had reached a reserved place, separated. He was now in the place where the Holy Ghost can speak. "I beseech you ... [to] present your bodies a living sacrifice" (Rom 12:1). Here is the mercy of God, the unfathomable, desirable will of God. The body presented a living sacrifice. It's presented—a living sacrifice, not a worn-out life. The body, soul, and spirit to be presented blameless at the coming of the Lord. The present life given—with no choice but God's will. So on the altar. Oh, Lord, not mine—thine now! Lord, use it for thy glory. We are through with kicks and won'ts—all! A living body, placed at God's disposal. A holy body, with the best mind. Without a thought outside holiness unto the Lord. God only asks for what you can give!

"Be not conformed to this world" (Rom 12:2). Be not conformed—moved by it—not a hermit or careless, but transformed—every hour more purely *transformed*—to prove what God's will is for you. It's a holy, acceptable will. No sourness or irritability, or that thing about you that nobody wants. It's an acceptable will. If you give, you give cheerfully; if you love, you love warmly; if you shake hands, people know you mean it. The whole life beautiful—cleaving unto God, rejoicing in hope. *Tribulation!* Meeting it with prayer. A blessing without a curse.

This kind of life is received by men, and is acceptable in the sight of God—and at the closing-up day, it has a sure reward. Let us pray and commit our whole way to God. Being not conformed, but transformed, proving God's good and acceptable and perfect will. Amen.

Originally published as "Transformed," in *Redemption Tidings* (England), October 1930, p. 3. Preached in London, August 1930.

An International Ministry

No Other Book but the Bible

The Union Pentecostal meetings held in Chicago, October 29–November 12 [1922], were times of blessed refreshing. The large crowds which gathered twice daily to hear the messages God gave through evangelist Smith Wigglesworth of Bradford, England, were evidence that they were feasting on the Word. "For fifty years," said Brother Wigglesworth, "I have read no other book but the Bible, which my wife taught me to read." And the originality and freshness of the God-given messages convinced his hearers that the price he paid to so shut himself up with the Word of God, was worthwhile. He paid many tributes to the wonderful Word, and his grasp of the Scriptures created a hunger in a number of ministers' hearts to know that Word in equal power.

He not only preaches the Word of God but acts it out literally, puts it into practice. To quote him, "God demands of every believer who has been baptized in the Holy Spirit that he should have some 'acts.' If you do not have them, you had better get face to face with God and demand from Him your acts."

When time was given for testimony in one of the services, people arose all over the house and testified to having been healed of many diseases.

"Our Union Meetings," *The Latter Rain Evangel* (Chicago), December 1922, p. 12.

30
The Day Faith Begins to Laugh

"In Isaac [laughter] shall thy seed be called" (Rom 9:7). Faith is the great inheritance, for "the just shall live by faith" (Rom 1:17). "My faith pure, my joy sure" (see Rom 4).

For twenty-five years Abraham waited for God to fulfill his promise to give him a son. He looked to God who never fails, and believed his Word. As we live in the Spirit, we live in the process of God's mind, and act according to his will.

Could a child be born? Yes! On the law of faith in God who had promised. Here is no limitation. "Therefore it is of faith, that it might be by grace" (Rom 4:16). Grace is God's inheritance in the soul that believes.

Faith always brings a fact and a fact brings joy.

Faith! Faith! Making us know God is, and that he is a rewarder of those who diligently seek him. God! Who quickeneth that which was dead, and calleth the things that are not as though they were. There is no want to those who trust God. He quickeneth the dead.

The more Abraham was pressed, the more he rejoiced. Being not weak in faith, he considered not his own body. He staggered not through unbelief, but was strong in faith, giving glory to God, that what God had promised he was able to perform. He became heir of the world through righteousness by faith. God quickened that which was dead. The

257

longer there was no hope, Abraham believed in hope. If we knew the value of trial, we should praise God for it. It is in the furnace of affliction that God gets us to the place where he can use us. Paul says of difficulty, "I therein do rejoice, yea, and will rejoice. For I know that this shall turn to my salvation through your prayer, and the supply of the Spirit of Jesus Christ ... that ... Christ shall be magnified in my body" (Phil 1:18-20).

Before God puts you in the furnace, he knows you will go through. It is never above what we are able to bear. If you know the baptism of the Holy Ghost is in the Scriptures, never rest until God gives it to you. If you know it is scriptural to be healed of every weakness—to be holy, pure, to overcome amid all conditions—never rest until you are an overcomer.

If you have seen the face of God and have had vision and revelation, never rest until you attain to it, that ye may apprehend with all saints. Holy men spake as God gave them power and utterance. We must be blameless amid the crooked positions of the world. Jesus is the type of sonship for our attainment. He was God's pattern, a firstfruit—clothed with power. We must go in his name—that when you lay hands on the sick, Satan has no power—and when you command in Jesus' name he has to go.

> *The walls are falling down,*
> *The walls are falling down;*
> *Oh praise the Lord—Praise ye his name,*
> *The walls are falling down.*

Let us take God's Word and stand upon it as our strength to resist the devil till he is forced to flee. Amen, Amen.

Originally published as "Faith's Laughter," in *Redemption Tidings* **(England), November 1930, p. 1.**

31
A Door of Utterance

"That God would open unto us a door of utterance, to speak the mystery of Christ, ... that I may make it manifest, as I ought to speak" (Col 4:3-4).

The Need for Utterance

Paul felt as we do, the need of utterance. He had plenty of language, but he wanted utterance. We can have inspiration operating, tongue, mind, heart—we need all these. God works thus! In this divine order to give forth the truth most needed for this time. But the supreme need of the hour is the need of prayer for utterance.

These men were sent forth by the power of the Holy Spirit. But they could not without unction open the door or give forth the right word for the hour. Paul and his helpers are unequal to meet the need. Then was something out of order? No! For "except the Lord keep the city, the watchman waketh but in vain" (Ps 127:1). We are dependent upon the Holy Spirit to breathe through us. Apart from this living breath of the Spirit, the message is ordinary and not extraordinary. The question is: How can we live in this place, thrown on omnipotent power with the Spirit of the Lord giving vent, speaking through us? It is not an easy thing; God said to David that it was good that the desire was in his heart. But that will not do for us, who live in the latter days, when God is pouring forth his Spirit and rivers are at our word (see Jn 7:37-38). What is needed is Mark 11:22-23: "Have faith in God ... he shall have whatsoever he saith."

In Genesis 1:3, God said: "Let there be light." Let God arise. Let God breathe his Holy Spirit through your caravan of nature, through your eye and tongue. The supernatural in the natural for the glory of God. God raised Paul for this ministry (Acts 26:18): "To open their eyes, and to turn them from darkness to light, and from the power of Satan unto God, that they may receive forgiveness of sins, and inheritance among them which are sanctified." What was the means? Jesus said: By the faith that is in me. The faith of God. In Isaiah 50:4-5, we read: "The Lord God hath given me the tongue of the learned, that I should know how to speak a word in season to him that is weary: he wakeneth morning by morning, he wakeneth mine ear to hear as the learned. The Lord God hath opened mine ear, and I was not rebellious."

Do you believe it? Oh! For more to believe God, "that the tongue of the dumb may sing" (see Is 35:6). When will they? When they believe and fulfill the conditions: oh, beloved, it is not easy. But Jesus died and rose again for the possibility. Have faith in God. Have the tongue of a ready writer, the whole man immersed in God that the Holy Spirit may operate and the dying world have the ministry of life for which it is famishing. Romans 8:11 says: "But if the Spirit of him that raised up Jesus from the dead dwell in you, he that raised up Christ from the dead shall also quicken your mortal bodies by his Spirit that dwelleth in you." As the dead body of Christ was quickened and brought out by the Holy Spirit.

Anointed Speech

The need is to have eyes to see and ears to hear, as well as speech. If any man speak, let him speak as the oracles of God. That's our order: speaking that which no man knoweth, save the Holy Spirit as the Spirit giveth divine utterance—a language which would never come at all, except the Holy Spirit gave utterance. It is taking the things of Christ and revealing them.

"The mystery of Christ." Colossians 4:3-4 says: "praying also for us, that God would open unto us a door of utterance, to speak the mystery of Christ, for which I am also in bonds: That I may make it manifest, as I ought to speak." Did God answer the prayer?—Yes! Paul writes in Romans 15:19, "Through mighty signs and wonders, by the power of the Spirit of God; so that from Jerusalem and round about unto Illyricum, I have fully preached the gospel of Christ." It was the grace of our Lord Jesus Christ, that great shepherd of the sheep that brought to us redemption. It was the grace of God, his favor and mercy—a lavished love, an undeserved favor. God brought salvation—we did not deserve it.

"Let your speech be alway with grace, seasoned with salt" (Col 4:6). Salt has three properties: (1) it smarts; (2) it is healing; and (3) it has preservation. So your words by the Spirit should be filled with grace, yet, cut to the heart, and bring preservation. We must be very careful to be salty. His Word shall not return void; it shall accomplish and it shall prosper—but our mouths must be clean and our desire wholly for God. Jesus used straight words. He said, "Ye hypocrites, ye whitened sepulchers" to the elite of the holiness movement of his day. To others he said: "If ye were Abraham's children, ye would do the works of Abraham.... Ye are of your father the devil, and the lusts of your father ye will do" (Jn 8:39, 44). His mouth was full of meekness and gentleness, yet so salty, because of their corruption. Unless you knew the charm of Christ, you might think you were out of the wheel of the working of his eternal power. Hear the prophet again—"A bruised reed shall he not break" (Is 42:3); to those for whom there is no lifting up, he comes as the balm of Gilead.

Colossians 4:6—"that ye may know how ye ought to answer every man." This is not easy to learn. It is only learned in the absorbed (eaten up) place of God. When we are there we seek to glorify God, and can give a chastening word full of power, to waken up and to save. Use the salt, beloved! Use conviction, use the healing for their preservation. How true we have to be! You are seasoned with salt. I love it! It is inspiring! Conviction! Thus the Holy Ghost writes upon the fleshy tables of the temple of the Spirit. Oh, Lord, enlarge our conception of our sense of thy presence in the temple, discerning the Lord's body in the midst.

> For he is so precious to me
> For he is so precious to me;
> 'Tis heaven below, my Redeemer to know.
> For he is so precious to me.

God Speaks Through Us

Our whole being should be so full of the life of our Lord, that the Holy Ghost can speak and act through us. Living always in him. Oh, the charm of his divine plan. Living out on God for his omnipotent place for future ministry. Crying out for the inspiration of the God of power. Acting in the

Holy Ghost. Breathing out life divine. The glory, miracles, wonders, working out the plan of the most High God. Eaten up—knowing nothing among men, save Jesus and him crucified. Unto thee, Oh God, be the glory and the honor and the power!

Can you wonder why it is I love him so! "And as I began to speak, the Holy Ghost fell on them, as on us at the beginning" (Acts 11:15).

> *Oh, be on fire, oh, be on fire,*
> *Oh, be on fire for God.*
> *Oh, be on fire, be all on fire,*
> *Be all on fire for God.*

Amen. Amen.

Originally published as "Utterance," in *Redemption Tidings* (England), January 1931, pp. 6–7. From an address given in Switzerland.

An International Ministry

Father and Son Healed in Norway

In 1921, Smith Wigglesworth visited Norway and Sweden as well as Denmark. Vast crowds attended the meetings. At times it was necessary to move into the open air, where stands were erected for the occasion, because the buildings were too small. A great number were saved and blessed. Pastor [Thomas] Barratt wrote at that time that all Norway was stirred. He said, "A man and his son came in a taxi to the meeting. Both had crutches. The father had been in bed two years and was unable to put his leg to the ground. He was ministered to. He dropped both crutches, walking and praising God. When the son saw this, he cried out, 'Help me, too.' And after a little while, father and son, without crutches and without taxi, walked away from the hall together. The wonder-working Jesus is just the same today."

Stanley H. Frodsham, *With Signs Following* (Springfield, Mo.: Gospel Publishing House, 1946), pp. 74–75. Used by permission.

32
The Glory From Above

In Matthew 20:20-23, the mother of Zebedee's children with her sons came

> worshipping him, and desiring a certain thing of him. And he said unto her, "What wilt thou?" She saith unto him, "Grant that these my two sons may sit, the one on thy right hand, and the other on the left, in thy kingdom." But Jesus answered and said, "Ye know not what ye ask. Are ye able to drink of the cup that I shall drink of, and to be baptized with the baptism that I am baptized with?" They say unto him, "We are able." And he saith unto them, "Ye shall drink indeed of my cup, and be baptized with the baptism that I am baptized with: but to sit on my right hand, and on my left, is not mine to give, but it shall be given to them for whom it is prepared of my Father."

The Life-Changing Word
We have here a wonderful subject: all of God's Word is life-giving. It is life and light. If we are poor, it is because we do not know the Word of God. God's Word is full of riches ever opening to us fresh avenues of divine life. It is the Spirit that quickeneth. Jesus said, "The words that I speak unto you, they are spirit, and they are life" (Jn 6:63). It has a mighty changing power effectively working in us. We need not

remain in the same place two days. It is the Word of God, and he giveth us rightly all things to enjoy. This Book is the copy of the Word—the original is in the glory: "In the beginning was the Word, and the Word was with God, and the Word was God" (Jn 1:1).

You will find the moment you reach the glory you will have the principle of the Word. The Author is there—the Author of faith is there. He is our life and fills us with illumination—the Holy Ghost unveiling unto us the Christ.

A brother came to see me to ask about the Holy Ghost. He was so anxious that his ministry should be a success. I pointed out to him the words of Jesus to his disciples, "The Holy Ghost is with you and shall be in you." I said to him, "You see the sun this morning—how it pours into the room from the outside? But if the light was inside how the light would shine forth outside illuminating the dark places."

When we receive the baptism in the Holy Ghost, we receive a new ministry with divine power and glory. "The kingdom of God is not meat and drink; but righteousness, and peace, and joy in the Holy Ghost" (Rom 14:17). The Holy Ghost reveals the Christ who reigns in every believer when Jesus is coronated, and Jesus is coronated when you receive the Holy Ghost.

Have you received the Holy Ghost since you believed? Jesus is king over your desires, and no man can call Jesus Lord but by the Holy Ghost. When the Holy Ghost comes in, Jesus is Lord—then his Word floods our souls, and the tide flows out to the needy, the vision increases. Hungrier than ever, nothing satisfies me but God. I like this word: "What wilt thou?" ..."Grant that these my two sons may sit, the one on thy right hand and the other on the left, when thou comest into thy kingdom." I am sure James and John had this desire, and you can have the same desire. Jesus is the mighty worker of desire. He moves people to desire. He said, "Ye know not what ye ask." Did they know? No! Did Mary know? No! But she said "be it unto me according to thy Word." James and John said, "We are able." Would they have said it if they had known?

On another occasion they asked, "What shall we do, that we might work the works of God?" (Jn 6:28). Jesus said, "believe on him whom he hath sent." I believe it is more than saying it. It is the life of God in the nature, that stretches out to believe and to receive. We can be so drawn into the love of the Spirit, the law of the Spirit of Life making us free from the law of sin and death. And you know you are in that which will never pass away. Jesus said, "I am come to send fire on the earth" (Lk 12:49). The father shall be divided against the son, the son against the father, and a man's foes shall be those of his own household.

I remember twenty-two years ago [1907] when I received the baptism of the Holy Ghost according to Acts 2:4, I sent home a wire (the Post Office was opposite my house), that I had received the baptism of the Holy Ghost and was speaking in other tongues. The news ran like fire—everybody seemed to know. When I arrived home, my wife said to me, "So you have received the baptism of the Holy Ghost and are speaking in tongues?" She said, "I want you to know I am baptized as much as you." Right in my house the war had begun. She said, "For twenty years I have been the preacher" (I could not preach; I had tried many a time). Preachers are God-made men and women. My wife said, "Next Sunday you go on the platform by yourself, and I'll see if there is anything in it."

During the next few days, I was under great pressure what I was to speak about; and as I went on the platform, Jesus said to me, "The Spirit of the Lord is upon thee" (see Lk 4:18). I don't know what I said, but my wife ... she got up, she sat down, she got up, she sat down. She said, "That is not my husband." No man can be filled with the Holy Ghost and be the same man. He is turned into another man.

The Cups
Yes, Jesus speaks of the cups, the cup of blessing and the cup of suffering. They go together. It is always the hundredfold but with persecutions also, but it's going all the way.

> *The cross is not greater than his grace.*
> *The storm cannot hide his blessed face.*
> *I am satisfied to know*
> *That, with Jesus here below,*
> *I can conquer ev'ry foe.*
>
> BALLINGTON BOOTH

Did John know what it meant? No! Thank God there is something we cannot resist, saying, "Lord, give me the baptism of the Holy Ghost." With your whole being you cry out for the living God, and you say, "Yes, Lord!"

Never mind any cost! I saw one man in a waiting meeting seeking the baptism of the Holy Ghost about to leave. I said, "Brother, why are you leaving?" "Oh," he said, "I must go home—I have something to do. I wrote a letter to my wife's brother, and I must say I am sorry." He told his wife what he was doing. She said, "You fool." The baptism of the Holy Ghost means a clean heart. The next night there he was at the meeting again. "Oh," he said, "it is too much this time." I said, "Brother, obey God at any cost. It does not matter how bitter the cup, God will give you grace."

He was a farmer, and was accustomed to send a check regularly for corn, but one time he missed, and he had put off paying his account. The blessing of God came upon his life. Oh yes, we must be eligible for this wonderful place in the glory. We must drink the cup, but it will mean the baptism; the baptism of the Holy Ghost means the fullness of the divine anointing.

Jesus returned in the power of the Spirit into Galilee. "This day," he said, "is this scripture fulfilled in your ears" (Lk 4:21). And there are days when the Spirit is mighty upon us and it's a "this day" now.

Once while I was in a ship going from Alexandria to Venice, and again the other day at Liverpool, I saw a crowd, some thousand people, and my heart was moved with compassion. I began to speak. All was still as death. The captain, crew, and passengers were as still as death as they listened to the message God gave to me for them. There are times when you know the Spirit of God is mighty upon you and you act, though to the onlooker it may seem out of place. But you have your orders, and you act, and the Holy Ghost bears witness to it (see Heb 2:4).

The Fire

Another time in Jerusalem at the place of wailing, the Spirit of the Lord moved me. I saw young men, many of them in the prime of manhood, beating their breasts, weeping bitterly, saying, "Lord, how long, Lord, how long?" I preached unto them Jesus. On the next day ten came to see me, and with them a rabbi. They said, "Where did the fire come from? When you preached we felt the fire. We have no fire in our synagogues."

Oh, brother, the baptism of the Holy Ghost is a fire of baptism. "He shall baptize you with the Holy Ghost, and with fire" (Mt 3:11). So I began to talk with them about God's promises of a Messiah, and how he was crucified at Calvary. God wants us so filled with the Holy Ghost that people feel the power—feel the fire.

At Alexandria I got on the ship. I wanted to preach, but I could not. I had not the language, and no interpreter. I read Acts 1:1: "Jesus began both to do and teach." To do and then to teach. I wanted to do, but how? I was ready, but I had no opportunity. Men cannot make the opportunity. He has to be ready. It is God that makes the opportunity, and just where I stood a man fell on the deck. His wife cried out, "My husband is dead." One ran for the doctor, but before he arrived I began to do. I said, "In the name of Jesus," and the man revived. There was much excitement and pointing at me—all wanted to know what had happened. I could not speak to them, but I found five people who could interpret me. And all on the ship heard the old story of Jesus and his love.

Don't forget, we have to begin to do, then to teach. There is no one that loves me like Jesus, and there is no one can heal me like he can. He is acquainted with my weakness. He knows all my sorrows. There is no one can heal me like him. Oh yes, it's a real baptism of fire and a real baptism of suffering. The suffering keeps you in balance.

Jesus Is Our Perfect Example

Jesus did the most astounding thing, making the people marvel. As he is we have to be. He fed five thousand. He healed the man born blind. Wherever Jesus went, the crowds came. The children came. He could not be hid—the crowds followed him. Blind Bartimeus heard the noise. "Who is it? Who is it?" "It's Jesus!" He cried, "Jesus! Jesus! Jesus! Thou Son of David, have mercy upon me." Jesus stopped, and he'll stop tonight. "Jesus, thou Son of David, have mercy on me." They said, "Hold thy peace." But presently it changed to "Be of good comfort, rise; he calleth thee." Jesus said, "What wilt thou?" (see Mk 10:46-52). What is your request? And he is here tonight. What wilt thou? Bartimeus cried and Jesus stood still and commanded him to be called—and Jesus is here tonight. Yes, it is a cup of blessing and a cup of suffering and the place prepared in the glory. May we so yield to God that the Holy Ghost can prepare us for the place—and the glory (see Acts 1:1-2), that we may begin to do and to teach until the day when we are taken up, having the same testing as he had. It is finished! Ministering the cup of blessing which means the cup of suffering.

Originally published as "The Given Glory," in *Redemption Tidings* (England), February 1931, pp. 6–7.

33
The Ministry of the Flaming Sword

This glorious inworking of Holy Ghost power is preparing us for the rapture [Second Coming of Jesus Christ]. Our greatest theme—the glory of the splendor of our Lord. His face! His tenderness! His sweetness! Making our hearts long to be forever with the Lord. Amen! So let it be! Romans 8:31-39:

> What shall we then say to these things? If God be for us, who can be against us?... Who shall separate us from the love of Christ? shall tribulation, or distress, or persecution, or famine, or nakedness, or peril, or sword?... Nay, in all these things we are more than conquerors through him that loved us. For I am persuaded that neither death, nor life, nor angels, nor principalities, nor powers, nor things present, nor things to come, nor height, nor depth, nor any other creature, shall be able to separate us from the love of God, which is in Christ Jesus our Lord.

Oh, the joy of the thought of it! What shall separate us from the love of Christ? A place of confidence, assurance, and rest, where God has perfect control over all human weakness and you stand as on the Mount of Transfiguration manifested and glorified as in the presence of God, able to say, I know all things are working together for good within me, silently destroying all that can be destroyed that he might have pre-eminence in the body. If God be for us who can be against us?

The Same Glory

God is bringing forth a new creation; the sons of God are to be manifested, and we must see our inheritance in the Holy Ghost. Nothing can separate us! What is it God wants us to know? Right in our earthly temple God has brought forth a son with power, with manifestation, with grace, crowned already in the earth, *crowned with glory*. "The glory which thou gavest me I have given them; that they may be one, even as we are one" (Jn 17:22). The Spirit of the Lord is showing me God must get a people who can see that from before the foundation of the world he has had them in his mind. God has been delivering us through all difficulty. Where sin abounded, he has brought in his grace; where disease came in to steal our life, God raised up a standard, and we are here having come through tribulation. God has been purifying us, strengthening us, equipping us with divine audacity by the power of almightiness—till we can say "What shall we say then to these things?"

Shall we dethrone what we know up to the present time has equipped us and brought us through? Shall we allow our hearts to fail us in the day of adversity? No! That which God has already strengthened and perfected!—weakness made strong!—corruption changed to purity! Knowing that in the tribulation and the fire God has purified us, what shall we say to *these* things? These light afflictions are working for us a far more exceeding and eternal weight of glory.

The New Creation

People have been in meetings where the glory of God has fallen and the expression of God has been upon everything, and fortifications have been made in the body. The next morning the power of Satan has assailed—but the spiritual life, the Son manifested, the glory of the new creation is already in our mortal body. Then the flesh, however, is a battleground for the enemy and is tested. But that which God is forming is greater than the mortal body. The spirit which is awakening into the glorious liberty of a son of God is greater. From perfection to perfection, it is this knowledge of what he has done. What shall we say? How shall we compare this with that which is to come?

The flesh profiteth nothing but the Spirit of the living God. Though worms destroy this body, I have another life greater than this life which shall look upon God—which shall see him in his perfection, which shall behold him in his glory—which shall be changed like unto him and be formed into him (see Jn 6:63; Jb 19:26-27). By the presence of God a new creation— a glorious celestial—shall so clothe us that we shall be there in the presence of his likeness. Knowing this, shall I give place to the devil? Shall I fear? Shall I let my feelings change the experience of the Word of God? Shall I trust in my fears? No! A million times, no! There has never been any good thing in the flesh, but God has quickened the spirit till we live a new life divine over all time and are eternally shaped for God.

What shall we say? Are you going to let the past, where God has wrought for you, bring you to a place of distress, or are you standing to your testing—"Now are we the sons of God." Are we going to remember how God has answered our prayers, brought light into our home, delivered us from carnality, and touched us when no power in the world could avail? What shall we say? Can anything be brought against the elect of God? I know in whom I have believed and I am persuaded that he who purposed us for God, will surely bring us to the place where we shall receive the Crown of Life through the faith that God has given us. God is in you mightily forming within you a new creation by the Spirit—to make you ready for the glory that shall be revealed in him.

One said to me the other day, "I am in terrible trouble; a man is cursing me all the time." If God be for us, who can be against us? God is never small in any of his blessings. He takes you into all he has. "He that spared not his own Son ... how shall he not with him freely give us all things?" (Rom 8:32). God has given us Jesus, the bosom of his love, the express image of his Person, so perfect in brilliance, purity, righteousness, and glory. I have seen him many times and it always changes me. Your struggle is one of the "all things." Many needs have broken my heart, but I could say to the troubled one, God is greater than your heart, greater than circumstances, greater than the thing that holds you. God will deliver you if you dare to believe him, but we have to press it in and in and in before we can get the people to believe God.

A dear woman was marvelously delivered and saved, but she said, "I am so addicted to smoking, what shall I do?" "Oh," I said, "Smoke night and day," and she said, "In our circumstances we take a glass of wine and it has a hold on me." "Oh," I said, "Drink all you can." It brought some solace to her, but she was in misery. She said, "We play cards." I said, "Play on!" But after being saved, she called her assistant and said, "Wire to London and stop the shipment of those cigarettes." The new life does not want it. It has no desire. The old is dethroned.

A clergyman came and said, "I have a terrible craving for tobacco." I said, "Is it the old man or the new?" He broke down. "I know it's the old," he said. Put off the old man with his deeds. Another said, "I have an unlawful affection for another." I said, "You want revelation. Seeing God has given you Jesus. He will give you all things. He will give you power over the thing, and it will be broken"—and God broke it. "Allow God to touch thy flesh." Now he has quickened thy spirit. Allow him to reign, for he shall reign until all is subdued. He is preeminently King in thy life over thy affection, thy will, thy desire, thy plans. He rules as Lord of Hosts over thee, in thee, through thee, to chasten thee and bring thee to the perfection of thy desired haven. It is Christ in thee. It is the glory. "Who shall separate us from the love of Christ?" Once things could separate us, but they no more can. We have a vision. What is the vision? Those days when we have eaten of the hidden manna.

The Sword

When I was baptized in the Holy Ghost, God showed me something about Adam and Eve when they transgressed and were turned out of the garden. At the gate was put a flaming sword, a sword of death if they entered in. But when I was baptized in the Holy Ghost, God put the Tree of Life right in me and a flaming sword outside to keep the devil from me— that I might eat all the time of the eternal bread. I am eating of this wonderful bread of life. It is the life in the body which has come to a perfect place to this life from which nothing can separate us. It is increasing tremendously, perpetually; rapture has something to do with it. In a moment this will clear out and leave the body. What is it? What shall separate us? Tribulations come, but they only press us in—press us nearer persecution, the finest thing that can come. There among the persecuted you get the ripest, the holiest, the purest, the most intent, filled with divine order—all these things work for us. Nothing comes but what is helpful. Trials lift you, distresses give you a heave and sigh, but God causes us to triumph. Greater is he that is *in* you than all the powers of darkness.

Whatever befalls you as you abide in him, is the good hand of God upon you so that you won't lose your inheritance. Every trial is a life—every burden a place of exchanging strength. God will work. "Who shall lay any thing to the charge of God's elect?" (Rom 8:33). People do it, but it makes no difference. God is for us. "Eye hath not seen, nor ear heard, neither have entered into the heart of man, the things which God hath prepared for them that love him" (1 Cor 2:9). But unto us it hath been revealed by the Spirit. Not a weapon that is formed against you can prosper (see Is 54:17). Know the wisdom and purpose of the great hand that is upon you. Glorify God in distresses and persecutions, for the Spirit of God is there made manifest. Be chastened! Be perfected! Press on to heights, lengths, depths, breadths. Faith is the victory—the hope is within you—the joy set before you. The peace which passeth all understanding. The knowledge that the flesh has withered in the presence of the purifying of the Word. He who has brought you hitherto will take you to the end. I have wept bitterly and mourned when I needed revelation of God, but I need not have done.

The Lord lifteth up and changeth and operateth, and makes body and soul till he can say, "There is no spot in thee" (Song 4:7). Yes, it was persecution, tribulation, and distress that drew us near. Lifting places—changing places—the operation of God by the Spirit.

Do not let us pass this way, but let God have his way.

God stretched out his hand—covered us with the mantle of his love and brought us nearer and nearer into the channel of his grace until our heart has moved and yielded, and so turned to the Lord that every moment has seen a divine place where God has met us and stretched out his arms and said, "See ye my face—look unto me." Behold and see what great love the Master has for you, to lead you to the fountain of living water. Yield! Be led! And let God be glorified! Amen.

From *Redemption Tidings* (England), April 1931, pp. 2–3.

An International Ministry

Boy Healed in London

While Smith Wigglesworth was conducting a meeting in London in 1925, a father brought his son to be healed. The boy was described as being "caged in irons"—which probably indicated he was unable to walk.

After listening to the message, the father picked up the boy and passed him to the next row of people, and in this way over the heads of the people he reached the platform. The boy's head and arms were held up by irons, his loins also were caged in the same way. He was prayed for in the name of Jesus. The boy cried out, "Daddy! Daddy! It's going all over me." Brother Wigglesworth said, "Take the irons off." They were taken off, and the boy stood upon the platform perfectly healed by the Lord Jesus. Hallelujah!

Walter H. Clifford, *Miracles of Healing,* published in India; reprinted in *Triumphs of Faith,* September 1925, pp. 213–14.

34
The Might of the Spirit

I invite you to turn to the first chapter of the Acts of the Apostles.

This morning I understand that our subject is "Power for Service," and "Power in Service." It is a very wonderful subject, and possibly we shall not be able today to define all its lines. But there is so much in it that we are comprehending now what was once blank; there is much now that we know about, that we are not feeling after, not thinking about, not speaking so much about as something not yet quite clear; but we are speaking the things we do know, and testifying to the things which we have seen.

Now we are on the Rock. We are understanding now what Peter received on the memorable day when our Lord said to him, "Thou art Peter, and upon this rock I will build my church; and the gates of hell shall not prevail against it" (Mt 16:18). We are standing now on the foundation, the Rock, Christ, the Word, the Living Word. The power is contained in substance there. Christ is the substance of our faith. He is the hope of our inheritance; he is the substance and sum of our whole convention, and outside that we are altogether outside the plan of the great ideal of this convention. *Christ the center.*

"Ye shall receive power, after that the Holy Ghost is come upon you" (Acts 1:8). Jesus was living in the knowledge of the power. The Spirit of the Lord was upon him. These are some of the important lines that I want, God breathing through me, to deal with today—the fact of power being there, the fact of a knowledge of the power, the fact of the substance being there, the fact of that which is being created, or breathed in, or formed by God himself in the individual.

We have come into a new order; we are dwelling in a place where Christ is the whole substance, where man is but the carcass or the clay, and the Word of God the temple. Within the temple there is a living principle laid down of rock, the Word of the Living God, formed in us, and a thousand times more mighty than "me," in thought, in language, in activity, in movement; there is an unction, a force, a power mightier than dynamite, stronger than the mightiest gun that has ever been made, and able to resist the greatest pressure that the devil can bring against it. Mighty power has no might against this almighty power. When we speak about evil power, we speak about mighty power; when we speak about almighty power, we speak about a substance of rock dynamite diffusing through the human, displaying its might and bringing everything into insignificance.

I want you to think well out what I am saying. I want us this morning to be able to lay everything down on the Word. "The people that do know their God shall be strong, and do exploits" (Dn 11:32). The Holy Ghost has come with one definite purpose, to reveal unto us the Father and the Son in all their different branches of helpfulness to humanity, displaying almighty power that the weak may be made strong; bringing sickness into such a display of the revelation of the blood of Christ, of the Atonement on Calvary, that the evil power of disease is conquered and cleared out.

A Holy Boldness

There is in this baptism of the Holy Ghost a holy boldness; not superstition, but a boldness which stands unflinchingly and really on what the Word of God says. To have holy boldness is to live in the Holy Ghost, to get to know the principles that are worked out by him. It says that "Jesus began to teach." He did not have to begin to teach in order that they might understand his plan, but he began to teach. Then I must understand that as he lived in this blessed, sweet fellowship with his Father, and worked and operated because his Father worked, therefore I must learn that the blessed principles of divine order are in me, and that I am existing only for him, so long as *I* am not. *He* is, and ought to be always in preeminence. Then there is no fear. Perfect love, perfect knowledge of God, of Jesus, brings me to the state where there is no fear.

Now there is another order which is Christ working in me and bringing every thought into subjection, every desire into a divine plan of desire, and now I am working on a new plan—Christ performing, and "me" ceasing, and the work accomplished.

You say "How?" I am going to mention a few things for the helpfulness of our morning. You cannot have holy boldness without you know God; and do not attempt to exercise it without you know him. Daniel would never have entered into the lions' den if he had not known God. What did the king say? The king said this: "Daniel,... is thy God, whom thou servest continually, able to deliver thee?" "O king, live for ever. My God hath sent his angel, and hath shut the lions' mouths, that they have not hurt me" (Dn 6:20-21). The mouths of the lions were not shut in the den; and yet they were. The lions' mouths were shut when the decree was signed. You will always find that victory is at the moment when you open the door of your heart to believing.

I landed one day in a place where there was a great deal of strife and friction. I had a letter of introduction to a stranger, and did not know a single person in the place. I brought a letter to this man and he read it, and he said, "This letter is from Brother ____ of Cleveland. I know him. The letter mentions much about you. There will be an open door for you here."

Instantly after that he said, "Go out and visit these different people." And he gave me their names. "Then come back to dinner." As soon as I got back, a little bit late, he said, "I am sorry you are late for dinner; we have had dinner, and for this reason. A young man has been here, heartbroken. He was going to marry a beautiful young woman. She is dying, and the doctor is by her side and cannot help her. That young man has promised to be here and will be here in a minute. You'd better get ready." "I am ready now."

Just as I commenced my dinner, in came this man, brokenhearted. I did not question him. I went with him, and we got to the house. The mother met me at the door, brokenhearted. I said to her, "Cheer up. Show me the girl, take me to her; it will be all right in a minute or two." I was taken right into the house upstairs, and there in bed the young woman lay. She was just a travailing, poor soul. I said to her, "It will be all right in a minute or two." Then I said, "Come out!" and instantly she was healed. Holy boldness!

What do you mean by holy boldness? We may say that there is a divine position where the human may dwell, and where he has such a knowledge of God that he knows God will not fail him. It is not a miracle, though it seems sometimes almost as if it has a measure of it. It does not act sometimes exactly as the human mind would have it to act. God does not act that way. It is very often in quite an opposite line altogether. What I want you to know is this: God has a plan for his child.

What came out of that case that I have just mentioned? There is the secret. The doctor came a short time after that girl had been healed, and could not understand it. He saw this young woman, and she was dressed and downstairs in ten minutes after having been made well. While she was dressing, four other people were definitely healed. What was God's purpose? That young doctor had been investigating this power of healing, and he could not find a single person who was able to heal thus. He said to the young woman, "Are you down [from the bedroom]?" "Yes." "Come here." "A young man"—she called me a young man—"from England has been brought, and I was instantly healed." "Come here"; and then he took her and pressed his long finger into the soft of that tumor. It would have made her scream had she still had appendicitis. But he could not feel any symptom, and he said, "This is God, this is God."

Anything else? Yes. They had built a new place there, and they had not it full. But the leader said, "I am going to prophesy that our place won't hold the people." Neither would it. Anything else? Yes, God healed over two hundred people in that place.

Brothers and sisters, it is not we. I am as conscious as anything that it is just as Jesus said in the fourteenth chapter of John's Gospel: "The words that I speak unto you I speak not of myself: but the Father that dwelleth in me, he doeth the works" (Jn 14:10). Is not that beautiful? Just think of it, some of you people who have been so busy in arranging plans for preaching. Think how wonderful it is when the Holy Ghost comes and takes possession, and just utters through you such things as are needed.

Do These Things Last?

Some people ask, "Do these things last?" Praise God, his truth never fails to last; it goes on lasting. I had a letter the other day from Albany, about seventy miles from Oregon [possibly referring to Portland]. This person had never written to me since I was there. The letter ran like this: "You remember my taking you to my wife's brother who had lost all power of reason and everything?" Drink and the power of the devil had laid hold on him. "My brother has been perfectly whole ever since and has never tasted alcohol."

"Ye shall have power." Glory to God; I realize this: that if I will be still, God can work; if I will be sure that I pay the price, and not come out of the divine order, God will surely work.

Let me say a word to your hearts. Most of us here this morning are diligently seeking God's best. We feel that we would pay any price for his best. God knows my heart. I have not an atom of desire outside the perfect will of God, and God knows that. But Wigglesworth, like everybody else, occasionally has to come to this: "What is up with me? I do not feel the unction"; and if there is anything to repent of I get right down before God and get it out. You cannot cover sins over, or cover faults over; you must get to the bottom of them. You cannot have the unction and the Holy Ghost power, and the life of Christ, and the manifest glory—it cannot come excepting through self-abasement, complete renunciation of self, with God only enthroned—and Wigglesworth dead. It must be of God, and if he will only examine the conditions and act upon them, I tell you things would come off wonderfully.

Message in tongues with interpretation: *The deliverances of the Lord are as high as the righteousness of heaven; the purity of his saints as white as the linen; and the divine principles of his gracious will can only flow out when he is enthroned within. Christ first, last, always Christ. Through Christ and by the name of Jesus, whatever you shall ask in my name I will do.*

I repeat, people sometimes say, "Do these things last; is this thing permanent?" The baptism of the Holy Ghost in my life is as a river flowing on. It happened eight years ago, and the tide rises higher and higher. Holiness, purity of heart, divine thoughts and revelations of God, are far in advance of what they were even a short time ago. We are living in a divine place where the Lord is blessedly having his way.

I want you to hear what I have to say about one or two things. Some people can have things rubbed out, but I want God Almighty to do something now that cannot be rubbed out. We are definitely told in the Word of God that if we ask of the Holy Spirit, he will give. We hear people give that out quite easily, but I find that many people who dwell upon that do not get it. I know when a man is baptized of the Holy Ghost. There is a kindred spirit with a person who is baptized of the Holy Ghost that there is not in any other person.

Jesus Requires Obedience

The Holy Ghost is given to those that *obey*. That obey what? What Jesus said. What did Jesus say? "Tarry ... until ye be endued with power from on high" (Lk 24:49). Is not that clear? That is Scripture. You need not have anything more scriptural than that. Now the reason why God the Holy Ghost brings me into this place this morning is because I love the church of God; and when I hear men and women who are saved as much as I am—when I hear them on a line that I know is not according to the Spirit of God, I know exactly what spirit they are of. God save us from building up on our own imagination. Let us build up on what the Word of God says. We shall never be strong except as we believe what God says. If God tells me that Paul was the chiefest of sinners, I say I will believe it, I will believe it forever. Whatever the Holy Ghost says through his Word, I believe it, and keep to it, and I will not move from it. And the Holy Ghost says I will have power after he comes upon me through Jesus.

Message in tongues with interpretation: *They that fear the Lord and they that keep his commandments shall have the goodness of the land; and they that will do his will shall know the doctrine, and God will declare unto their hearts the perfectness of his way. For there is a way that seemeth right unto a man, but the way of that is death; but the way of righteousness bringeth to pass that God's Word is true.*

Knowing Your Place

I am so pleased because there is a thought coming into my heart that you ought all to know. I believe there is a great need today of finding our place in the Holy Ghost. It would save us from such a lot of burdens and many things.

I am going to give you a little illustration about a dear woman at our house who looks after my affairs. Everlastingly she becomes a real slave servant. I often think she does so much that is not needed. She is a slave servant; that is her disposition. There are many of them. We have a lot in our place that God has been blessing, and who have come out to speak for him in different places. She thought she ought to do the same. There were many invitations, and she accepted one of these invitations. She looked timid and said she had to take this service.

I got up the needed boldness and set to work to strip away that which was causing this timidity. With her heart full, she went out and got someone else, and instantly she found relief. She came back with her face beaming. "What's up?" I asked. She said, "I've got relieved." The burden was gone. Some people, just because they have been baptized with the Holy Ghost and with fire, think they have to go and be preachers. It is a thousand pities that it is so. It is good that that desire is in your heart, but it may not be God's purpose for you. If you would get to know your place in the Holy Ghost, it would save you from struggles and burdens, and relieve the whole situation. Get to know your place in the Holy Ghost and God will bless you.

There are hearts here crushed because they are not able to sing like our Welsh brother. But it would not do for us all to be like him. We should be breaking all the pots in the house if we were all like him. *We* have all to get to know our position in the Holy Ghost. God can work it so beautifully, and harmonize it so that there will not be a thing out of order. God will put you in the place you are to occupy, if you will ask and trust him for it; and you will live in the Holy Ghost so that his glory shall be always upon you. If you miss it, say, like David, you can pray, "Restore unto me the joy of thy salvation" (Ps 51:12). If you feel out of touch with God, get back to Calvary, keep near the cross; let the God of glory glorify himself in you.

It is marvelous how all the gifts of the Spirit may be manifested in some people. Everybody acquainted with me knows that I was short of speech and slow at everything, and all out of order. My wife used to preach, and I carried the babies and the boots and everything. Then there came a time when my wife could not be there and I was forced to roll in somehow, and I rolled in, and was very glad to roll out many a time. But it is marvelous now. As a vocation God has allowed every one of the nine gifts to be ministered through me. There is not a single gift but what has been ministered through me. What I mean is this. You won't hear me say that I have these gifts. But, living in the Holy Ghost, you are in a place in which God can manifest anything at any needed moment. You may live in that glorious attitude, and then it is heaven to live, it is heaven to eat, it is heaven to sleep, it is heaven all the time; and when heaven comes, it will never be a breaking of the casket, but only more fullness, for already the kingdom of heaven is within.

My speech is a heart speech this morning. It is useless speaking unless I speak from my heart. I have put my hands to this work, and I feel that God the Holy Ghost has done something, and I want just to speak about it in closing. I know you will believe it; I know it is true. God has helped me to go into different places and bring about revivals. Over and over again, revivals begin with people who are baptized, and God does great things.

Last night there was in one of these rooms a preacher. There he was. He knelt down. He was as stiff as a board. You want to have discernment to see whether there is reality. He was frightened to let go. I said, "Come, brother, receive the Holy Ghost." "I cannot." "You are not in earnest, you are not real; there is no business about you, you must begin to move. Receive the Holy Ghost." Then with a knowledge that he was being really stirred up, according to God's divine order I put my hands on him and said, "Receive the Holy Ghost," and God the Holy Ghost shook him from top to bottom, inside out, and what a wonderful baptism he had!

Do You Want the Holy Ghost?

Brothers and sisters, do you want the Holy Ghost? Some hymns are sung about the breath of the Holy Ghost. We read that Jesus breathed upon them (see Jn 20:22), and they received the unction in the breathing. As people breathe in the Holy Ghost they become so possessed with the power of God that they have no possessions in themselves; they simply fall into God, and God takes possession of everything—hands, and feet, and body, and tongue for the glory of God. My heart yearns for you to be so filled with the divine power of the Holy Ghost that you will go back from these meetings into your own meetings and assemblies in the order of God—not taking notice of your fullness, but having the fact remaining in you that you have power, and letting the Word of God so act upon the power that God will let it flow through you to others. By what way? His way. You cannot baptize people, but his way can do it. How? Receive ye the Holy Ghost; let him have his way.

From *Flames Of Fire* (England), September 1916. An address at the London Conference on Friday morning.

35
The Spirit of the Lord Is Upon Me

Turn with me to the fourth chapter of Luke, verse 18: "The Spirit of the Lord is upon me, because he hath anointed me to preach the gospel to the poor; he hath sent me to heal the brokenhearted, to preach deliverance to the captives, and recovering of sight to the blind, to set at liberty them that are bruised."

Jesus took up the book in the temple and read these words, and he impressed the fact because of the manifestation of the work he was doing. I believe God is bringing us to a place where we know the Spirit of the Lord is upon us. If we have not arrived at that place, God wants to bring us to the fact of what Jesus said in John 14:16: "I will pray the Father, and he shall give you another Comforter, that he may abide with you for ever." Because the Spirit of the Lord came upon him who is our head, we must see to it that we receive the same anointing, and that the same Spirit is upon us. The devil will cause us to lose the victory if we allow ourselves to be defeated by him. But it is a fact that the Spirit of the Lord is upon us, and as for me, I have no message apart from the message he will give, and I believe then the signs he speaks of will follow.

God Sent Jesus Forth

I believe that Jesus was the "sent forth" one from God, and the propitiation for the sins of the whole world, and we see the manifestation of the Spirit resting upon him so that his ministry was with power. May God awaken us to the fact that this is the only place where there is any ministry of power. In asking the Lord what to say to this people, it came to me to arouse them to the fact that the Comforter has come. He is come; and he has come to abide forever. Are you going to be defeated by the devil? No, for the Comforter has come that we may receive and give forth the signs which must follow, so that we may not by any means be deceived by the wiles of the devil.

No Limit in the Spirit

There is no limit as to what we may become if we dwell and live in the Spirit. In the Spirit of prayer we are taken from earth right away into heaven. In the Spirit the Word of God seems to unfold in a wonderful way, and it is only in the Spirit that the love of God is shed abroad in us. We feel as we speak in the Spirit that the fire which burned in the hearts of the two men on their way to Emmaus, when Jesus walked with them, is burning in our heart. It is sure to come to pass when we walk with him, our hearts will burn; it is the same power of the Spirit. They could not understand it then, but a few hours later they saw him break the bread, and their eyes were opened. But beloved, our hearts ought to always burn. There is a place where we can live in the unction and the clothing of the Spirit, where our words will be clothed with power. "Be not drunk with wine, ... but be filled with the Spirit" (Eph 5:18). It is a wonderful privilege.

I see that it was necessary for John to be in the Spirit on the Isle of Patmos for the revelation to be made clear to him. What does it mean to this generation for us to be kept in the

Spirit? All human reasoning and all human knowledge cannot be compared to the power of the life that is lived in the Spirit. We have power to loose, and power to bind in the Spirit. There is a place where the Holy Ghost can put us where we cannot be anywhere else but in the Spirit. But if we breathe his thoughts into our thoughts, and live in the unction of the Holy Spirit as he lived, then there will be evidences that we are in him; and his works we will do. But it is only in the Spirit.

I read in Matthew's Gospel of a power which we have not yet claimed, and we shall not be able to claim this manifestation of the Spirit unless we live in the Spirit. He says, I will give you power to bind and I will give you power to loose (see Mt 16:19). When are you able to bind and able to loose? It is only in the Spirit. You cannot bind things in the human or with the natural mind. This power was never off from Jesus. I feel as I preach to you tonight that there is a great lack of it in most of us. God help us! "The Spirit of the Lord is upon me." Beloved, there was a great purpose in this Spirit being on him, and there is a special purpose in your being baptized in the Spirit. We must not forget that we are members of his body and by this wonderful baptismal power, we are partakers of his divine nature.

God Keeps Us From Evil

In a vision I saw Adam and Eve driven out of the garden and a flaming sword at every side to keep them from entering the garden. But I saw that all around me was a flaming sword keeping me from evil. It seemed this would be true if I would claim it, and I said, "Lord, I will." The flaming sword was around about me delivering me from the power of hell. So we are preserved from evil. He is like a wall of fire around about us; then why should we fear? What a wonderful salvation! What a wonderful deliverer!

Notice Ezekiel chapter 37. The only need of Ezekiel was to be in the Spirit, and while he was in the Spirit it came to him to prophesy to the dry bones and say, "O ye dry bones, hear the word of the Lord" (Ez 37:4). And as he prophesies according to the Lord's command, he sees an "exceeding great army" rising up about him (see Ez 37:10). The prophet obeyed God's command, and all we have to do is exactly this, obey God. What is impossible with man is possible with God.

I pray God that your spirit, soul, and body may be preserved holy, and that you may be always on fire, and always ready with the unction on you. If this is not so, we are out of divine order, and we ought to cry to him until the glory comes back upon us. "The Spirit of the Lord is upon me." There must have been a reason why it was upon him. First of all, it says here, "because he hath anointed me to preach the gospel to the poor; he hath sent me to heal the brokenhearted" (what a gospel!), "to preach deliverance to the captives" (what a wonderful Spirit was upon him!), "and recovering of sight to the blind, to set at liberty them that are bruised, to preach the acceptable year of the Lord" (Lk 4:18-19).

You missionaries that are going to India and Africa and China and other places have a wonderful gospel to take to these people who know nothing about God, a gospel of salvation and healing and deliverance. If you want to know how it works, look at Paul among the barbarians; when the viper came out of the fire and lit on Paul's hand, they watched to see him swell up and die, but when he neither swelled up or died, they said, "These are gods" (see Acts 28:6). When you go forth to these dark lands where the Holy Ghost has sent you to preach the unsearchable riches of Christ, to loose the bands of Satan and set the captives free, be sure you can say, "The Spirit of the Lord is upon me." And remember that Christ is made unto us not only salvation but wisdom and redemption.

> *Filled with God,*
> *yes, filled with God,*
> *pardoned and cleansed,*
> *and filled with God.*

Filled with God leaves no room for doubting or fearing. We have no idea of all that means, to be filled with God. It means emptied of self. Do you know what it means to be filled with God? It means you have no fear; for when you are filled with God you are filled with love, and perfect love casts out fear.

Manifestation of the Power

I want to know more about this manifestation of the power of the Holy Spirit. Let us follow Paul further; here we find the chief of the island had the bloody flux, and when Paul ministered to him he was healed, and they loaded Paul with everything to take away (see Acts 28:10).

When we think the church is so poor and needy, we forget that the spirit of intercession can unlock every safe in the world. What did God do for the children of Israel? He took them to vineyards and lands flowing with milk and honey, and all they did was to walk in and take possession. If we will only live in the Spirit and the unction of the Spirit, there will be no lack. There is only lack where faith is not substance, but the

Lord says faith is the substance, and whatsoever is not of faith is sin. Things will surely come to pass if you will believe this. You do not have to pray to try to bring him down; he is down. You do not have to try to bring him here; he is here. If we will obey the Lord, there is nothing he will not give us since he has given us Jesus. The Spirit will have to reveal to us that fact that because he has given us Jesus, he has given us *all things*.

"The Spirit of the Lord is upon me." It is true, we must be filled with the Spirit. Father, teach us what that means! It was only because he had a knowledge of it that he could stand and say before those men, to the demon, "Come out of him."

Who is the man that is willing to lay down all, that he may have God's all? Begin to seek and don't stop seeking until you know the Spirit of the Lord is upon you. "I thank Thee, Father, thou hast hid these things from the wise and prudent, and revealed them unto babes." If you are in the "babe" class tonight, the Spirit must have revealed to you your lack. We need to seek with all our hearts. We need to be made flames of fire.

From *Triumphs of Faith* (Oakland, Calif.), September 1914, pp. 204–06. An address at the Elim Grove Camp Meeting, Cazadero, California. Reported by Miss Sadie Cody.

An International Ministry

Preaching in Dallas

Smith Wigglesworth's morning services were the greatest that have ever been held in Dallas among our pentecostal people. How was it, why was it, that the people crowded in the Peak and Garland church to hear this man? He wasn't sensational, no special songs, he did not play a guitar or crack any funny jokes and yet the people came. A man past his seventies, and yet he aroused Dallas as no other preacher has. Our ministers from over the field came in like they come to a district convention. One morning we counted over forty-five pastors and evangelists from the fields; some drove nearly four hundred miles to be there. Just to sit and listen to a plumber now filled with the Holy Ghost.

There is a lesson for us. We must confess that we have tried to improve on Pentecost. There is no use denying it, we have compromised to some extent in Pentecost. There can be no modern Pentecost. The thing is either Pentecost or it is something else. Our people have been fed on sensationalism, high-rated evangelism, until they are weak, many frail in spirit. We personally, can see where we have failed God in letting down the standard, but we are encouraged to let go and let God.

From a clipping titled "A Close-up of Smith Wigglesworth," from *The Religious Press*, written by an "M. S." in Dallas, probably in the 1930s.

36
Concerning Spiritual Gifts

Whenever I have come in touch with people who have acknowledged the Lord Jesus, I have known whether they knew anything about the Spirit of God, for every spirit which is of God testifies of Jesus, and you will always be able to tell by that their spiritual condition. If they do not confess that Jesus was manifested in the flesh, you may know that they have not the Spirit of God. Beloved, on the contrary, we find out that every spirit that confesses that Jesus is the Lord, is by the Holy Ghost.

Diversities of Gifts

"There are diversities of operations, but it is the same God which worketh all in all. But the manifestation of the Spirit is given to every man to profit withal" (1 Cor 12:6-7). Everyone who has received the Holy Ghost has within him great possibilities and unlimited power; also great possessions, not only of things which are present, but also of things which are to come. The Holy Ghost has power to equip you for every emergency. The reason people are not thus equipped is that they do not receive him and do not yield to him; they are timid and doubt, and in the measure that they doubt, they go down. But if you yield to his leadings and do not doubt, it will lead you to success and victory; you will grow in grace and will have not only a controlling power, but you will have a revealing power of the mind and purposes which God has for you.

I see where all things are in the power of the Holy Ghost, and I must not fail to give you the same truth. We must remember that we have entered into the manifestation of the glory of God, and in that is great power and strength.

Many might be far ahead of where they are this morning, but they have doubted. If by any means the enemy can come in and make you believe a lie, he will do so. We have had to struggle to maintain our standing in our salvation, for the enemy would beat us out of that if possible. It is in the closeness of the association and oneness with Christ where there is no fear, but perfect confidence all the time. The child of God need not go back a day for his experience, for the presence of the Lord is with him and the Holy Ghost is in him and in mighty power, if he will believe; and I see that we should stir one another up and provoke one another to good works.

Knowing What You Believe

The pentecostal people have a "know" in their experience. We know that we have the Spirit abiding within and if we are not moved upon by the Spirit, we move the Spirit; that is what we mean by stirring up the Spirit. And yet it is not we, but the living faith within us; it is the Spirit who stirs himself up. Where are we living? I do not mean in the natural order. We are a spiritual people, a royal priesthood, a holy people (see 1 Pt 2:9).

If we find that there is unbelief in us we must search our hearts to see why it is there. Where there is a living faith, there is no unbelief, and we go on from faith to faith until it becomes as natural to live there as can be. But if you try to live faith before you are just, you will fail, for "the just shall live by

faith" (Rom 1:17), and when you are just, it is a natural consequence for you to live by faith. It is easy; it is joyful; it is more
than that, it is our life, and spiritual inheritance.

Allow the Spirit to Stir You

"For to one is given by the Spirit the word of wisdom; to
another the word of knowledge by the same Spirit" (1 Cor
12:8). If the Spirit can stir you up this morning, you will come
short in no gift. God wants you to see that we need not come
behind in any gift, and wants to bring us to a place where we
will be on fire because of what he has called us to. We ought
always to move the tent every night; we cannot stay in one
place; the land is before us; there are wonderful possessions.
He says, "They are yours; go in and claim them."

Paul prayed that we might be "able to comprehend with all
saints" (Eph 3:18), and I see that place where Paul was in the
Holy Ghost and I believe that God is calling us today to comprehend as much as Paul comprehended. It is in the perfect
will of God that we should possess the needed gifts, but there
must be unity between God and you. When the gifts are in evidence, the whole church is built up, Christ being the head.
Jesus said, "I delight to do thy will, O my God" (Ps 40:8), and
as we surrender in that way God will be delighted to hand to
us the gift which is necessary. The more we realize that God
has furnished us with a gift, the more completely we will be
united with Jesus, so that people will be conscious of him
rather than of his gift.

Oh, beloved, if it is not all of the Holy Ghost and if we are
not so lost and controlled in the ministry of the gift, that it is
only to be Jesus, it will all be a failure and come to naught.
There was none so self-conscious as they who said, "In thy

name [we] have cast out devils" (Mt 7:22). They were so controlled by the natural and the thought that they had done it all, that God was not in it. But when he comes forth and does it, it is all right.

There is a place in the Holy Ghost where we will not allow unbelief to affect us, for God has all power in heaven and earth. And now that I am in the secret knowledge of this power I stand in a place where my faith is not to be limited, because I have the knowledge that he is in me and I in him.

Some of you come from your homes with broken hearts; you have a longing for something to strengthen you in conditions which exist there, and a power to make these conditions different. You say you are unequally yoked together; you have a mighty power that is greater than all natural power. You can take victory over your homes, and your husbands and children, and you must do it in the Lord's way.

Suppose you do see many things that ought to be different; if it is your cross you must take it and win the victory for God; it can be done, for greater is he that is in you than all the power of hell. I reckon that any man filled with the Holy Ghost is equal to a legion of devils any day.

A man in Glasgow got up and said, "I have power to cast out devils." A man full of devils got up and came to him, and this man did everything he could, but could not cast out the devils. Do you want to cast out devils? You be sure it is the Holy Ghost that does it. You know that spirit of divination followed Paul three days. The Holy Ghost has his dwelling place within me and is stirring up my heart and life to adore Jesus. Other things must be left behind; I must adore him.

Ask and Receive

God says, "Every one that asketh receiveth" (Mt 7:8). What do you ask for? What is the motive? In the fourth chapter of James we read that they asked amiss, that they might consume it on their own lusts. There is a need for the gifts, and God will reveal to you what you ought to have, and you ought never to be satisfied until you receive it.

It is important that we know we can do nothing of ourselves; but we may know that we are clothed with the power of God so we are not in the natural man in a sense, but as we go forth in this power, things will take place as they took place in the days of the disciples.

When I received the new birth at eight years of age, it was so precious and lovely; I have never lost the knowledge of my acceptance with God since that time. Brothers and sisters, there was a work that God wrought in me when I tarried for the baptism which has been wonderful. I was in a strange position; I had testified to having received the baptism of the Holy Spirit for sixteen years and had the anointing of the Spirit; I could not speak without it. My wife would come to me and say, "They are waiting for you to come out and speak to the people." I would say, "I cannot and will not come without the anointing of the Spirit." I can see now I was calling the anointing the baptism; but when the Holy Spirit came into my body until I could not give satisfaction to the glory that was in me, God took this tongue, and I spoke as the Spirit gave utterance which brought perfect satisfaction to me. When he comes in he abides. I then began to reach out as the Holy Ghost showed me.

The Call of Elisha

In the call of Elisha, God saw the young man's willingness to obey (see 2 Kgs 2:1-15). The twelve yoke of oxen, the plow, and all soon came to naught and all bridges had to be burned behind him. Brother, the Lord has called you. Are you separated from the old things? You cannot go without. As Elisha went on with Elijah, he heard the wonderful things of his ministry, and he was longing for the time when he would take his master's place. The time was coming. His master said to him, "I am going to Gilgal today; I want you to remain here." "Master," he said, "I must go with you." I find that other people knew something about it for they said to him, "Do you know the master is going to be taken away from you today?" He said, "Hold your peace, I know it." Later on the master said, "I want to go on to Bethel; you stay here." But Elisha says, "No, I will not leave thee."

Something had been revealed to Elisha. Perhaps God is drawing you to do something; you feel it. Then Elijah said, "The Lord hath sent me to Jordan; you stay here." It was the spirit of the old man that was stirring up the young man. If you see zeal in somebody else, get on a stretch for it; it is for you. I am recognizing that God is wanting all the members of his body joined together; and he makes us feel in these days when a person is failing to go on with God, we must have that member.

When they came to the Jordan, Elijah switched his mantle over it, and they passed over, and no doubt Elisha said, "I must follow his steps." And when they had gone over, the old man said, "You have done well, you would not stay back; what is the real desire in your heart? I feel I am going to leave you; ask what you like now before I leave you." "Master," he says, "I have seen all that you have done; Master, I want twice as much as you have." I believe it is the fainthearted that do not get much. As they went on up the hill, down comes the chariot of fire, nearer and nearer, and when it lights, the old man jumps in, and the young man says, "Father, Father, Father," and down comes the mantle.

What have you asked for? Are you satisfied to go on in the old way now when the Holy Spirit has come to give you an unlimited supply of power, and he says, "What will you have?" We see Peter so filled with the Holy Ghost that his shadow falling on sick people heals them. What do you want? He asked and he got it.

Elisha came down and he said, "I don't feel any different," but he had the knowledge that feelings are not to be counted for anything. (Some of you are looking at your feelings all the time.) He came to the waters as an ordinary man, then in the knowledge that he possessed the mantle (not in any feelings about it) he said, "Where is the God of Elijah?" And he put his feet down. When you put your feet down and say you are going to have a double portion, you will get it. After he had crossed, there were the young men again (they always come where there is power) and they said, "The spirit of Elijah doth rest upon Elisha."

The Gifts Are for You
You are to have the gifts, but you are to claim them. Then the Lord will certainly change your life, and you will be new men and women.

Are you asking for a double portion this morning? I trust that no one shall come behind in any gift. You say, "I have asked; do you think God will be pleased to have me ask again?" Yes, go before him; ask again, and we may this morning go forth in the spirit of the mantle, and it shall be no longer I, but the Holy Ghost. And we shall see and know his power because we believe.

Originally published as "Spiritual Gifts," in *Triumphs of Faith* (Oakland, Calif.), November 1914, pp. 248–52. An address at the Los Angeles Pentecostal Convention. Reported by Miss Sadie Cody.

37
Sons and Joint-Heirs

I used to have a hard heart, and God had to break and break and break me. I used to be critical of people who preached divine healing and did certain things which I thought they could not do. Then God began to put me through a testing and to break me; I went down before God, and then the hardness was taken away and all bitterness. I believe God wants to get all the grit and hardness out of us.

"If the Spirit of him that raised up Jesus from the dead dwell in you, he that raised up Christ from the dead shall also quicken your mortal bodies by his Spirit that dwelleth in you" (Rom 8:11). The power of God here is dealing with our "mortal bodies," but I see the power of the Spirit today wants to quicken us both in spirit and body. "If ye live after the flesh, ye shall die: but if ye *through the spirit* do mortify the deeds of the body, ye shall live. For as many as are led by the Spirit of God, they are the sons of God. For ye have not received the spirit of bondage again to fear; but ye have received the Spirit of adoption, whereby we cry, Abba, Father.... And if children, then heirs; heirs of God, and joint-heirs with Christ" (Rom 8:13-17, emphasis added).

We Are Sons, Daughters, and Joint-Heirs

The thought that specially comes to me today is that of sonship. The Spirit brings us to a place where we see that we are sons of God. And because of this glorious position, we are not only sons but heirs, and not only heirs, but joint-heirs. And because of that, I want you to see that all the promises of God are yea and amen to you through Jesus in the Holy Ghost. If the Spirit of God that raised Jesus from the dead is in you, that power of the Spirit is going to quicken your mortal body. And it brings me into a living place to believe that as an adopted child I may lay hold of the promises. I see two wonderful things: I see deliverance for the body, and I see also the power of the Spirit in sonship is raising me up, and pressing me onward to translation through faith in the Lord Jesus Christ.

Fellowship With the Father

I want to read three verses in the seventeenth chapter of John: "These words spake Jesus, and lifted up his eyes to heaven, and said, Father, the hour is come; glorify thy Son, that thy Son also may glorify thee: As thou hast given him power over all flesh, that he should give eternal life to as many as thou hast given him. And this is life eternal, that they might know thee the only true God, and Jesus Christ, whom thou hast sent" (Jn 17:1-3). It is no small thing to be brought into fellowship with the Father through Jesus Christ. The Spirit that is in you not only puts to death all other power, but he is showing us our privilege and bringing us into a faith that we can claim all we need. The moment a man comes into the knowledge of Christ, he is made an heir of heaven. But by the Spirit he is being changed into the image of the Son of God, and it is in that image that we can definitely look into the face of the Father and see that the things we ask for are done.

"If children, then heirs; heirs of God, and joint-heirs with

Christ; if so be that we suffer with him, that we may be also glorified together. For I reckon that the sufferings of this present time are not worthy to be compared with the glory which shall be revealed in us" (Rom 8:17-18). And the glory is not only going to be revealed, but it is already revealed in us. We are being changed from glory to glory. I want you to go away from this camp meeting in the knowledge of your sonship. I want you to go away knowing that the Spirit which raised up Jesus from the dead is dwelling in your mortal body, and making you a son. We shall be like him for we shall see him as he is. It does not mean that we shall have faces like Jesus, but have the same Spirit. When they look at us and see the glory, they will say, "Yes, it is the same Spirit." For they will see the luster of the glory of Jesus Christ. Beloved, we are being changed. "For the earnest expectation of the creature waiteth for the manifestation of the sons of God" (Rom 8:19). Every one of us that is born of God, and has the power of the Holy Spirit in him, is longing for the manifestation of the sonship.

You say, when shall these things come forth? So Paul gets into the expectation of it and says, "The whole creation groaneth and travaileth in pain together until now.... Even we ourselves groan ... waiting for the adoption, to wit, the redemption of our body" (Rom 8:22-23).

Earthquake Shakes the Camp

Brothers and sisters, within me this afternoon, there is a cry and a longing for deliverance. Praise God, it is coming! There is a true sense even now in which you may live in the resurrection power. The Holy Spirit is working in us and bringing us to a condition where we know he is doing a work in us. I never felt so near heaven as last night when the house was shaking with an earthquake, and I thought my Lord might come. More than crossing the sea and seeing my children, I would rather see Jesus. "For the creature was made subject to vanity" (Rom 8:20). Praise God, we are delivered by the power of the Spirit. "Because the creature itself also shall be delivered from the bondage of corruption into the glorious liberty of the children of God" (Rom 8:21). Do not say, how can this be and that be? The sovereign grace and power of God are equal to all these things. I am so wonderfully and graciously changed by the power of the Holy Spirit, that I know there is a bigger man in me than the natural man.

Benefits of the Baptism in the Spirit

"And not only they, but ourselves also, which have the first-fruits of the Spirit, even we ourselves groan within ourselves, waiting for the adoption" (Rom 8:23). Brothers and sisters, are you really waiting? The baptism of the Holy Spirit links heaven to earth, and God wants us to be so filled with the Spirit, and walk in the Spirit, that while we live here on earth our heads will be right up in heaven. Brothers and sisters, the Spirit can give you patience to wait.

The baptism in the Holy Ghost is the essential power in the body which will bring rest from all your weariness, and give you a hopeful expectation that each day may be the day we go up with him. We must not be foolish people, folding our hands and giving up everything. I find there is no time like the present to be up and active. "The Spirit also helpeth our infirmities" (Rom 8:26). We have need for our infirmities to be helped by the Spirit, in order that the body should not be taxed out of measure. The Holy Spirit himself will pray through you and bring to your remembrance the things you ought to pray for, according to the mind of the Spirit.

Is there a person in this place who says, "I have no need of the Holy Ghost"? A young man came into the meeting last night, and I asked him where he stood. He said, "I am satisfied." I said, "You are in a sad condition; there is nothing anywhere for a man who is satisfied. It is only the hungry and thirsty that God says shall receive and shall be filled." "Blessed are they which do hunger and thirst after righteousness: for they shall be filled" (Mt 5:6).

Becoming Like Jesus

The highest purpose God has for us is that we shall be transformed into the image of his Son. We have seen in a measure God's purpose in filling us with his Spirit, that he might bring about in us the image of his Son. "For whom he did foreknow, he also did predestinate to be conformed to the image of his Son, that he might be the firstborn among many brethren. Moreover whom he did predestinate, them he also called: and whom he called, them he also justified: and whom he justified, them he also glorified" (Rom 8:29-30).

Where are you this afternoon; are you standing on that? I believe there are two classes of people, the whosoever will and the whosoever won't. I want you to examine yourselves this afternoon and see where you stand, and if you stand on these truths which God has given, you will be amazed to see how God will make everything move so that you may be conformed to the image of his Son. Galatians 1:15 says, "But when it pleased God, who separated me from my mother's womb, and called me by his grace, to reveal his Son in me, that I might preach him among the heathen."

It is a sad thing today to see how people are astonished at

the workings of God. Millions of years ago he purposed in his heart to do this mighty thing in us. Are you going to refuse it, or are you going to yield? I thank God he predestinated me to be saved, and it is a case of whosoever will, and whosoever will not believe. You see it is a mystery, but God purposed it before the foundation of the world. And if you yield, he will put in you a living faith, and you cannot get away from the power of it. Oh, brothers and sisters, let us come a little nearer.

How amazing it is that we can be so transformed that the thoughts of Christ will be first in our minds. How blessed that when everybody around you is interested in everything else, you are thinking about Jesus Christ. Brothers and sisters, let us get a little nearer still. I want to say this afternoon it is the purpose of God that you should rise into the place of sonship. Don't miss the purpose God has in his heart for you. If you could only realize that God wants to make of you the first-fruits, and separate you unto himself. God has lifted some of you up over and over again. It is amazing how God in his mercy has restored and restored. "And whom he called, them he also justified: and whom he justified, them he also glorified." The glorification is still going on, and is going to exceed what it is now.

What Do You Need Today?

Within your heart this afternoon there surely must be a response to this call. "What shall we then say to these things? If God be for us, who can be against us?" (Rom 8:31). It does not matter who is against us. If there are millions against you, God has purposed it and will bring you right through to glory. "What shall we then say to these things?" Human wisdom has to stand still. It is with the heart that man believeth unto righteousness. "He that spared not his own Son, but delivered him up for us all, how shall he not with him also freely give us all things?" (Rom 8:32). Brothers and sisters, what do you want? That is the question. What have you come here for? We have seen God work in horribly diseased bodies. Our God is able to heal and to "freely give us *all things*."

"Who shall lay any thing to the charge of God's elect?" (Rom 8:33). I tell you, it is a bad business for the man that puts his hand upon God's anointed. "Who is he that condemneth?" (Rom 8:34). How much of that there is today: brother condemning brother, everybody condemning one another. You also go about condemning yourself. The devil is the accuser of the brethren. But there is power in the blood to free us and keep us and to bring us healing. Do not let the enemy cripple you and bind you.

Why don't you believe God's Word? There is a blessed place for you in the Holy Ghost. Instead of condemning you, Christ is interceding for you. "For I am persuaded, that neither death, nor life, nor angels, nor principalities, nor powers, nor things present, nor things to come, nor height, nor depth, nor any other creature, shall be able to separate us from the love of God, which is in Christ Jesus our Lord" (Rom 8:38-39).

Beloved, you are in a wonderful place. I want you to take home this afternoon the knowledge that because God has called you and chosen you, he wants you to know today that you have power with him, and because you are sons, and joint-heirs, you have a right to healing for your bodies, and to be delivered from all the power of the enemy.

From *Triumphs of Faith* (Oakland, Calif.), February 1915, pp. 34–38. An address at Cazadero Camp Meeting. The Cazadero

Camp is in the giant redwoods in Northern California. It was operated by George and Carrie Judd Montgomery. Reported by Miss Sadie Cody. Revised by *Triumphs of Faith* editor, Carrie Judd Montgomery.

An International Ministry

A Close-Up of Smith Wigglesworth

Smith Wigglesworth is a peculiar man. The way he speaks and the way he conducts himself shows that he is being led by other than man's plans. One beautiful thing about him is that he knows himself and can control himself at all times. As you look in his face you see a perfect peace, a rest, an assurance. Seldom have we witnessed such expressions as were seen on his face as the Lord would pour from his lips messages in "tongues." We are not saying these things to gain his friendship and respect, for we have already learned that he will not read anything about himself. Truly this man has learned the secret of being where God would have him. Brother Salter told us that Brother Wigglesworth has never read his own book, *Ever Increasing Faith,* written a few years ago. It was easy to approach this kindly man for he was friendly.

From a clipping titled "A Close-up of Smith Wigglesworth," *The Religious Press,* written by an "M. S." in Dallas, probably in the 1930s.

38
Immersed in the Holy Ghost

The baptism of the Holy Ghost is a great beginning. The greatest difficulty today with us is to be held in the place where it shall be God only—it is so easy to get our own mind to work. The working of the Holy Ghost is so different. I believe there is a mind of Christ, and we may be so immersed in the Spirit that we are all the day asking, "What wilt thou have me to do?" (Acts 9:6).

This has been a day in the Holy Ghost. The last three months have been the greatest days of my life. I used to think if I could see such and such things worked, I should be satisfied; but I have seen greater things than I ever expected to see, and I am more hungry to see greater things yet. The great thing at conventions is to get us so immersed in God that we may see signs and wonders in the name of the Lord Jesus; a place where death has taken place and we are not, for God has taken us. If God has taken hold of us, we will be changed by his power and might. You can depend on it, the Ethiopian will be changed. I find God has a plan to turn the world upside down.

When I have been at my wits' end, and have seen God open the door, I have felt I should never doubt God again. I have been taken to another place that was worse still. There is no place for us, and yet a place where God is, where the Holy Ghost is just showing forth and displaying his graces; a place where we will never come out, where we are always immersed in the Spirit, the glory of God being seen upon us. It is wonderful!

Power Behind the Scenes

There is a power behind the scenes that moves things. God can work in such a marvelous way. I believe we have yet to learn what it would be with a pentecostal church in England that understood truly the work of intercession. I believe God the Holy Ghost wants to teach us that it is not only the people on the platform who can move things by prayer. You people, the Lord can move things through you. We have to learn the power of the breath of the Holy Ghost. If I am filled with the Holy Ghost, he will formulate the word that will come into my heart. The sound of my voice is only by the breath that goes through it.

When I was in a little room at Bern, waiting for my passport, I found a lot of people, but I couldn't speak to them, so I got hold of three men and pulled them unto me. They stared, but I got them on their knees. Then we prayed, and the revival began. I couldn't talk to them, but I could show them the way to talk to Someone else.

God will move upon the people to make them see the glory of God just as it was when Jesus walked in this world, and I believe the Holy Ghost will do special wonders and miracles in these last days.

I was taken to see a young woman who was very ill. The young man who showed me the way said, "I am afraid we shall not be able to do much here, because of her mother, and the doctors are coming." I said, "This is what God has brought me here for." And when I prayed, the young woman was instantly healed by the power of God. God the Holy Ghost says in our hearts today that it is only he who can do it. After the healing we got crowds, and I ministered to the sick among them for two hours.

The secret for the future is living and moving in the power of the Holy Ghost. One thing I rejoice in is that there need not be an hour or a moment when I do not know the Holy Ghost is upon me. Oh, this glorious life in God is beyond expression; it is God manifest in the flesh. Oh, this glorious unction of the Holy Ghost—that we move by the Spirit. He should be our continual life. The Holy Ghost has the last thoughts of anything that God wants to give. Glory to God for the Holy Ghost! We must see that we live in the place where we say, "What wilt thou have me to do?" And see that we are in the place where he can work in us to will and to do of his good pleasure.

From *Triumphs of Faith* (Oakland, Calif.), May 1921, pp. 113–14. Reprinted from *Confidence* (Sunderland, England).

39
Filled With God

I want to read to you, in the beginning, the second chapter of Hebrews. Now, this, like every other scripture, is all very important for us. You could scarcely, at the beginning, pick any special scripture out of this we have read, it is all so full of truth, it means so much to us, and we must understand that God, in these times, wants to bring us into perfect life, that we need never, under any circumstances, go outside of his Word for anything.

God's Fullness

Some people only come with a very small thought concerning God's fullness, and a lot of people are satisfied with a thimbleful, and you can just imagine God saying, "Oh, if they only knew how much they *could* take away!" Other people come with a larger vessel, and they go away satisfied, but you can feel how much God is longing for us to have such a desire for more, such a longing as only *God himself* can satisfy.

I suppose you women would have a good idea of what I mean from the illustration of a screaming child being taken about from one to another, but never satisfied till it gets to the bosom of its mother. You will find that there is no peace, no help, no source of strength, no power, no life, nothing can satisfy the cry of the child of God but the Word of God. God has a special way of satisfying the cry of his children. He is waiting to open to us the windows of heaven until he has so moved in the depths of our hearts that everything unlike himself has been destroyed.

No one in this place need go away dry, dry. God wants you to be filled. My brother, my sister, God wants you today to be like a watered garden, filled with the fragrance of his own heavenly joy, till you know at last you have touched immensity. The Son of God came for no other purpose than to lift and lift, and mold and fashion and remold, until we are just after his mind.

I know that the dry ground can have floods, and may God save me from ever wanting anything less than a flood. I will not stoop for small things when I have such a big God. Through the blood of Christ's atonement we may have riches and riches. We need the warming atmosphere of the Spirit's power to bring us closer and closer until nothing but God can satisfy, and then we may have some idea of what God has left after we have taken all that we can. It is only like a sparrow taking a drink of the ocean and then looking around and saying, "What a vast ocean! What a lot more I could have taken if I had only had room."

You may have sometimes things you can use, and not know it. Don't you know that you could be dying of thirst right in a river of plenty? There was once a vessel in the mouth of the Amazon River. They thought they were still in the ocean, and they were dying of thirst, some of them nearly mad. They saw a ship and asked if they would give them some water, for some of them were dying of thirst, and they replied, "Dip your bucket right over; you are in the mouth of the river." There are any amount of people today in the midst of a great river of life, but they are dying of thirst, because they do not dip down and take it.

Dear brother, you may have the Word, but you need an awakened spirit. The Word is not alive until it is moved upon by the Spirit of God, and in the right sense it becomes Spirit and life when it is touched by his hand alone.

Oh, beloved, there is a stream that maketh glad the city of God. There is a stream of life that makes everything move (see Ps 46:4). There is a touch of divine life and likeness through the Word of God that comes nowhere else. There is a death which has no life in it; and there is a death-likeness with Christ which is full of life.

The Need for Spiritual Power

Oh, beloved, there is no such thing as an end to God's beginnings. But we must be in it; we must know it. It is not a touch; it is not a breath; it is the almighty God; it is a Person; it is the Holy One dwelling in the temple not made with hands. Oh, beloved, he touches and it is done. He is the same God over all, rich unto all who call upon him. Pentecost is the last thing that God has to touch the earth with. The baptism is the last thing; if you do not get this you are living in a weak and impoverished condition, which is no good to yourself or anybody else. May God move us on to a place where there is no measure to this fullness that he wants to give us. God exalted Jesus and gave him a name above every name. You notice that everything has been put under him.

It is about eight years since I was in Oakland, and in that time I have seen thousands and thousands healed by the power of God. Last year in Sweden, the last five months of the year, we had over seven thousand people saved by the power of God. The tide is rolling in; let us see to it today that we get right out into the tide, for it will hold you up. The bosom of God's love is the center of all things. Get your eyes off yourself; lift them up high and see the Lord, for in the Lord there is everlasting strength.

If you went to see a doctor, the more you told him the more he would know, but when you come to Doctor Jesus, he knows all from the beginning, and he never gives you the wrong medicine. I went to see a person today, and someone said, "Here is a person who has been poisoned through and through by a doctor giving him the wrong medicine." Jesus sends his healing power and brings his restoring grace, and so there is nothing to fear. The only thing that is wrong is your wrong conception of the mightiness of his redemption.

Dealing With Satanic Origins

He was wounded that he might be touched with a feeling of your infirmities (see Heb 4:15). He took your flesh and laid it upon the cross that he might destroy him that had the power of death, that is the devil, and deliver them who through fear of death were all their lifetime subject to bondage. You will find that almost all the ailments that you are heir to come on satanic lines, and they must be dealt with as satanic; they must be cast out. Do not listen to what Satan says to you, for the devil is a liar from the beginning (see Jn 8:44). If people would only listen to the truth of God they would find out they were over the devil, over all satanic forces. They would realize that every evil spirit was subject to them; they would find out that they were always in the place of triumph; and they would "reign in life" by King Jesus.

Never live in a less place than where God has called you to, and he has called you up on high to live with him. God has designed that everything shall be subject to man. Through Christ he has given you power over all the power of the enemy. He has wrought out your eternal redemption.

Restoring Sight to the Blind

I was finishing a meeting one day in Switzerland. And when we had finished the meeting and had ministered to all the sick, we went out to see some people. Two boys came to us and said that there was a blind man present at the meeting this afternoon who had heard all the words of the preacher. But he said he was surprised that he had not been prayed for. They went on to say this blind man had heard so much that he would not leave that place until he could see. I said, "This is positively unique. God will do something today for that man."

We got to the place. This blind man said he never had seen; he was born blind, but because of the Word preached in the afternoon he was not going home until he could see. If ever I have joy it is when I have a lot of people who will not be satisfied until they get all they have come for. With great joy I anointed him that day and laid hands on his eyes, and then immediately God opened his eyes. It was very strange how he acted. There were some electric lights. First he counted them; then he counted us. Oh, the ecstatic pleasure that every moment was created in that man because of his sight! It made us all feel like weeping and dancing and shouting. Then he pulled out his watch, and said that for years he had been feeling the watch for the time, but the raised figures, but now he could look at it and tell us the time. Then, looking as if he was awakened from some deep sleep, or some long, strange dream, he awakened to the fact that he had never seen the face of his father and mother, and he went to the door and rushed out. At night he was the first in the meeting. All the people knew him as the blind man, and I had to give him a long time to talk about his new sight.

Beloved, I wonder how much you want to take away today. You could not carry it if it were substance, but there is something about the grace and the power and the blessings of God that can be carried, no matter how big they are. Oh, what a Savior; what a place we are in, by grace, that he may come in to commune with us. He is willing to say to every heart, "Peace, be still," and to every weak body, "Be strong."

Are you going halfway; or are you going right to the end? Be not today deceived by Satan, but believe God.

From *Triumphs of Faith* (Oakland, Calif.), August 1922, pp. 184–86. Extracts from an address delivered at Mrs. Montgomery's meeting, Danish Hall, Oakland, California. Reported by Miss Mabel Bingham.

An International Ministry

On the Road With Wigglesworth

Smith Wigglesworth wrote the letter below to his friends George and Carrie Judd Montgomery in 1928. Mrs. Montgomery reprinted it in her June 1928 Triumphs of Faith *so her readers could keep up with Wigglesworth's ministry.*

To My Beloved Brother and Sister Montgomery:

I am in the midst of a real revival: over one thousand people saved and blessed. I am here in Switzerland for six weeks, and then leave on May 24th for Whitsuntide Convention, London. After that Mr. and Mrs. Salter [his daughter and son-in-law] and myself have a call to a Church of England in the heart of London. A tent is to be put up near the vicarage, and I am to preach in the church on Sundays. There is a great cloud of constant intercession going up for these meetings. God is doing great things all the time.

May God preserve you as a testimony to your living faith. "This is the victory that overcometh the world, even our faith" (1 Jn 5:4).

Yours in our risen, glorious Lord,

Smith Wigglesworth

40
You've Been Named in a Will

I believe the Lord would be very pleased this morning to have us look at the first chapter of 2 Peter, that we may see what the mind of the Lord is concerning us in this passage of Scripture.

I believe the Lord wants us to know our inheritance this morning. You know there is such a thing as having something left to you. For instance, many people make wills, and they leave executors to carry out their wills. When the person is dead, very often those people that have had the property left to them never get it, because of unfaithful stewards who have been left in charge.

Understanding Our Lord's Will

But there is one will that has been left, and he that made the whole will is our Lord Jesus Christ. After he was dead, he rose to carry out his own will. And now we may have all that has been left to us by him, all the inheritances, all the blessings, all the power, all the life, and all the victory. All the promises are ours because he is risen.

Because he is risen, and is our faithful High Priest, he is here to help us this morning to understand these divine principles that we have been reading. I pray God that we may have a clear knowledge of what he means for us in these days, for he has called us to great banquets, and we must always have a good appetite at the Lord's banquets.

It is a serious thing to come to a banquet of the Lord and have an anemic stomach that cannot take anything. We must have great appetites, longing desires, hungry and thirsty souls when we come to the Lord's table. Then we can have what is laid up for us: we can be strengthened by the might of the power of God in the inner man. May the Lord take us into his treasures now. Suppose we turn to the third verse:

"According as his divine power hath given unto us all things that pertain unto life and godliness, through the knowledge of him that hath called us to glory and virtue" (2 Pt 1:3).

We will find the main portion of truth this morning in the unfolding of the Christ. All the fullness is in him. All the glories surround him. All the divine virtue flows from him. And God is bringing us into the place that we may understand what he means by "pertain[ing] unto life and godliness, through the knowledge of him."

Virtue Can Remain

God has brought us from one step to another. The first days he gave us a glimpse of the faith which was given to us. Next he gave us assurance of the faith on the principles of Christ's being the foundation of all things. Now the Lord wants to show us how this virtue can remain in us. Paul speaks to us in the third chapter of Ephesians of the effectual working of the power of God, which is the Holy Ghost, the divine incoming which is to fill the whole spirit, soul, and body with life, virtue, grace, power, and faith. There are no limitations. He is the executive of the kingdom of heaven. He is the healing power in our body as we open ourselves to him.

So, beloved, God wants us to see this day that we must have a personal incoming of this life of God, this Holy Ghost. And I want you to think what it really means to receive the Holy Ghost. We are born again of the incorruptible Word, which is Christ. It is an incorruptible Word; it liveth and abideth forever, and we are born again of that incorruptible power. We must be made divine in order to understand things which are divine; even the mind must be "the mind of Christ," and the very inner moving and crying must be of the divine plan, for God has come to change us into the same image.

Just as he was in the world, so are we to be; and as he is, so are we. Whatever God has designed for man, we must claim it now—power now, blessing now, God now, heaven now, glory now, virtue now.

It is the Spirit that worketh in us all these divine plans, that he may build us on the foundations of the living Word, which quickeneth, moveth, and builds higher with love. He wants us to go higher and higher. Oh, for a heavenly sight this morning, a divine touch of God, of Jesus. One touch of deity, one flash of light, one moment in the presence of him, one touch of the infinite; it makes us mighty in a moment to see all things as he sees them. Oh, it is that which God hath for me. I must never cease till I reach that which he has for me, for I must be for others as he wants me to be.

God Has a Plan for You

Take the sixth chapter of Acts and you see Stephen, "A man full of faith, and of the Holy Ghost" (v. 5). And you see Barnabas and read of him. Barnabas was a good man filled with the Holy Ghost and faith (see Acts 11:22-24). God has a plan and you can get into that plan only by *holiness*. It seems there is a pure place, a pure heart that sees God. There is a divine place of purity where the unclean never put their feet. But God has a way. It is called "the way of holiness," and he can bring us into that place. He has a divine longing to bring us into that place where we hear the voice of God, see the form of God, understand the way of God, and we walk in communion with God. These are the places where divine virtue flows.

There is a life which seems right to men, but oh, it is not that life. There is another life which is only taken in and lived out, moved in by God alone. There is a virtue, a truth. God must manifest his power till everything we touch moves at the power of God. Paul knew it; the apostles had a clear conception of it; Jesus spoke about it. The woman felt it as she touched him in the skirts of his garment. There is a transmitting condition; there is a power that goes through the human body to another body. It is in perfect conjunction with the Scriptures that we lay hands on the sick, and they shall recover.

Mysteries of the Gospel

There is a truth in John's Gospel; sometimes I think we have never understood it, but maybe God has revealed it to some of us, and I would like to give it to you this morning. John's Gospel has many wonderful things to say to us. I will read from John 3:11: "Verily, verily, I say unto thee, we speak that we do know, and testify that we have seen; and ye receive not our witness. If I have told you earthly things, and ye believe not, how shall ye believe, if I tell you of heavenly things? And no man hath ascended up to heaven, but he that came down from heaven, even the Son of man which is in heaven" (Jn 3:11-13).

If I told you earthly things, and you cannot understand them, suppose I tell you heavenly things? He says the Son of Man cometh down, the Son of Man is down, and yet the Son of Man is up above.

Now, you see that electric light there is only showing forth the brilliancy because of the dynamo. It has a receiver and transmitter. There you have the naked wires, but the power of the dynamo is sending forth through those naked wires brilliancy.

In the glory there are all the powers of God. Every man who is born of God is receiving life from God. Inside the vessel is the bare wire with revelation, and illumination, and in order to keep it perfect it is always returning from whence it came. It cometh down, it is down, it is always the same.

And so is everyone that is born of God. He is kept alive by a power which he cannot see but feel, which power is generated in the glory, and comes down into earthen vessels, and is received back to the throne of God. And all the time we are receiving and transmitting—just as we stop for a moment to place our hands upon a needy case, the supernatural goes through the case, and brings forth life. So there is a divine glory, a divine nature, a perfect knowledge in the glory.

The Holy Ghost is the great incentive to us all. He receives; he disburses and reechoes the wonderful manifestations. So we must have life in this glorious order of the Spirit, united, illuminated, transformed all the time by this glorious regenerating power of the Spirit of the life of God. May God open the door for us this morning to see that it is for us all, such a manifestation of the life and power of God to be given us till there shall be neither barrenness nor unfruitfulness, but a bending unto all his will. Hallelujah!

It is that which God has designed from the beginning. It is no new thing. It is as old as God. It lasts as long as eternity. We are, we shall be forever with him. He has created us for this purpose that we should be the sons of God with power, with promise, with life, for all the world.

Do not tell me that we have the fullness of the Spirit; it is an immeasurable measure. It comes in floods we cannot contain. The more of this joy the saints of God get, the more they require, the more they desire. It is God in you that longs for all the fullness of God to come into you. Praise his name.

Originally published as "Our Inheritance," in *Triumphs of Faith* (Oakland, Calif.), April 1923, pp. 75–78. An address delivered at Glad Tidings Hall, San Francisco, California. Revised and condensed.

41
Glory and Virtue

I want you to see this morning two words that are closely connected, beautiful words and full of blessing this moment for us. Let me read them: "Through the knowledge of him that hath called us to *glory and virtue*" (2 Pt 1:3, emphasis added). People have a great misunderstanding about glory, though they often use the word.

The Spirit's Manifestation

There are three things that ought to take place in the baptism of the Holy Spirit. It was a necessity that the moving by the mighty rushing wind should be made manifest in the Upper Room, also that they should be clothed with tongues as of fire. Then that the body should receive, not only fire, but also the rushing wind; the personality of the Spirit is in the wind, and the manifestation of the glory is in the wind, or breath of God.

The inward man receives the Holy Ghost instantly with great joy and blessedness. He cannot express it. Then the power of the Spirit, this breath of God, takes of the things of Jesus and sends forth as a river the utterances of the Spirit. Again, when the body is filled with joy, sometimes so inexpressible, being thrown on the canvas of the mind, the canvas of the mind has great power to move the operation of the tongue to bring out the very depths of the inward heart's power, love, and joy to us. By the same process the Spirit, which is the breath of God, brings forth the manifestation of the glory.

Peter speaks in 2 Peter 1:16-17: "For we have not followed cunningly devised fables, when we made known unto you the power and coming of our Lord Jesus Christ, but were eyewitnesses of his majesty. For he received from God the Father honour and glory, when there came such a voice to him from the excellent glory."

Sometimes people wonder why it is that the Holy Ghost is always expressing himself in words. It cannot be otherwise; you could not understand it otherwise. You cannot understand God by shakings, and yet shakings may be in perfect order sometimes. But you can always tell when the Spirit moves, and brings forth the utterances. They are always the utterances that shall magnify God. The Holy Ghost has a perfect plan. He comes right through every man who is so filled, and brings divine utterances that we may understand what the mind of the Lord is.

Rejoicing Brings the Glory

Perhaps I might take you to three expressions in the Bible upon the glory. Psalm 16:9: "Therefore my heart is glad, and my glory rejoiceth." Something has made the rejoicing bring forth the glory. It was because his heart was glad. Turn to Psalm 108:1: "O God, my heart is fixed; I will sing and give praise, even with my glory." You see when the body is filled with the power of God, then the only thing that can express the glory is the tongue. Glory is presence and the presence always comes by the tongue, which brings forth the revelations of God.

You find in Acts 2:25-26 another side to this: "For David

speaketh concerning him, I foresaw the Lord always before my face, for he is on my right hand, that I should not be moved: Therefore did my heart rejoice, and my tongue was glad." God first brings into us his power, then he gives us verbal expressions by the same Spirit, the manifestation out of us just as it is within us. "Out of the abundance of the heart the mouth speaketh" (Mt 12:34).

Virtue has to be transmitted, and glory has to be expressed. So God, by filling us with the Holy Ghost, has brought into us this glory, that out of us may come forth the glory. The Holy Ghost understands everything Christ has in the glory and brings through the heart of man God's latest thought. The world's needs, our manifestations, revivals, all conditions, are first settled in heaven, then worked out on the earth. So we must be in touch with God Almighty to bring out on the face of the earth all the things that God has in the heavens. This is an ideal for us, and God help us not to forsake the sense of holy communion, entering into the closet in privacy, that publicly he may manifest his glory.

We must see the face of the Lord and understand his workings. There are things that God says to me that I know must take place. It does not matter what people say. I have been face to face with some of the most trying moments of men's lives, when it meant so much if I kept the vision, and held fast to what God had said. A man must be in an immovable condition, and the voice of God must mean to him more than what he sees, feels, or what people say. He must have an originality born in heaven, transmitted or expressed in some way. We must bring heaven to earth.

God Provides Things of Life and Godliness
Turn to 2 Peter 1:3: "According as his divine power hath given unto us all things that pertain unto life and godliness, through the knowledge of him that hath called us to glory and virtue." Oh, this is a lovely verse. There is so much depth in it for us. It is all real from heaven. It is as divinely appointed for this meeting as when the Holy Ghost was upon Peter, and he brings it out for us. It is to me life; it is like the breath; it moves me. I must live in this grace. "According as his divine power," there it is again, "hath given unto us all things that pertain unto life and godliness." Oh, what wonderful things he has given us, "through the knowledge of him that hath called us to glory and virtue." You cannot get away from him. He is the center of all things. He moves the earth, transforms beings, can live in every mind, plan every thought. Oh, he is there all the time.

A Rally Call for the Saints
You will find that Paul is full of the might of the Spirit breathing through him, and yet he comes to a place where he feels he must stop. For there are greater things than he can even utter only by prayer, the almighty breathing through the human soul.

In the last of Ephesians 3, are these words which no human man could ever think or plan with pen and ink, so mighty, so of God when it speaks about his being able to do all things, "exceeding abundantly above all that we ask or think" (v. 20). The mighty God of revelation! The Holy Ghost gave these words of grandeur to stir our hearts, to move our affections, to transform us altogether. This is ideal! This is God. Shall we teach them? Shall we have them? Oh, they are ours. God has never put anything over on a pole where you could not reach it. He has brought his plan down to man, and if we are prepared this morning, oh, what there is for us! I feel sometimes we have just as much as we can digest, yet there are such divine nuggets of precious truth held before our hearts, it makes you understand that there are yet heights, and depths, and lengths, and breadths of the knowledge of God laid up for us. We might truly say,

> *My heavenly bank, my heavenly bank,*
> *The house of God, treasure and store.*
> *I have plenty in here; I'm a real millionaire.*

Glory! Never to be poverty-struck any more. An inward knowledge of a greater bank than ever the Rothcnilds, or any other, has known about. It is stored up, nugget upon nugget, weights of glory, expressions of the invisible Christ to be seen by men.

The Answer to Our Longing Hearts

God is shaking the earth to its foundations, and making us to understand that there is a principle in the Scriptures that may bring to man freedom from the natural order, and bring him into a place of holiness, righteousness, and peace of God which passeth all human understanding. We must reach it. Praise God! God has brought us in on purpose to take us on. He has brought us here this morning, and you say, "How shall I be able to get all that is laid up for me?" Brother, sister, I know no other way—a broken and contrite heart he will not despise.

What do you want this morning? Be definite in your

seeking. God knows what you need, and that one thing is for you this morning. Set it in your minds that you will know this morning the powers of the world to come.

"Ask, and it shall be given you; seek, and ye shall find; knock, and it shall be opened unto you: For every one that asketh receiveth; and he that seeketh findeth; and to him that knocketh it shall be opened" (Mt 7:7-8).

From *Triumphs of Faith* (Oakland, Calif.), May 1923, pp. 105–07, 119. An address delivered at Glad Tidings Hall, San Francisco, California. Condensed and revised.

An International Ministry

Wigglesworth Testifies of His Healing

For three years I have been suffering from pains in the bladder, often passing much blood. It has truly been a trial of faith in the furnace of affliction with continuous pain night and day, for weeks at a time, hoping against hope (see Rom 4:18). For about forty-five years I have believed in divine healing, and for over thirty years have been helping needy sufferers, and my preaching has been to establish faith among saints.

What will seem strange to some is the fact that while I continued to help others and they received health and healing, I was still held in this terrible grip of pain and suffering. Some months ago I consulted a doctor, and he said I was in a dangerous state, and advised me to have an X ray. This showed a stone in the bladder the size of a large bean. The doctor said nothing but an operation could remove this. I said that hundreds were praying for me.

On October 4 [1933], about four P.M. God worked a miracle. For hours I passed grit and sharp stones, some one-fourth to three-eighths inches long, of a sharp granite appearance, nine of which I have kept to show if necessary. I have been refusing calls [to minister] for three years on account of this suffering. James 1:2-3 has been a blessing to me: "Count it all joy ... knowing this, that the trying of your faith worketh patience."

Now I am full of praise to God for the miracle he has

wrought in me. To him be all the glory! I believe the future will be greater than the past to help those who are sick and suffering.

Smith Wigglesworth, "Wonderfully Healed," *Triumphs of Faith* (Oakland, Calif.), January 1934, p. 11.

42

Overcoming

In the fifth chapter of the first Epistle of John we have essential truths that give us a clear discernment of our position in Christ. God wants us to be so built up in truth, righteousness, and the life of God that every person with whom we come into contact may know of a truth that we are of God; and we who are of God can assure our hearts before him and we can have perfect confidence. We must not look at the Word as only a written word. The Word is a live fact to work in the human body living truths, changing it, moving it till the person is a living fact of God's inheritance, till he is in the body reigning. In conversation or activity, the man is a product of God.

Let us look at the first verse of this chapter: "Whosoever believeth that Jesus is the Christ is born of God: and every one that loveth him that begat loveth him also that is begotten of him." What is the outcome of being born of God? God's life is God's truth, God's walk, God's communion, fellowship, oneness, likemindedness. All that pertains to almightiness, righteousness, and truth comes forth of this new birth, and in it, through it, and by it, we have a perfect regenerated position. Again it is an impartation of love and expression of himself, for God is love. The first revelation of light of the new creation within the soul is so pure, so unadulterated, so perfect, and so righteous. Go back to when you first believed in your heart: you felt so holy, you felt you loved so much, you were in a paradise of wonderment. Another fact was this: that for days and days there was something so remarkable that came over your life you had no desire for sin.

Catching the Breath of the Spirit

We want to be so established in God that nothing in this world shall be able to move us from our perfect position. See how much God has for us in the world. God wants people who are mighty in the Spirit, who are full of power. God has great designs for man. He has determined by his power and his grace, through his Son, to bring many sons unto glory, clothed upon with the Holy One from heaven. God is jealous over us this morning. How he longs for us to catch the breath of his Spirit. How he longs for us to be moved in union with himself that there may not be a thought in heaven but that the Holy Ghost could breathe through the natural and so chasten it by his divine power that you should have a new faith, or a revelation of God. "For whatsoever is born of God overcometh the world: and this is the victory that overcometh the world, even our faith. Who is he that overcometh the world, but he that believeth that Jesus is the Son of God?" (Jn 5:4-5). It is most beautiful! We shall have to come into divine measurement, divine revelation. The possibilities are ours.

Revealed Unto Babes

Nothing happens to the believer but what is good for him. "All things work together for good to them that love God," but we must not forget the rest of this verse: "To them who are the called according to his purpose" (Rom 8:28).

Remember, you are called according to his purpose in the working out of the power of God within you for the salvation of others. God has called and saved you for a purpose. Look, beloved, I want you to be without carefulness. Hear what the Scripture says, "Thou hast hid these things from the wise and prudent, and hast revealed them unto babes: even so, Father; for so it seemed good in thy sight" (Lk 10:21).

The first thing that God really does with a newborn child is to keep him as a child. There are wonderful things for children. The difference between a child and the wise and prudent is this: the prudent man is too careful. The wise man knows too much. But the babies! We have had babies and sometimes have had to pull the bottle back lest they take the bottle with the milk, they were so ravenous. The child cannot dress itself but God clothes it. He has a special raiment for children, white and beautiful. The babe cannot talk but it is lovely to know that you will take no thought what you shall say. The Holy Ghost can speak through you. He loves his children. Oh, how beautifully he looks after his children; how kind and good he is.

He that believes that Jesus is the Son of God, overcomes the world, because Jesus is so holy and you become his habitation. Jesus is so sweet, his love passes all understanding. His wisdom passes all knowledge and therefore he comes to you with the wisdom of God and not of this world. He comes to you with peace, not as this world giveth. He comes to you with boundless blessing, with measure pressed down and running over. God is a rewarder of all men that diligently seek him, for they that seek him shall lack no good thing. Surely the Lord is not going to send you away empty. He wants to satisfy your longing soul with good things.

Brother, where are your bounds this morning? There are heights and depths and lengths and breadths to the love of God. The Word of God contains the principles of life. I live not, but another mightier than I liveth in me. The desires have gone into the desires of God. It is lovely. Oh, how God loves his children.

I'll never forget when we had our first baby. He was asleep in the cradle. We both went to him and my wife said, "I cannot bear to have him sleep any longer. I want him." And I remember waking the baby because she wanted him. "If ye then, being evil, know how to give good gifts unto your children: how much more shall your heavenly Father give the Holy Spirit to them that ask him?" (Lk 11:13). Ah, he is such a lovely Father.

Truly Believing and Trusting God
One time I thought I had the Holy Ghost. Now I know the Holy Ghost has got me. There is a difference between our hanging on to God and God lifting us up. There is a difference between my having a desire and God's desire filling my soul. There is a difference between natural compassion and the compassion of Jesus that never fails. Human faith fails but the faith of Jesus never fails. Oh, beloved, I see through these glorious truths a new dawning: assemblies loving one another, all of one accord. Until that time comes there will be deficiencies. "By this shall all men know that ye are my disciples, if ye have love one to another" (Jn 13:35). Love is the secret and center of the divine position. Build upon God.

You ask what is the gift of faith? It is where God moves you to believe. Here is a man called Elijah with like passions as we have. The sins of the people were grieving the heart of God and the whole house of Ahab was in an evil state. But God moved upon this man Elijah and gave him an inward cry: "There shall not be dew nor rain these years, but according to my word" (1 Kgs 17:1). "And it rained not on the earth by the space of three years and six months" (Jas 5:17). Oh, if we dared believe God! A man of like passions as we are, stirred with almightiness. "And he prayed again, and the heaven gave rain, and the earth brought forth her fruit" (Jas 5:18).

Brother, sister, you are now in the robing room. God is adding another day for you to come into line, for you to lay aside everything that has hindered you, for you to forget the people. And I ask you how many want to touch God for faith that cannot be denied? I have learned this day if I dare put up my hands in faith, God will fill them. Come on, beloved, seek God and let us get a little touch of heaven this morning.

From *Triumphs of Faith* (Oakland, Calif.), July 1924, pp. 154–56. Address given at the Pentecostal camp meeting, Berkeley, California, June 1924. Abridged by the *Triumphs of Faith* editor, by author's permission.

43
Possession of the Rest

We have in Hebrews 4:1-15 one of those divine truths which is so forceful in all of its bearings to us in this morning's meeting. God wants us all to see that we must not come short of that blessed rest which is spoken to us. I am not speaking about the rest there is through being saved, although it is a very blessed rest; I am not speaking about the rest we have in the body because pains have passed away, nor of the rest because of no sin, when sanctification has worked in a wonderful way by the blood.

But God wants me to speak about the rest where you cease from your own works, and where the Holy Spirit begins to work in you and where you know that you are not your own, but absolutely possessed by God.

A Different Type of Rest
Beloved, I ask you to diligently follow me on these lines this morning, because there are so many people who are at unrest, they have no rest—untested on so many lines. I believe that God can bring us into a place of rest this day, where we will cease from our own works, where we will cease from our own planning, where we will cease from our own human individuality, which so interferes with God's power within us. God wants to fill the body with himself—yes, to fill the bodies so full of himself when he takes us into his plan.

353

Then, beloved, I notice here that many people fall short of coming into line with this divine blessing because of unbelief. Last time I was in Wellington, I met people who had been Christians, breaking bread for years, but filled with unbelief. They will not have the right way of the Lord. They break bread, but they won't toe the line. God save us from such a position. Now it is unbelief, nothing else; but when the Holy Ghost comes, then unbelief is moved away, and they are humble, brokenhearted, thirsty, and they want God. May God keep us humble, and hungry for the Living Bread. God is showing me that you cannot have this blessed power upon you without you become hungry.

If you turn to the Scriptures, you will find that the whole of Israel is a plan for us to see that God would have taken them on to many victories but could not because of unbelief. They were eligible for all the fullness of God, but there was not a single person entered but Joshua and Caleb. The reason they went in was because they had another spirit. Have you never read it? Joshua and Caleb had another spirit. The Spirit was so mighty upon Joshua and Caleb that they had no fear; the Holy Spirit upon them had such a dignity of reverence to God that those two people brought the bunches of grapes and presented them before the people. There were ten other people sent out; they had not received the Spirit, and came back murmuring.

Is there a message here for us? I am speaking about the people who get the Holy Ghost and go on, not the people who remain stationary, but those who go forward. When these ten people came they were murmuring. What was it? They had no rest.

"There remaineth therefore a rest to the people of God"

(Heb 4:9), and the people who enter into that rest cease from their own works, and God begins to work. These ten people said, "We shall become prey to them, and our children shall be slain by them"; and God said, through Moses, "Your children shall go in, and ye shall be shut out" (see Nm 14). It was only unbelief.

I pray God the Holy Ghost that you will search your hearts and the Word, and see if you have received this Spirit. What is it? The Holy Spirit. It is to be filled with the Holy Ghost, filled with the life of the Spirit, that which we call unction, revelation, force. What do I call force? Force is that position in the power of the Spirit where, instead of wavering, you go through, instead of judgment you receive truth. May God help us.

The Holy Ghost Reveals the Word
I want to give you a very important point about the Holy Ghost this morning. The Holy Ghost manifests the Word in the body. "For the word of God is quick, and powerful, and sharper than any two-edged sword, piercing even to the dividing asunder of soul and spirit, and of the joints and marrow, and is a discerner of the thoughts and intents of the heart" (Heb 4:12).

I want to deal now with the breath of the Spirit on the Word of God; that will give you rest. I want to give it to you so that you may understand it. Concerning the breath of the Holy Ghost, we have in the second chapter of Acts one of the most divine elementary revelations. When the Holy Ghost came like a mighty rushing wind and filled the place where they were, cloven tongues of fire sat upon each of them, and they were filled with this ... wind? breath? power? Person?

They were filled with God, the Third Person; the Holy Ghost filled their bodies. I have seen people filled with the Holy Ghost who used to be absolutely helpless, and when the power of God took their bodies, they became like young men instead of old withered people, through the power of the Holy Ghost; but now I am going to show you the reason. The Word of God is quick and powerful. Paul said, "You hath he quickened ..." (Eph 2:1). Powerful to the pulling down of the strongholds of Satan.

I would like you to read 2 Corinthians 10:4, 5: "For the weapons of our warfare are not carnal, but mighty through God to the pulling down of strongholds; casting down imaginations, and every high thing that exalteth itself against the knowledge of God, and bringing into captivity every thought to the obedience of Christ." Now, the Holy Ghost will take the Word, making it powerful in you till every evil thing that presents itself against the obedience and fullness of Christ would absolutely wither away. I want to show you this morning the need of the baptism of the Holy Ghost, by which you know there is such a thing as perfect rest, a perfect Sabbath coming to your life when you are filled with the Holy Ghost, and I want you to see perfect rest in the place. I want you to see Jesus. He was filled with the Holy Ghost. He lay asleep, filled with the Holy Ghost, and the storm began so terribly, and filled the ship with water, till they cried, "Master, we perish." Then he arose [filled with the Holy Ghost], and rebuked the wind. He asked, "Where is your faith?" (see Lk 8:24-25).

"There remaineth ... a rest to the people of God" (Heb 4:9). God wants you to enter into that rest. "For he that is entered into his rest, he also hath ceased from his own works, as God did from his. Let us labour therefore to enter into that rest, lest any man fall after the same example of unbelief" (vv. 10-11). Enter into rest, get filled with the Holy Ghost, and unbelief will depart. When they entered in, they were safe from unbelief, and unbelief is sin. It is the greatest sin, because it hinders you from all blessing.

An Encouragement

Let me encourage you. God is a God of encouragement. Now I want to take you to the thirteenth verse. "Neither is there any creature that is not manifest in his sight: but all things are naked and opened to the eyes of him with whom we have to do." No creature is hid from his sight; all are naked before him. Now when God speaks of nakedness, he does not mean that he looks at flesh without clothing. It is not your body, it is Christ clothing upon you within, and you have no spot. He looks at your nakedness, at your weaknesses, at your sorrow of heart. He is looking into you right now, and what does he see? "Seeing then that we have a great high priest, that is passed into the heavens, Jesus the Son of God, let us hold fast our profession." (v. 14).

What is our profession? I have heard so many people testifying about their profession; some said, "Thank God, I am healed." "Thank God, he has saved me." "Thank God, he has cleansed me." "Thank God, he has baptized me with the Holy Ghost." That is my profession—is it yours? That is the profession of the Bible, and God wants you to make it your profession.

You have to have a *whole* Christ, a *full* redemption, you have to be filled with the Holy Ghost, just a channel for him to flow through: Oh, the glorious liberty of the gospel of God's power.

> *Heaven has begun with me,*
> *I am happy, now, and free,*
> *Since the Comforter has come,*
> *Since the Comforter has come.*

It's all there. I know that God has designed this fullness, this rest, this perfect rest. I know he has designed it, and there ought not to be a wrinkle, a spot, a blemish (see Eph 5:27). Praise the Lord for such a wonderful, glorious, inheritance through him who loved us. Hallelujah.

From *Triumphs of Faith* (Oakland, Calif.), March 1925, pp. 53–57. Reprinted from the *New Zealand Evangel*. Portions of an address given in the Town Hall, Wellington, New Zealand.

An International Ministry

1935 Meetings in San Francisco

It is frankly admitted on every side that the Wigglesworth-Salter* services held from January 29 to February 10 were a great spiritual stimulus. Faith rose steadily as the meetings progressed. The meetings grew in number and in power. A large number of persons were built up in the most holy faith. Many since the close of the services have testified to the miraculous healings. God was in our midst and still is. We shall never be the same again.

Brother Wigglesworth was very lowly in spirit, much more gentle and mellow, and had been wondrously renewed by God in his body.** Approaching his seventy-sixth birthday, his vigor seems unabated. We praise God for both his and the Salters' ministry in the Lord. The question and answers in the morning services proved very attractive to the students of the Bible Institute and to many others.

It is estimated that almost, if not quite two thousand persons were present on the last Sunday night of the campaign.

The outstanding thought perhaps was that absolute holiness of heart and life measures the power we shall have with God. It is therefore up to us to die to self and sin, and abide in Him continually.

Robert Craig, *Glad Tidings* (San Francisco), reprinted in *Triumphs of Faith*, March 1935, p. 72. Craig and his wife Mary pastored Glad Tidings Temple, San Francisco, and founded what is now Bethany College, Scotts Valley, California.

*Smith Wigglesworth and his daughter Alice and her husband James Salter.

**Wigglesworth had been healed of a very painful condition two years earlier (see "Wigglesworth Testifies of His Healing," p. 345). Some who had seen Wigglesworth before and after his healing observed that he empathized more with the sick after suffering himself. Craig could be referring to the change.

44
Flames of Fire

Praise the Lord! I am sure anyone would have great liberty in preaching in this convention! I believe God the Holy Ghost can so bring into our hearts these truths that we shall live in the top place of expectation. There may be much variation in these meetings, but I believe God will give us the desire of our hearts. I am so glad to be here; my heart is full on so many lines.

The message to me this morning was very fine. I know that only God can satisfy my thirst. I know that the man who is to be possessed with a zeal for God's work can only possess it as he is thirsty after God. Jesus had a great longing, a great passion. It was the zeal of the house of God. I believe this morning God wants to bring us to a place where we shall realize there is a revolution coming in our lives.

Kicking Off a Spiritual Revolution
Oh, beloved, it seems to me that we shall never be anywhere for God until there has been perfect revolution in our whole being.

It was a tremendous thought for me to know that I had received the Holy Ghost. But I am coming to a great wonderment of splendor to know that the Holy Ghost has at last got me! And the revolution has had such an effect upon my life that everything is of new order—a reviving process—a divine mark right within the inner heart. It is certainly an incision without a mark but God puts his stamp into the hidden desires and cravings, and the whole thing is a great plan of a divine creation—the thirst of God after the image of the one he first created. It was forfeited, but it is now being brought back to its beginning. It may only be in its infancy; but oh, the development since last year of God's incarnation in my whole soul! Nothing less will please the Lord, only a constant, full burnt offering for God, where he is in absolute and utter authority over my whole being, until I am living, thinking, acting in the power of the Holy Ghost. Praise the Lord!

It is worthy of thought this morning, to allow God to bring a powerful might to so burst upon all our natural desires and longings that we may at last come on to a plane of the divine plan where God breathes his own breath and makes his own food and eats and drinks with us and lives within us—an overflowing measure that shall never be taken away.

There is something in this pentecostal work for God that it seems a continual decreasing with an increasing measure to take over the measureless measure! I am satisfied in my heart this morning that the hand of God is upon us. If we could only believe—if we could only believe to see the glory of the salvation that God has for us in the person of Jesus!

A Flame of Fire

Let us read the first chapter of Hebrews—it is full of holy vision. The word that I have for you this morning is in the seventh verse: "And of the angels he saith, Who maketh his angels spirits, and his ministers a flame of fire."

His ministers are to be flames of fire! This means so much

for us this morning. It seems to me that no man with a vision, especially a vision by the Spirit's power, can read that wonderful verse—that divine truth—without being kindled to such a flame of fire for his Lord that it seems as if it would burn up everything that would interfere with his progress. A flame of fire! A perpetual fire; a constant fire; a constant burning; a holy inward flame which is exactly that which God's Son was in the world manifesting for us all. I can see this—that *God has nothing less for us than to be flames!*

The import of our message is that the Holy Ghost has come to make Jesus king. It seems to me that the seed, which is an eternal seed, that life which was given to us when we believed, was of such a nature of the resurrection power that I see a new creation rising with a kingly position, and I see that when the Holy Ghost comes, he comes to crown Jesus king.

So, beloved, it is not only the King within, but all the glories of the kingly manifestations which are brought forth. So I see this, that even that alone would cause you to feel a burning after Jesus; a longing, a passion after him. Oh, for him to so work in us, melting us until a new order rises, moved with compassion! There is something about the message that I want you to catch this morning. It does not seem to me that God can in any way even make us to be anything, but I do see that we can so come into a place in the order of God that he sets us up where the vision becomes so much brighter and where the Lord is in his glory with all his beatitudes and gifts, and all his glory seems to fill the soul who is absolutely dead to self and alive to him. There is so much talk about death, but I do see that there is a death which is so deep in God that out of that death God brings the splendor of his life and all his glory.

On Fire—Always

A remarkable evidence of being a flame of fire for God came when I was traveling from Egypt to Italy. It is quite true when I tell you that on the ship and everywhere God has been with me. A man on the ship suddenly collapsed; his wife was in a terrible state and everybody else seemed to be. Some said that it had come to the end, but oh, to be a flame—to be indwelt by the living Christ!

We are a back number if we have to pray for power, if we have to wait until we feel a sense of his presence. The baptism of the Holy Ghost should empower you for any emergency. "Ye shall receive power, after that the Holy Ghost is come upon you" (Acts 1:8). Within you there is a greater power than there is in the world (see 1 Jn 4:4). Oh, to be awakened out of our unbelief into a place of daring for God! On the authority of the blessed Book!

So in the name of Jesus I rebuked the devil, and to the astonishment of the man's wife and himself he was able to stand. He said, "What is this? It is going all over me. I have never felt anything like this before," for from the crown of his head to the soles of his feet the power of God shook him.

In season and out of season (see 2 Tm 4:2), God has for us an authority over the powers of the devil—over all the power of the enemy. Oh, that we may live in the place where the glory excelleth! I would that we could all see *him* this morning. God says to us through this lovely word in Hebrews 1:3, "Who being the brightness of his glory, and the express image of his person, and upholding *all things* by the Word of his power, when he had by himself purged our sins, sat down on the right hand of the Majesty on high" (emphasis added).

It would make anyone a flame of fire. Praise God, it is a fact!

Jesus is in our body, and he is the exprcss image of God, and he has come to our human weakness to change us into a divine substance so that by the power of his might we may not only overcome, but rejoice in the fact that we are more than over-comers. God wants to have the last part more than overcomers!

Beloved, all I speak this morning is burning in my soul. The baptism of the Spirit has come for nothing less than to eat the whole of my life. It set up Jesus as king, and nothing can stand in his holy presence when he is made king. Every-thing will wither before him. I am realizing this. I feel I come to a convention like this to stir you up and to help you to know that this inheritance of the Spirit is given to every man to profit withal. Praise the Lord! And in the Holy Ghost order we have to come behind with no gifts, but I love the thought that all the gifts are of no qualification or service to us if the Giver does not work the gift. If he is working the gift, and it is there in operation, and you are there only as an instrument or a voice or a temple, he fills the temple, he fills the bill! Oh, it is lovely! He dwells inside! He lives; he moves; he reveals. He causes us to forget our sorrow and rejoice with joy unspeakable and full of glory. "The brightness of his glory and the express image of God."

We must not forget that we must make this a personal thing. When God made the angels, he made them sing. All that were in the heavens did obedience to this wonderful royal King, and, beloved, we must see that this Word this morning is a personal experience. I look at the Scriptures, and I say, "Oh, Lord, it *must* be mine if you give it to me—you must make it mine." This is how I talk to him, so he knows my language well! And I am the thirstiest man in the world, and he has a reservoir specially for me and for us all. We sometimes get to a place where we say, "Lord, it is no good, nothing you have shown me yet has moved me sufficiently. You will have to do something like you did in the Bible, something that will make the people marvel." But he will yet show you things that you may marvel (see Jn 5:20).

This same Jesus has come for one purpose, that he might so be made manifest in us that the world shall see him, and we must be burning and shining lights to reflect such a Holy Jesus. We cannot do it with cold, indifferent experiences, and we never shall. I come across those people at times who always "have a good report" (see Heb 11:2, 39), but oh, for a pentecostal ring in our hearts all the time! Oh, what do you have, brother, sister?

It is his purpose to take you into the Promised Land. What an inward burning—what an inward craving God can give! It is a taste of the heavenlies! And we want more! More of these wonderful joys until God has absolutely put his stamp upon everyone by the power of his presence.

From *Triumphs of Faith* (Oakland, Calif.), October 1926, pp. 230–33. Extracts from an address; reprinted from *Redemption Tidings*.

45
When the Holy Ghost Has Control

B eloved, the Lord would have us to know in these days that there is a fullness of God where all other powers must cease to be. I beseech you this afternoon to know that the baptism in the Holy Spirit is to so possess us that we may be continually full of his utterances, and revelations, and divine perception. I beseech you that you may be so remarkably controlled by the Spirit of God that you may live and move in a glorious sphere of usefulness for his glory.

We Receive What Jesus Promised

If we will read John's Gospel, we will see that Jesus predicted all that we are getting today in the Holy Ghost. He said that the Holy Ghost would take of the things of his Word and reveal them unto us—he should live out in us all the life of the Lord Jesus Christ. If we could only think what this really means! Talk about graduation! Come into the graduation of the Holy Ghost and you will simply outstrip everything they have in any college in the land. You would leave that which is as cold as ice and move out into the sunshine. God the Holy Ghost desires us to have such a fullness of the Spirit that we shall not be ignorant, neither will we have mystic conceptions, but we will have a clear, unmistakable revelation of all the mind of God for these days.

I beseech you, beloved, in the name of Jesus, that you should see that you must come right into all the mind of God. Jesus verily said, "But ye shall receive power, after that the Holy Ghost is come upon you" (Acts 1:8). And I want you to know that "He shewed himself alive after his passion by many infallible proofs, being seen of them forty days, and speaking of the things pertaining to the kingdom of God" (Acts 1:3). He is all the time unfolding to every one of us the power of his resurrection. Remember, the baptism of the Holy Ghost is resurrection. If you can touch this ideal with its resurrection power, you will see that nothing earthly can remain. Resurrection is to breathe in you Christ's life and to cause you to know that you are quickened by the Spirit in the life of Jesus. Oh, the word "resurrection"! I wish I could say it just on parallel lines with the name of Jesus. They very harmoniously go together. Jesus is resurrection and to know Jesus in this resurrection power is simply to see that you have no more to be dead, but "alive unto God" by the Spirit.

We must see that we are no good unless God takes charge of us. But when he gets entire control of us, what a plan for our lives! What a wonderful open door for God! Oh, brethren, we must see this ideal by the Spirit! What shall we do? Do? You dare not do anything but "go through." Submit to the power of God. If you yield, other people are saved. When you know the power of resurrection, other people will be raised out of death and be taken out of all kinds of evil into a blessed life through the Spirit. Beloved, we must see that this baptism of the Spirit is greater than all. Remember, when I talk about resurrection, I talk about one of the greatest things in the Scriptures because resurrection is an evidence that we have wakened up to a new line of truth that cannot cease to be, but will always go on with greater force and increasing power with God.

A New Day for Believers

See to it that this day makes you press on with a new order of the Spirit, so that you can never be where you were before. This is a new day for us all. You say, "What about the people who are already baptized?" Oh, this is a new day also for those who have been baptized, for the Spirit is an unlimited source of power. There is nothing stationary in God. God has no place for a man who is stationary. The man who is going to catch the fire, hold for the truth, always be on the watchtower, is the man who is going to be a beacon for all saints having a light greater than his natural order. I must see that God's grace and God's life and his Spirit are mightier than the man a million times. When you are baptized in the Holy Ghost you are on an extraordinary plane. You are brought into line with the mind of God. If you want the quickening that moves your body till you know that you are all renewed, it is in the Holy Ghost. And while I say so much about the Holy Ghost today, I withdraw everything that does not put our Lord Jesus Christ in the place he belongs. When I speak about the Holy Ghost, it is always with reference to the revelation of Jesus. The Holy Ghost only is the revealer of the mighty Christ who has all for us, so that we may never know any weakness, but all limitations are gone. Glory to God!

A Yielded Vessel Is Filled

The Holy Ghost never comes until there is a place ready for him. The Holy Ghost can only come into our bodies (his temples) when they are fully yielded to him. It does not matter what kind of a building you get—you cannot count the building being a substitute for the temple of the Holy Ghost. You will all have to be temples of the Holy Ghost to have the building anything like the Holy Ghost order.

On the day of Pentecost, the Holy Ghost could not come until the apostles and those that were with them in the Upper Room were all of one mind and one heart, all of "one accord" with each other and with God (see Acts 1:14). You will notice that Jesus said, "I thank Thee, O Father, Lord of heaven and earth, because thou hast hid these things from the wise and prudent, and hast revealed them unto babes" (Mt 11:25). This is the mind and plan of God for all who desire to seek the Holy Ghost.

What is the difference between the wise and prudent man and a baby? If you have the "babe" spirit this afternoon and will yield to God and let him have his way, he will fill you with the Holy Ghost. The natural man cannot receive the Spirit of God, but when you get into a supernatural place, then you will receive the mind of God. Oh, beloved, if we can only be babes today, great things will take place in the line and thought of the Spirit of God. The Lord wants us all to be so in likemindedness with him that he can put his seal upon us.

Originally published as "The Baptism in the Holy Ghost," in *Triumphs of Faith* (Oakland, Calif.), November 1927, pp. 244–46. Extracts from an address, condensed and revised by the editor of *Triumphs of Faith*.

An International Ministry

A Personal Experience in Sydney

A large auditorium was procured in the city to continue the [Wigglesworth] campaign, with meetings each morning and night for the space of one month.

My older sister was paralyzed down one side of her body. She was brought to the meeting and was instantly healed allowing her actually to run to catch a train, though previously she had been confined to her home. For the next 30 years she served the Lord with me in true dedication.

My brother had lived a wild and reckless life which had left him in a dying state with incurable ailments and more importantly, without salvation. He was persuaded to attend the revival meetings where he was called to the front by the preacher. Looking him over, Brother Wigglesworth said, "Your woeful condition is the result of your sinful life. Nevertheless, God in His compassion has showed me He is going to heal you completely." My brother, strangely humbled, said, "But I have no faith," to which Smith Wigglesworth rejoined, "Well I 'ave." (It was a fact that Brother Wigglesworth could take away an "H" from his son 'Arold, to add to his daughter Halice.) He went away saved, healed, and rejoicing in the Lord. Subsequently, he married a Christian wife and raised a family of talented children, all serving and living for God.

P.B. Duncan, *The Charismatic Tide,* published by author, pp. 4–5. Used by permission.

46
Wilt Thou Be Made Whole?

I believe the Word of God is so powerful that it can transform any and every life. There is power in God's Word to make that which does not appear to appear. There is executive power in the Word that proceeds from his lips. The psalmist tells us, "He sent his word, and healed them" (Ps 107:20), and do you think that word has diminished in its power? I tell you nay, but God's word can bring things to pass today as of old.

The psalmist said, "Before I was afflicted I went astray: but now have I kept thy word." And again, "It is good for me that I have been afflicted; that I might learn thy statutes" (Ps 119:67, 71). And if our afflictions will bring us to the place where we see that we cannot live by bread alone, but must partake of every word that proceedeth out of the mouth of God, they will have served a blessed purpose. But I want you to realize that there is a life of purity, a life made clean through the word he has spoken, in which, through faith, you can glorify God with a body that is free from sickness, as well as with a spirit set free from the bondage of Satan.

Think about the pathetic case around the pool. Here they lay, a great multitude of impotent folk, of blind, halt, withered, around that pool, waiting for the moving of the water (from Jn 5:2-9). Did Jesus heal everybody? He left many around that pool unhealed. There were doubtless many who had their eyes on the pool and who had no eyes for Jesus. There are many today who have their confidence all the time in things seen. If they would only get their eyes on God instead of on natural things, how quickly they would be helped.

Are These Blessings for Everyone?

The question arises: Are salvation and healing for all? They are for all who will press right in and get their portion. You remember the case of the Syrophenician woman who wanted the devil cast out of her daughter. Jesus said to her, "Let the children first be filled: for it is not meet to take the children's bread, and to cast it unto the dogs" (Mk 7:27). Note that healing and deliverance are here spoken of by the Master as "the children's bread"; so, if you are a child of God, you can surely press in for your portion.

The Syrophenician woman purposed to get from the Lord what she was after, and she said, "Yes, Lord: yet the dogs under the table eat of the children's crumbs." Jesus was stirred as he saw the faith of this woman, and he told her, "For this saying go thy way; the devil is gone out of thy daughter" (Mk 7:28-29). Today there are many children of God refusing their blood-purchased portion of health in Christ and throwing it away, while sinners are pressing through and picking it up from under the table, as it were, and are finding the cure not only for their bodies but for their spirits and souls as well. The Syrophenician woman went home and found that the devil had indeed gone out of her daughter. Today there is bread, there is life, there is health for every child of God through his all-powerful Word.

Instructions for the Sick

"Is any sick among you? let him call for the elders of the church; and let them pray over him, anointing him with oil in the name of the Lord: And the prayer of faith shall save the sick, and the Lord shall raise him up; and if he have committed sins, they shall be forgiven him" (Jas 5:14-15).

We have in this precious word a real basis for the truth of healing. In this scripture God gives very definite instructions to the sick. If you are sick, your part is to call for the elders of the church; it is their part to anoint and pray for you in faith, and then the whole situation rests with the Lord. When you have been anointed and prayed for, you can rest assured that the Lord will raise you up. It is the Word of God.

I believe that we all can see that the church cannot play with this business. If any turn away from these clear instructions they are in a place of tremendous danger. Those who refuse to obey, do so to their unspeakable loss.

James tells us in connection with this, "If any of you do err from the truth, and one convert him; Let him know, that he which converteth the sinner from the error of his way shall save a soul from death" (Jas 5:19-20). Many turn away from the Lord, as did King Asa, who sought the physicians in his sickness and consequently died; and I take it that this passage means that if one induces another to turn back to the Lord, he will save such from death and God will forgive a multitude of sins that they have committed. This scripture can also have a large application on the line of salvation. If you turn away from any part of God's truth, the enemy will certainly get an advantage over you.

Does the Lord meet those who look to him for healing and obey the instructions set forth in James? Most assuredly. Let me tell you a story to show how he will undertake for the most extreme case.

The Role of the Word in Healing

The Word can drive every disease away from your body. It is your portion in Christ who himself is our bread, our life, our health, our all in all. And though you may be deep in sin, you can come to him in repentance, and he will forgive and cleanse and heal you. His words are spirit and life to those who will receive them. There is a promise in the last verse in Joel, "I will cleanse their blood that I have not cleansed" (3:21). This is as much as to say he will provide new life within. The life of Jesus Christ, God's Son, can so purify men's hearts and minds that they become entirely transformed, spirit, soul, and body.

There they are round the pool; and this man had been there a long time. His infirmity was of thirty-eight years' standing (see Jn 5:5). Now and again an opportunity would come, as the angel stirred the waters, but his heart would be made sick as he saw another step in and be healed before him. But one day Jesus was passing that way, and seeing him lying there in that sad condition, inquired, "Wilt thou be made whole?" (v. 6). Jesus said it, and his word is from everlasting to everlasting. This is his word to you, poor, tried, and tested one today. You may say, like this poor impotent man, "I have missed every opportunity up till now." Never mind about that—*Wilt thou be made whole?*

I visited a woman who had been suffering for many years. She was all twisted up with rheumatism and had been two years in bed. I said to her, "What makes you lie here?" She said, "I've come to the conclusion that I have a thorn in the flcsh." I said, "To what wonderful degree of righteousness have you attained that you have to have a thorn in the flesh? Have you had such an abundance of divine revelations that there is danger of your being exalted above measure?" She said, "I believe it is the Lord who is causing me to suffer." I said, "You believe it is the Lord's will for you to suffer, and you are trying to get out of it as quickly as you can. There are doctor's bottles all over the place. Get out of your hiding place and confess that you are a sinner. If you'll get rid of your self-righteousness, God will do something for you. Drop the idea that you are so holy that God has got to afflict you. Sin is the cause of your sickness and not righteousness. Disease is not caused by righteousness, but by sin."

A Perfect Atonement

There is healing through the blood of Christ and deliverance for every captive. God never intended his children to live in misery because of some affliction that comes directly from the devil. A perfect atonement was made at Calvary. I believe that Jesus bore my sins, and I am free from them all. I am justified from all things if I dare believe. He himself took our infirmities and bore our sicknesses; and if I dare believe, I can be healed.

See this poor, helpless man at the pool. "Wilt thou be made whole?" But there is a difficulty in the way. The man has one eye on the pool and one on Jesus. There are many people getting cross-eyed this way these days; they have one eye on the doctor and one on Jesus. If you will only look to Christ and put both your eyes on him you can be made every whit whole, spirit, soul, and body. It is the word of the living God that they that believe should be justified, made free from all things.

And whom the Son sets free is free indeed.

You say, "Oh, if I only could believe!" He understands. Jesus *knew* he had been a long time in that case. He is full of compassion. He knows that kidney trouble, he knows those corns, he knows that neuralgia. There is nothing he does not know. He only wants a chance to show himself merciful and gracious to you. But he wants to encourage you to believe him. If thou canst only believe, thou canst be saved and healed. Dare to believe that Jesus was wounded for your transgressions, was bruised for your iniquities, was chastised that you might have peace, and that by his stripes there is healing for you right here and now (see 1 Pt 2:24). You have failed because you have not believed him. Cry out to him even now: "Lord, I believe; help thou mine unbelief" (Mk 9:24).

Testimonies of Healing

I was in Long Beach, California, one day, and with a friend, was passing a hotel. He told me of a doctor there who had a diseased leg; that he had been suffering from it for six years, and could not get out. We went up to his room and found four doctors there. I said, "Well, doctor, I see you have plenty on, I'll call again another day." I was passing at another time, and the Spirit said, "Go join thyself to him." Poor doctor! He surely was in a bad condition. He said, "I have been like this for six years, and nothing human can help me." I said, "You need God Almighty." People are trying to patch up their lives, but you cannot do anything without God. I talked to him for awhile about the Lord, and then prayed for him. I cried, "Come out of him, in the name of Jesus." The doctor cried, "It's all gone!"

Oh, if we only knew Jesus! One touch of his mightiness

meets the need of every crooked thing. The trouble is to get people to believe him. The simplicity of this salvation is so wonderful. One touch of living faith in him is all that is required, and wholeness is your portion.

I was in Long Beach about six weeks later, and the sick were coming for prayer. Among those filling up the aisle was the doctor. I said, "What is the trouble?" He said, "Diabetes, but it will be all right tonight. I know it will be all right." There is no such thing as the Lord's not meeting your need. There are no "ifs" or "mays"; his promises are all "shalls." All things are possible to him that believeth. Oh, the name of Jesus! There is power in that name to meet every condition of human need.

At that meeting there was an old man helping his son to the altar. He said, "He has fits—many every day." Then there was a woman with a cancer. Oh, what sin has done! We read that when God brought forth his people from Egypt, "there was not one feeble person among their tribes." No disease! All healed by the power of God! I believe that God wants a people like that today.

I prayed for the sister who had the cancer and she said, "I know I'm free and that God has delivered me." Then they brought the boy with the fits, and I commanded the evil spirits to leave in the name of Jesus. Then I prayed for the doctor. At the next night's meeting the house was full. I called out, "Now, doctor, what about the diabetes?" He said, "It has gone." Then I said to the old man, "What about your son?" He said, "He hasn't had any fits since." We have a God who answers prayer.

Turn Your Eyes Upon Jesus

Jesus meant this man at the pool to be a testimony forever. When he had both eyes on Jesus, he said to him, "Do the impossible thing. Rise, take up thy bed, and walk." Jesus called on the man with the withered hand to do the impossible—to stretch forth his hand. The man did the impossible thing—he stretched out his hand, and it was made every whit whole. And so with this impotent man—he began to rise, and he found the power of God moving within. He wrapped up his bed and began to walk off. It was the Sabbath day, and there were some of those folks around who think much more of a day than they do of the Lord; and they began to make a fuss. When the power of God is in manifestation, a protest will always come from some hypocrites. Jesus knew all about what the man was going through and met him again; and this time he said to him, "Behold, thou art made whole: sin no more, lest a worse thing come unto thee" (Jn 5:14).

There is a close relationship between sin and sickness. How many know that their sickness is a direct result of sin? I hope that no one will come to be prayed for who is living in sin. But if you will obey God and repent of your sin and quit it, God will meet you, and neither your sickness nor your sin will remain. "The prayer of faith shall save the sick, and the Lord shall raise him up; and if he have committed sins, they shall be forgiven him" (Jas 5:15).

Faith is just the open door through which the Lord comes. Do not say, "I was healed by faith." Faith does not save. God saves through that open door. Healing comes the same way. You believe, and the virtue of Christ comes. Healing is for the glory of God. I am here because God healed me when I was dying; and I have been all round the world preaching this full redemption, doing all I can to bring glory to the wonderful name of Jesus, through whom I was healed.

"Sin no more, lest a worse thing come upon thee." The Lord told us in one place (see Lk 11:24-26) about an evil spirit going out from a man. The house that he left got all swept and garnished, but it received no new occupant. And that evil spirit, with seven other spirits more wicked than himself, went back to that unoccupied house, and the last stage of the man was worse than the first. The Lord heals you for his glory and that from henceforth your life shall glorify him. But this man remained stationary. He did not magnify God. He did not seek to be filled with the Spirit. And his last state became worse than the first.

Healing Is for His Glory
The Lord would so cleanse the motives and desires of our hearts that we will seek but one thing only and that is, his glory. I went to a certain place one day and the Lord said, "This is for my glory." A young man had been sick for a long time, confined to his bed in an utterly hopeless condition. He was fed only with a spoon, and was never dressed. The weather was damp, and so I said to the people of the house, "I wish you would put the young man's clothes by the fire to air." At first they would not take any notice of my request, but because I was persistent, they at last got out his clothes, and, when they were aired, I took them into his room.

The Lord said to me, "You will have nothing to do with this." And I just lay out prostrate on the floor. The Lord showed me that he was going to shake the place with his glory. The very bed shook. I laid my hands on the young man in the name of Jesus, and the power fell in such a way that I fell with my face to the floor. In about a quarter of an hour the young man got up and walked up and down praising God. He dressed himself and then went out to the room where his father and mother were. He said, "God has healed me." Both the father and mother fell prostrate to the floor as the power of God surged through that room.

There was a woman in the house who had been in an asylum for lunacy, and her condition was so bad that they were about to take her back. But the power of God healed her too.

The power of God is just the same today as of old. Men need to be taken back to the old paths, to the old-time faith, to believe God's Word and every "Thus saith the Lord" therein. The Spirit of the Lord is moving in these days. God is coming forth. If you want to be in the rising tide, you must accept all God has said.

"Wilt thou be made whole?" It is Jesus who asks this question. Give him your answer. He will hear and he will answer.

From *The Bridal Call Foursquare* (Los Angeles), September 1927, pp. 19–20, 32. (It is more than likely that this sermon was preached at Aimee Semple McPherson's Angelus Temple, Los Angeles.)

47
The Evidence of the Baptism of the Spirit

There is much controversy today as regards the genuineness of the pentecostal work, but there is nothing so convincing as the fact that over fifteen years ago [1908] a revival on Holy Ghost lines began and has never ceased. You will find that in every clime throughout the world God has poured out his Spirit in a remarkable way in a line parallel with the glorious revival that inaugurated the church of the first century. People, who could not understand what God was doing when he kept them concentrated in prayer, wondered as these days were being brought about by the Holy Ghost and found themselves in exactly the same place and entering into an identical experience as the apostles.

The Promise of the Father
Our Lord Jesus said to his disciples, "Behold, I send the promise of my Father upon you: but tarry ye in the city of Jerusalem, until ye be endued with power from on high" (Lk 24:49). God promised through the prophet Joel, "I will pour out my spirit upon all flesh ... upon the servants and upon the handmaids in those days will I pour out my spirit" (Jl 2:28-29).

You know, beloved, it had to be something on the line of solid facts to move me. I was as certain as possible that I had received the Holy Ghost, and was absolutely rigid in this conviction. When this pentecostal outpouring began in England

I went to Sunderland and met with the people who had assembled for the purpose of receiving the Holy Ghost. I was continuously in those meetings, causing disturbances until the people wished I had never come. They said that I was disturbing the whole condition. But I was hungry and thirsty for God and had gone to Sunderland because I heard that God was pouring out his Spirit in a new way. I heard that God had now visited his people, had manifested his power, and that people were speaking in tongues as on the day of Pentecost.

When I got to this place I said, "I cannot understand this meeting. I have left a meeting in Bradford all on fire for God. The fire fell last night and we were all laid out under the power of God. I have come here for tongues, and I don't hear them—I don't hear anything."

"Oh!" they said, "when you get baptized with the Holy Ghost you will speak in tongues." "Oh, is that it?" said I. "When the presence of God came upon me, my tongue was loosened, and really I felt as I went in the open air to preach that I had a new tongue." "Ah, no," they said, "that is not it." "What is it, then?" I asked. They said, "When you get baptized in the Holy Ghost—" "I am baptized," I interjected, "and there is no one here who can persuade me that I am not baptized." So I was up against them and they were up against me.

I remember a man getting up and saying, "You know, brothers and sisters, I was here three weeks and then the Lord baptized me with the Holy Ghost and I began to speak with tongues." I said, "Let us hear it. That's what I'm here for." But he would not talk in tongues. I was doing what others are doing today, confusing the twelfth chapter of 1 Corinthians with the second chapter of Acts. These two chapters deal with different things, one with the gifts of the Spirit, and the other with the baptism of the Spirit with the accompanying sign. I did not understand this and so I said to the man, "Let's hear you speak in tongues." But he could not. He had not received the "gift" of tongues, but the baptism.

As the days passed I became more and more hungry. I had opposed the meetings so much, but the Lord was gracious, and I shall ever remember that last day—the day I was to leave. God was with me so much that last night. They were to have a meeting and I went, but I could not rest. I went to the parsonage, and there in the library I said to Mrs. Boddy,* "I cannot rest any longer, I must have these tongues." She replied, "Brother Wigglesworth, it is not the tongues you need but the baptism. If you will allow God to baptize you, the other will be all right." "My dear sister, I know I am baptized," I said. "You know that I have to leave here at four o'clock; please lay hands on me that I may receive the tongues."

"The Fire's Falling"

She rose up and laid her hands on me and the fire fell. I said, "The fire's falling." Then came a persistent knock at the door, and she had to go out. That was the best thing that could have happened, for I was *alone with God.* Then he gave me a revelation. Oh, it was wonderful. He showed me an empty cross and Jesus glorified. I do thank God that the cross is empty, that Christ is no more on the cross. It was there that he bore the curse, for it is written, "Cursed is every one that hangeth on a tree." He became sin for us that we might be

---

*Mary Boddy, Mrs. A.A. Boddy. A.A. Boddy (Mary's husband) was a Pentecostal Anglican priest and editor of *Confidence.* J.T. Boddy was an American Pentecostal and editor of the *Pentecostal Evangel.*

made the righteousness of God in him, and now, there he is in the glory. Then I saw that God had purified me. It seemed that God gave me a new vision, and I saw a perfect being within me with mouth open, saying, "Clean, Clean! Clean!" When I began to repeat it I found myself speaking in other tongues. The joy was so great that when I came to utter it my tongue failed, and I began to worship God in other tongues as the Spirit gave me utterance.

It was all as beautiful and peaceful as when Jesus said, "Peace, be still!" and the tranquillity of that moment and the joy surpassed anything I had ever known up to that moment. But, hallelujah! These days have grown with greater, mightier, more wonderful divine manifestations and power. That was but the beginning. There is no end to this kind of beginning. You will never get an end to the Holy Ghost till you are landed in the glory—till you are right in the presence of God forever. And even then we shall ever be conscious of his presence.

The Bible Evidence

What had I received? I had received the Bible evidence. This Bible evidence is wonderful to me. I knew I had received the very evidence of the Spirit's incoming that the apostles received on the day of Pentecost. I knew that everything I had had up to that time was in the nature of an anointing, bringing me in line with God in preparation, but now I knew I had the biblical baptism in the Spirit. It had the backing of the Scriptures and you are never right if you have not a foundation for your testimony in the Word of God.

For many years I have thrown out a challenge to any person who can prove to me that he had the baptism without speaking in tongues as the Spirit gives utterance—to prove it by the Word that he has been baptized in the Holy Ghost without the Bible evidence. But so far no one has accepted the challenge. I say this only because so many were like I was, having a rigid idea that they have received the baptism without the Bible evidence. The Lord Jesus wants those who preach the Word to have the Word in evidence. Don't be misled by anything else. Have a Bible proof for all you have, and then you will be in a place where no man can move you.

I was so full of joy that I wired home to say that I had received the Holy Ghost. As soon as I got home, my boy came running up to me and said, "Father, have you received the Holy Ghost?" I said, "Yes, my boy." He said, "Let's hear you speak in tongues." But I could not. Why? I had received the baptism in the Spirit with the speaking in tongues as the Bible evidence according to Acts 2:4, and had not received the gift of tongues according to 1 Corinthians 12. I had received the Giver of all gifts. At some time later when I was helping some souls to seek and receive the baptism of the Spirit, God gave me the gift of tongues so that I could speak at any time.

Witnesses to the Experience

I want to take you to the Scriptures to prove my position. There are businessmen here, and they know that in cases of law, where there are two clear witnesses they could win a case before any judge in Australia. On the clear evidence of two witnesses, any judge will give a verdict. What has God given us? Three clear witnesses on the baptism in the Holy Spirit—more than are necessary in the law courts.

The first is in Acts 2:4: "They were all filled with the Holy Ghost, and began to speak with other tongues, as the Spirit gave them utterance." Here we have the original pattern. And God gave to Peter an eternal word that couples this experience with the promise that went before. "This is that." And God wants you to have *that*—nothing less than *that.* He wants you to receive the baptism in the Holy Spirit according to this original pentecostal pattern.

In Acts 10 we have another witness. Peter is in the house of Cornelius. Cornelius had had a vision of an holy angel and had sent for Peter. A person said to me one day, "You don't admit that I am filled and baptized with the Holy Ghost. Why, I was ten days and ten nights on my back before the Lord and he was flooding my soul with joy." I said, "Praise the Lord, sister, that was only the beginning. The disciples were tarrying that time, and they were still, and the mighty power of God fell upon them then and the Bible tells what happened when the power fell." And that is just what happened in the house of Cornelius. The Holy Ghost fell on all those who heard the word "and they of the circumcision which believed were astonished, as many as came with Peter, because that on the Gentiles was poured out the gift of the Holy Ghost" (v. 45). What convinced these prejudiced Jews that the Holy Ghost had come? "For they heard them speak with tongues, and magnify God" (v. 46). There was no other way for them to know. This evidence could not be contradicted. It is the Bible evidence.

If some people in this district had an angel come and talk to them as Cornelius had, they would say that they knew they were baptized. Do not be fooled by anything. Be sure that what you receive is according to the Word of God.

We have heard two witnesses and that is sufficient to satisfy the world. But God goes one better. Let us look at Acts 19:6,

"And when Paul had laid his hands upon them, the Holy Ghost came on them; and they spake with tongues, and prophesied." These Ephesians received Bible evidence identical to that the apostles had received at the beginning and they prophesied in addition. Three times the Scriptures show us this evidence of the baptism in the Spirit. *I do not magnify tongues.* No, by God's grace, *I magnify the Giver of tongues.* And I magnify above all him whom the Holy Ghost has come to reveal to us, the Lord Jesus Christ. He it is who sends the Holy Spirit, and I magnify him because he makes no difference between us and those at the beginning.

The Purpose of Tongues

But what are the tongues for? Look at the second verse of 1 Corinthians 14, and you will see a very blessed truth. Oh, hallelujah! Have you been there, beloved? I tell you, God wants to take you there. "He that speaketh in an unknown tongue speaketh not unto men, but unto God: for no man understandeth him; howbeit in the spirit he speaketh mysteries." It goes on to say, "He that speaketh in an unknown tongue edifieth himself" (v. 4).

Enter into the promises of God. It is your inheritance. You will do more in one year if you are really filled with the Holy Ghost than you could do in fifty years apart from him. I pray that you may be so filled with him that it will not be possible for you to move without a revival of some kind resulting.

Word And Work (Framingham, Mass.), January 1924, pp. 4–5. (A similar sermon is published in *World Pentecost*, #3, 1974, pp. 14–15). Evidently this sermon was preached in Australia.

An International Ministry

God at Work in South Africa

Basil Crompton was a young assistant pastor in South Africa when he was asked to chauffeur Smith Wigglesworth during his 1936 visit to South Africa. They became close friends and coworkers, and Wigglesworth even tried to find a suitable wife for the young single preacher during the time he spent in South Africa. Here is a report Crompton gave concerning the Wigglesworth style.

I saw a man coming forward on crutches, unable to put his sore foot to the floor. Wigglesworth commanded him to stamp his foot on the ground; and when he hesitated, commanded him a second time, very loudly and with great authority. This time he obeyed, stamped his foot hard and then, throwing away his crutches, he walked off the platform without help.

I saw many wheelchair cases get up and walk. But I think what impressed me most was that in many instances he didn't pray fervently but simply obeyed God's voice without question, saying only, "Get out of your chair." Or sometimes he would say just, "Walk!"... And without exception everyone did.

I was also present on many other occasions when people who were totally blind were healed as he laid his hands on their eyes. I saw the deaf and dumb healed. So many glorious miracles occurred that I couldn't always remember exactly what happened at all the meetings.

Quoted in *God in Action,* by Cathy Crompton, Crompton Ministries, Port Elizabeth, South Africa, p. 41. Published in 1993. Used by permission.

48
Ye Shall Receive Power

"Ye shall receive power, after that the Holy Ghost is come upon you" (Acts 1:8). The disciples had been asking whether the Lord would at that time restore again the kingdom to Israel. Christ told them that it was not for them to know the times and seasons which the Father had put in his own power, but he promised them that when they received the Holy Ghost they should receive power to witness for him in all the world. To receive the Holy Ghost is to receive power with God, and power with men.

The Good and Evil Powers

There is a power of God and there is a power which is of Satan. When the Holy Spirit fell in the early days, a number of spiritists came to our meetings. They thought we had received something like they had and they were coming to have a good time. They filled the two front rows of our mission. When the power of God fell, these imitators began their shaking and muttering under the power of the devil. The Spirit of the Lord came mightily upon me and I cried, "Now, you devils, clear out of this!" And out they went. I followed them right out into the street and then they turned round and cursed me. There was power from below, but it was no match for the power of the Holy Ghost, and they soon had to retreat.

The Lord wants all saved people to receive power from on

high—power to witness, power to act, power to live, and power to show forth the divine manifestation of God within. The power of God will take you out of your own plans and put you into the plan of God. You will be unmantled and divested of that which is purely of yourself and put into a divine order. The Lord will change you and put his mind where yours was, and thus enable you to have the mind of Christ. Instead of your laboring according to your own plan, it will be God working in you and through you to do his own good pleasure through the power of the Spirit within. Someone has said that you are no good until you have your "I" knocked out. Christ must reign within, and the life in the Holy Ghost means at all times the subjection of your own will to make way for the working out of the good and acceptable and perfect will of God within.

Tarrying for the Baptism

The Lord Jesus gave commandment that the disciples should tarry until they were endued with power from on high, and in Acts 2 we read how the Spirit of God came. He comes the same way today and we don't know of the Holy Ghost coming any other way.

I was holding a meeting, once, in London, and at the close a man came to me and said, "We are not allowed to hold meetings in this hall after eleven o'clock, and we would like you to come home with us—I am hungry for God." The wife said she, too, was hungry, and so I agreed to go with them. At about 12:30 we arrived at their house. The man began stirring up the fire and said, "Now we will have a good supper." I said to them, "I did not come here for your warm fire, your supper, or your bed. I came here because I thought you were hungry to get more of God."

We got down to pray and at about 3:30 the Lord baptized the wife and she spoke in tongues as the Spirit gave utterance. At about five o'clock I spoke to the husband and asked how he was getting on. He replied, "God has broken my iron, stubborn will." He had not received the baptism, but God had wrought a mighty work within him.

The following day, at his business, everyone could tell that a great change had come to him. Before, he had been a walking terror. The men who labored for him had looked upon him as a regular devil because of the way he acted; but coming into contact with the power of God that night completely changed him.

Before this night he had made a religious profession, but he had never truly entered into the experience of the new birth until that night when the power of God surged so mightily through his home. A short while afterwards I went to this man's home, and his two sons ran to me and kissed me, saying, "We have a new father." Previous to this these boys had often said to their mother, "Mother, we cannot stand it in the home any longer. We will have to leave." But the Lord changed the whole situation that night as we prayed together. On the second visit the Lord baptized this man in the Holy Ghost. The Holy Spirit will reveal false positions, pull the mask off any refuge of lies, and clean up and remove all false conditions. When the Holy Spirit came in, that man's house and business and he himself were entirely changed.

When the Holy Spirit comes, he comes to empower you to be an effective witness. At one time we were holding some special meetings and I was out distributing bills. I went into a shoemaker's store and there was a man with a green shade over his eyes and also a cloth. My heart looked up to the Lord and I had the witness within that he was ready to change any condition. The man was crying, "Oh! Oh! Oh!" I asked, "What's the trouble?" He told me he was suffering with great inflammation and burning. I said, "I rebuke this condition in Jesus' name." Instantly the Lord healed him. He took off the shade and cloth and said, "Look, it is all gone." I believe the Lord wants us to enter into real activity and dare to do for him. "Ye shall receive power, after that the Holy Ghost is come upon you."

The Holy Spirit Will Come

At one time a woman wrote and asked if I could go and help her. She said that she was blind, having two blood clots behind her eyes. When I reached the house they brought the blind woman to me. We were together for some time and then the power of God fell. Rushing to the window, she exclaimed, "I can see! Oh, I can see! The blood is gone, I can see." She then inquired about receiving the Holy Spirit and confessed that for ten years she had been fighting our position. She said, "I could not bear these tongues, but God has settled the whole thing today. I now want the baptism in the Holy Ghost." The Lord graciously baptized her in the Spirit.

The Holy Spirit will come when a man is cleansed. There must be a purging of the old life. I never saw anyone baptized who was not clean within. I never saw a man baptized who smoked. We take it for granted that anyone who is seeking the fullness of the Spirit is free from such things as these. You cannot expect the Third Person of the Trinity to come into an unclean temple. There first must be a confession of all that is wrong and a cleansing in the precious blood of Jesus Christ.

I remember being in a meeting at one time, where there was a man seeking the baptism, and he looked like he was in trouble. He was very restless, and finally he said to me, "I will have to go." I said, "What's up?" He said, "God is unveiling things to me, and I feel so unworthy." I said, "Repent of everything that is wrong." He continued to tarry and the Lord continued to search his heart. These times of waiting on God for the fullness of the Spirit are times when he searches the heart and tries the reins.

Later the man said to me, "I have a hard thing to do, the hardest thing I ever had to do." I said to him, "Tell the Lord you will do it, and never mind the consequences," and the next morning he had to take a ride of thirty miles and go with a bag of gold to a certain party with whom he dealt. This man had a hundred head of cattle and he bought all his feed at a certain place. He always paid his accounts on a certain day, but one day he missed. He was always so punctual in paying his accounts that when later the people of his firm went over their books, they thought they must have made a mistake in not crediting the man with the money and so they sent him a receipt. The man never intended not to pay the account, but if you defer to do a right thing, the devil will see that you never do it. But when that man was seeking the Lord that night the Lord dealt with him on this point, and he had to go and straighten the thing the next morning. He paid the account and then the Lord baptized him in the Spirit. They that bear the vessels of the Lord must be clean, must be holy.

The Holy Spirit Reveals Jesus

When the Holy Spirit comes he always brings a rich revelation of Christ. Christ becomes so real to you that when, under the power of the Spirit, you begin to express your love and praise to him, you find yourself speaking in another tongue. Oh, it is wonderful! At one time I belonged to a class who believed that they had received the baptism in the Spirit without the speaking in tongues. There are many folks like that today, but if you can go with them to a prayer meeting you will find them asking the Lord again and again to baptize them in the Spirit. Why all this asking if they really have received the baptism? I have never heard anyone who has received the baptism in the Holy Spirit after the original pattern asking the Lord to give them the Holy Ghost. They know of a surety that he has come.

I was once traveling from Belgium to England. As I landed I received a request to stop at a place between Harwich and Colchester. The people were telling me of a special case they wanted me to pray for. They said, "We have a brother here who believes in the Lord, and he is paralyzed from the loins downward. He cannot stand on his legs and he has been twenty years in this condition."

They took me to this man and as I saw him there in his chair I put the question to him, "What is the greatest desire in your heart?" He said, "Oh, if I could only receive the Holy Ghost!" I was somewhat surprised at this answer, and I laid my hands on his head and said, "Receive ye the Holy Ghost." Instantly the power of God fell upon him and he began breathing very heavily. He rolled off the chair and there he lay like a bag of potatoes, utterly helpless. I like anything that God does. I like to watch God working. There he was with his great, fat body, and his head was working just as though it was on a swivel. Then to our joy he began speaking in tongues. I had my eyes on every bit of him and as I saw the condition of his legs I said, "Those legs can never carry that body."

Then I looked up and said, "Lord, tell me what to do." The Holy Ghost is the executive of Jesus Christ and the Father. If you want to know the mind of God you must have the Holy Ghost to bring God's latest thought to you and to tell you what to do. The Lord said to me, "Command him in my name to walk." But I missed it, of course. I said to the people there, "Let's see if we can lift him up." But we could not lift him: he was like a ton weight. I cried, "Oh Lord, forgive me." I repented of doing the wrong thing, and then the Lord said to me again, "Command him to walk." I said to him, "Arise in the name of Jesus." His legs were immediately strengthened. Did he walk? He ran all around. A month after this he walked ten miles and back. He has a pentecostal work now. When the power of the Holy Ghost is present, things will happen.

There is more for us all yet, praise the Lord. This is only the beginning. So far we have only touched the fringe of things. There is so much more for us if we will but yield to God.

Do you want to receive the Spirit? "If ye then, being evil, know how to give good gifts unto your children: how much more shall your heavenly Father give the Holy Spirit to them that ask him?" (Lk 11:13). I am a father and I want to give my boys the very best. We human fathers are but finite, but our heavenly Father is infinite. There is no limit to the power and blessing he has laid up for them that love him. Be filled with the Spirit.

From *Word and Work* (Framingham, Mass.), January 1930, pp. 2, 14–15.

Time Line of Smith Wigglesworth's Life

Because no known Wigglesworth diaries are available, we have compiled this time line from various books, advertisements, posters, magazine articles, and correspondence. Readers having additions or corrections may write to the editors in care of Servant Publications, P.O. Box 8617, Ann Arbor, MI 48107.

1859   Born in Menston, Yorkshire, England, June 10. Baptized in Anglican Church, December 4.

1865   Worked in the fields at age six, pulling and cleaning turnips.

1866   At age seven began working in woolen mill twelve hours a day. No time for school.

1867   Converted in Menston Methodist Church, where John Wesley had preached.

1872   Confirmed in Anglican Church, September 5, at age thirteen. Moved to Bradford.

1875   Associated with Salvation Army and Plymouth Brethren.

1876   Baptized by immersion at age seventeen.

1879   Worked with poor children in Liverpool through

gospel services and feeding program. Supported himself as a plumber.

1882 Married Mary Jane "Polly" Featherstone. Their five children were Alice, Seth, Harold, Ernest, and George.

1889 He and Polly founded Bowland Street Mission, Bradford. Placed a flag outside proclaiming "Christ Died for Our Sins" on one side and "I Am the Lord that Healeth Thee" on the other.

1907 Baptized in the Holy Spirit October 28, 1907, at Sunderland through the laying on of hands. Began preaching but continued his plumbing business for income. He was 48 years old.

1912 Sunderland *Daily Echo,* May 31, reported Wigglesworth's healing meeting at All Saints Church.

1913 His wife Polly died in January. The London *Daily Mirror,* May 16, published front-page story along with four photographs of seaside baptismal service conducted by Wigglesworth.

1914 Traveled to the United States via Canada. Spoke at Stone Church in Chicago during June. Two months later preached for George and Carrie Judd Montgomery at Cazadero, located in redwood country about sixty miles north of San Francisco. Wigglesworth ordained by M.M. Pinson and Robert Craig, August 1. World War I began in Europe, which hampered travel.

1915 Back in England for Easter convention. Preached in London at first pentecostal Whitsuntide meeting. His son George died.

1920 Ministered in Europe for six months: France, Switzerland, Scandinavian countries. Jailed in Switzerland twice.

1921 Conducted meetings in Stockholm for Lewis Pethrus in April. Was arrested for laying hands on the sick. Charges dismissed with the order that he not lay hands on the sick in a mass meeting that Whitmonday.

1922 Traveled to Australia and New Zealand via Sri Lanka. Arrived in North Melbourne, Australia, February 16, 1922, with meeting that night. Preached in Wellington, New Zealand, in May. Wellington's *Dominion* published lengthy report under banner headlines, "Faith Healing. Extraordinary Scenes at Town Hall. The Deaf Made to Hear." Newspaper *Sun* in Christchurch was very critical of meetings held at the invitation of Sydenham Gospel Mission. Went on to Dunedin (Settlers Hall and Princess Theater). Reported in Dunedin's *Evening Star,* June 15, 1922. Stayed in Dunedin until end of June. Returned to Wellington, where he began meetings in July. *Dominion* reporters checked out healing affidavits. Started San Diego, California, meetings October 2. "Dare to Believe God" was his theme for Union Pentecostal meetings in Chicago, October 29-

November 12. He celebrated his sixty-second birthday this week (and would preach another 25 years).

1923　Returned to New Zealand in October. Held meetings in Auckland, Palmerton North, Blenheim, and went on to Wellington on December 16. Attended Pentecostal Convention December 23–30.

1923　Returned to the United States for preaching tour, which included stops in Berkeley, California, and Springfield, Missouri.

1924　Received ministerial credits with the United States Assemblies of God at age sixty-five. Under his "special calling," he marked "evangelist-teacher." Gospel Publishing House published *Ever-Increasing Faith*.

1925　Traveled to South Africa during the year. Started meeting in Phoenix with H.L. Faulkner, Apostolic Temple, February 8; preached at Maria Woodworth-Etter Tabernacle, Indianapolis, February 14. Held meetings in England and Switzerland. Preached in Bethel Temple, Los Angeles.

1927　Returned to Australia and New Zealand. Was at Richmond Temple, Melbourne, during the spring. Testimonies of healings in 1922 meetings given.

1927　Conducted meetings in Aimee Semple McPherson's Angelus Temple in the fall and other churches in Southern California. Preached at Glad Tidings Temple, San Francisco, October 26–November 6; also at Carrie Judd Montgomery's Monday meeting, October 31.

1928   In the spring went to Switzerland, then returned to England for Whitsuntide convention. Put up a tent in London to minister with the Church of England.

1930   Ministered in the United States, including meetings with Robert and Marie Brown in New York. Sailed for home April 19.

1930-33 Suffered with kidney stones. Refused to seek medical help.

1932   Asked the Lord for fifteen more years. Held meetings in Eureka Springs, Arkansas, August 29–September 12.

1933   Healed of kidney stones, October 4.

1934   Returned to the United States in the fall.

1935   Wigglesworth—now 76 years old—and the Salters ministered at Glad Tidings Temple, San Francisco, January 29–February 10.

1936   Traveled to South Africa. Gave prophecy concerning David du Plessis.

1938   Gospel Publishing House published *Faith That Prevails.*

1939-47 Ministry confined to England because of World War II and his increasing age.

1947   Smith Wigglesworth died March 12, 1947, at Glad Tidings Hall, Wakefield, Yorkshire. Funeral held at Elim Church in Bradford, March 17. Would have been eighty-eight in June. Deaths of contemporary ministers included Stephen Jeffreys and A.J. Tomlinson, 1943; Aimee Semple McPherson, 1944; Carrie Judd Montgomery, 1946; Charles Price, 1947; E.W. Kenyon and Robert Brown, 1948.

1947-50 Other evangelists began salvation-healing ministries, including Kathryn Kuhlman, Oral Roberts, William Branham, Jack Coe, and A.A. Allen.

1948 Stanley H. Frodsham wrote *Smith Wigglesworth, Apostle of Faith.*

1959 One hundredth anniversary of Wigglesworth's birth.

1972 William Hacking wrote *Reminiscences of Smith Wigglesworth* (reprinted in 1981 as *Smith Wigglesworth Remembered*).

1982 Albert Hibbert wrote *Smith Wigglesworth: The Secret of His Power.*

1983 Colin C. Whittaker wrote *Seven Pentecostal Pioneers,* including a chapter on Smith Wigglesworth.

1987 Jack Hywel-Davies wrote *Baptised by Fire* (reprinted in 1987 as *The Life of Smith Wigglesworth*).

1989 George Stormont wrote *A Man Who Walked with God* (Wigglesworth).

1990 Roberts Liardon compiled *Cry of the Spirit.*

1993 P.J. Madden compiled and wrote *The Wigglesworth Standard.*

1994 Wayne Warner compiled *The Anointing of His Spirit.*

1996   Wayne Warner compiled and edited *Only Believe*.

1997   Roberts Liardon compiled *The Complete Wigglesworth*.

1997   Judith Couchman compiled *Dare to Believe*.

1999   Wayne Warner and Joyce Lee compiled *The Essential Smith Wigglesworth* on the 140th anniversary of his birth.

Other Books of Interest

The Life of Smith Wigglesworth: *One Man, One Holy Passion*
JACK HYWEL-DAVIES
The Life of Smith Wigglesworth paints a striking portrait of this passionate man of God, whose simplicity, single-minded devotion to his call, and complete faith in God's Word plunged him into a central role in the modern charismatic movement. *171 pp, $9.99*

The Anointing of His Spirit
SMITH WIGGLESWORTH
The Anointing of His Spirit captures Wigglesworth's message of faith. Readers will find the heart of a man who cried out to God on behalf of others, praying powerfully and effectively for healing and provision. *200 pp, $10.99*

Dare to Believe
SMITH WIGGLESWORTH
The third volume in the "Life Messages of Great Christians" series, *Dare to Believe* is a compelling collection of excerpts from the best of Wigglesworth's teachings. Topics include living by faith, receiving God's power, living in righteousness, and following God's call. *180 pp, $10.99*

Only Believe! *120 Daily Devotions*
SMITH WIGGLESWORTH
"Only believe all things are possible," say the words to one of Wigglesworth's favorite songs. The legendary preacher cast out demons, healed the sick, and stirred up a passion for God in the hearts of thousands. This collection of devotional excerpts from his sermons will encourage the reader to new heights of faith. *200 pp, $10.99*

Available from your local Christian bookstore

or from Servant Publications
PO Box 8617, Ann Arbor, MI 48107
Please send payment plus $3.25 per book for shipping and handling.